Miracles & Divine Intervention

Chicken Soup for the Soul: Miracles & Divine Intervention
101 Stories of Faith and Hope
Amy Newmark

Published by Chicken Soup for the Soul, LLC www.chickensoup.com

The publisher gratefully acknowledges the many publishers and individuals who granted Chicken Soup for the Soul permission to reprint the cited material.

Front and back cover photo of gothic arches courtesy of iStockphoto.com/jacquesvandinteren (©jacquesvandinteren), photo of woman courtesy of iStockphoto.com/kieferpix (©kieferpix)
Back cover and interior photo of dove courtesy of iStockphoto.com/kieferpix (©kieferpix)
Photo of Amy Newmark courtesy of Susan Morrow at SwickPix

Cover and Interior by Daniel Zaccari

Distributed to the booktrade by Simon & Schuster. SAN: 200-2442

Publisher's Cataloging-In-Publication Data
(Prepared by The Donohue Group, Inc.)

Names: Newmark, Amy, compiler.
Title: Chicken soup for the soul : miracles & divine intervention : 101 stories of faith and hope / [compiled by] Amy Newmark.
Other Titles: Miracles & divine intervention : 101 stories of faith and hope | Miracles and divine intervention : 101 stories of faith and hope
Description: [Cos Cob, Connecticut] : Chicken Soup for the Soul, LLC, [2021]
Identifiers: ISBN 9781611590739 | ISBN 9781611593136 (ebook)
Subjects: LCSH: Miracles--Literary collections. | Miracles--Anecdotes. | Providence and government of God--Literary collections. | Providence and government of God--Anecdotes. | Faith--Literary collections. | Faith--Anecdotes. | LCGFT: Anecdotes.
Classification: LCC BL487 .C45 2021 (print) | LCC BL487 (ebook) | DDC 202.117/02--dc23
Library of Congress Control Number: 2020947975

PRINTED IN THE UNITED STATES OF AMERICA
on acid∞free paper

25 24 23 22 21 01 02 03 04 05 06 07 08 09 10 11

Miracles & Divine Intervention

101 Stories of Faith and Hope

Amy Newmark

Chicken Soup for the Soul, LLC
Cos Cob, CT

Changing the world one story at a time®

www.chickensoup.com

Table of Contents

1

~Heaven-Sent~

2

~Coincidences & Synchronicities~

❸

~Messages from Heaven~

❹

~How Did That Happen?~

❺

~Angels Among Us~

❻

~Divine Timing~

❼

~Dreams & Premonitions~

8

~Miraculous Connections~

9

~Love That Doesn't Die~

10

~Holiday Miracles~

Chapter 1

Heaven-Sent

Mr. Gaines to the Rescue

You should never feel alone.
There's always someone to turn to.
It is the guardian angel
who is watching over you.
~K. Sue

My husband Joe had been sent to Iran for a tour of duty. He would be getting out of the Army before Christmas, but he was still a soldier now, and he had to go.

"Come to Kansas," my sister Alice urged when I told her. "Load up the kids; we have plenty of room in the house, and they'll love it here."

Relief washed over me as she spoke. I hadn't realized how badly I had wished for the invitation. Two-year-old Anthony was a handful, and the baby was teething and fussy most of the day. With Joe's departure, I had to handle everything alone.

The trip from our home in Missouri to Kansas would take us approximately seven and a half hours. We had made it almost to the Kansas state line when I pulled into a rest stop to change and feed the kids, and let Anthony run around a bit. He was tired of being strapped in his car seat and he was fussing almost as much as the baby. While Anthony munched on his apple slices and raisins, and the baby pulled hungrily on her bottle, I called to let Alice know that

I had finally reached Kansas. Nobody picked up the phone, and when the answering machine came on, instead of the customary greeting, Alice had recorded a message for me. Her mother-in-law had suffered a heart attack in another city, and she and her husband were rushing to be with her. However, she assured me, she would be home before I arrived the next day. It was getting late, and I was weary of driving. I would check into a motel and rest before undertaking the last leg of my journey.

The next morning as I checked out of the motel, the young man behind the counter gave me his well-practiced, polite smile. "Be careful, miss. One of our famous Kansas summer storms is brewing. I hope you don't have far to go."

As I loaded the kids, I calculated how long it would take me to reach Alice's place. With feedings and changings, it would probably not be before noon. I used the payphone in the lobby and dialed her number, but I reached the answering machine again and heard the same message. I wasn't concerned because I still had a few hours to drive and I figured she was probably on her way home.

The longer I drove the darker the sky became, and the strong winds began to buffet my small car. I gripped the steering wheel as I fought to keep the car in my lane. The rain began to stream down in torrents and lightning lit up the sky. The thunder was so loud that it even made me jump, and soon the kids were howling right along with the wind. I kept peering through the windshield, hoping to spot a payphone somewhere. If I could reach Alice, I could let her know that the storm had slowed us down but I should arrive at her house within an hour. I finally spotted one outside a small two-pump service station. I got soaking wet only to reach the answering machine yet again. But according to the radio, storms had sprung up throughout the state. Alice and her husband were probably delayed by the storms too. Hopefully, they would be home when we arrived.

By the time I reached Alice's house, all three of us were exhausted and hungry. The baby had cried herself to sleep after taking her last bottle, and Anthony was giving me his best pout. I was so weary that I hadn't noticed how dark the house was. My heart sank. Nobody was home. I couldn't get into the house, and the kids needed to be changed, fed and comforted. It had been a hard trip.

I looked at Anthony, who seemed to be too weary to even cry anymore. "Honey, I'm going to look for a key. It's okay. Soon you can get out of your car seat and run all you want to. And I'm sure that Aunt Alice left us lots of good food to eat."

I checked under the doormat, the flowerpots, and above the door, anywhere that someone might hide a key. I was near tears myself. Suddenly, I heard a sound like someone softly clearing his throat. An older gentleman in a heavy parka and boots was crossing the yard next door and coming toward me. I was taken aback by the way he was dressed in the summer, but I was glad to see anyone at this point.

"I'm Alice's sister," I said as he drew near. "She must have forgotten to leave a key for me." I glanced at my car. "My kids are tired and hungry." I shrugged helplessly. What could this stranger do for me?

He gave me a kind, understanding smile. "I've had a key to Alice's house for years. I keep an eye on things when they are gone." He stuck out his hand. "I'm Mr. Gaines." He added with a big grin, "To the rescue."

When Alice and her husband arrived a couple of hours later, she was astonished to see me in the house. "I've been so worried about you and the kids. How did you get inside? I would have left a key for you, but we felt sure we would be home before you arrived. We had car trouble in Lynchburg, and of course the storm slowed us down, too."

I gave her a surprised look. "Mr. Gaines from next door let us in. He said you gave him a key a long time ago."

Alice and her husband exchanged astonished looks. Alice shook her head. "What did he look like?"

I shrugged. "Around seventy-five years old, I'd say. Snow-white hair. Thin. But he was dressed oddly for the weather. He was wearing heavy winter clothing and boots. I thought he must have dementia."

Alice plopped down on the sofa as all the color left her face. "That's Mr. Gaines, our next-door neighbor. And we did give him a key to the house." She shivered and gave me a wide-eyed look. "He had a heart attack last winter while shoveling snow from his driveway." Her voice dropped to barely above a whisper. "He died."

"Mr. Gaines was always helping people," Alice's husband added. "He would do anything for anybody when he was alive."

Apparently, he managed to come back and do one more good deed.

— Elizabeth Atwater —

Another Way Home

The wind of heaven is that which blows
between a horse's ears.
~Arabian Proverb

George was having a good day—sitting up in bed fifteen days after his hospital admission for pain management—when Anne, our patient advocate for the past two years, came into his room. "I'm glad to see more color back in your cheeks and less pain in those baby-blue eyes, George." Anne had a way of making this horrible disease a little easier for us to manage by knowing just what to say and when to say it.

"Are you flirting with me, young lady, with my wife right here in the room? Shame on you." George joked with her but knew that I needed to hear Anne's comments almost as much as he did. It had been a rough couple of months, and anything positive, even if it was just about his rosy cheeks, was welcome.

"Did you see that? Ladies, turn around… look at the TV… the Hindenburg… it just blew up!" George anxiously shouted as he grabbed for the remote to make the sound louder.

I looked frantically at Anne, not knowing what to say or do. It was August 2008. The Hindenburg disaster had taken place in May 1937. But Anne knew just how to handle it. She turned and looked up at the TV just long enough, and then she simply changed the subject while I stood there wondering if the cancer had spread to his brain.

Anne asked me to step out into the hall where she reassured me that this behavior was not unusual. She urged me to go along with whatever bizarre things George might say or do. It was a result of the high dose of morphine he was on. She reminded me that he'd spent the prior day calling everyone on his contact list to come get him because he was being discharged.

The morphine was doing its job: keeping the pain manageable. That drip had unique powers, though; it could take George back fifty years or it could take George into his future… but to properly do its job, it had to totally obliterate the present.

Anne went off to her office, and I went back into my husband's room.

"Hon, go look out the window. Maybe you'll see the horses that just flew past. They were the biggest horses I've ever seen… Why, they could have even been Clydesdales!"

I went to the window and looked down eight floors to Manhattan's busy First Avenue. As I looked at the street crowded with cabs and buses, I crossed my fingers and told my husband that I'd caught a glimpse of the horses turning onto 68th Street.

George fell into a morphine-induced sleep the next day and died three days later, still in the hospital. He had wanted to die at home, preferably 200 miles away at our upstate house on the river that we called our "camp."

It was the end of a whirlwind week when three close friends and I rode up to the camp to carry out George's wish to have his ashes scattered in the river. Our elderly next-door neighbors, Harry and Jean, were unable to come to the service or the funeral, so I invited them to join us at the riverside to say their goodbyes. As I dropped the ashes into the river, they caused a bubbling effect in the water, like George was actually taking his last breath there. I felt a warm shiver rush through me. As we were walking back into the camp to have lunch, Harry took my arm and said he wanted to show me something.

"Lin, you've got to see this. Last week, these tremendous horses ran through your back yard. They were so big! Look at the prints they left in your lawn."

Looking down at several large dents in the grass, I realized that

George had made one final call last week. The one for those horses that took him home.

I asked Harry to repeat what he had just said.

"It was Tuesday. There were four of them. Don't know where they came from. Never saw anything like it before, and I've lived next door for thirty years."

All I could say was "Thanks, Harry," taking comfort in the fact that George got his final wish. Those horses he saw outside his hospital window that Tuesday the prior week were the same ones that brought his heart and soul home here to his final resting place. He even took his last breath in the river that he so loved with me right there with him. The bubbles were proof of that.

I stood in our yard and looked upward toward the heavens just long enough to say a proper goodbye to my husband.

—Linda Monaco Behrens—

The Letter

Honest plain words best pierce the ear of grief.
~William Shakespeare

The 6 a.m. knock at our front door on February 12, 2004, startled me from my sleep. I had crashed the night before on the living-room sofa. I thought I must have been dreaming until I heard the knock again, followed by a loud voice calling, "Sergeant Major Tainsh," the rank and name of my husband, a retired U.S. Marine.

I called out to David. "I'm on the way," he said.

The porch light revealed two soldiers. David opened the door. "We know why you're here," he said.

"Sergeant Major and Mrs. Tainsh, on behalf of the President of the United States, we regret to inform you that your son, Sergeant Patrick Tainsh, was killed in action."

In the surreal moments that followed, the soldiers managed to steer us to seats in the living room. We soon learned that Patrick, an Army Cavalry Scout, and others in the unit had been ambushed while on a night mission. Patrick had succumbed to his injuries.

Ten days after the knock, David and I sat with our remaining son in a packed chapel. We choked on tears through the twenty-one-gun salute held outside the chapel's opened doors, taps, and acceptance of a folded flag.

Patrick was my "bonus son." We had entered each other's lives when he was thirteen. Transitions and the death of his birth mom when he was sixteen had led him down a road of drug use, homelessness and rehabilitation that eventually took him to the Army.

Day after day, I journaled about him. I wrote to capture Patrick's voice, his smile, our family struggles and joys, our struggles to cope with grief, and Patrick's redemption. In time, I shared my stories with the writing group that I facilitated at a bookstore. They said my words would help military families. They encouraged me to continue. Eleven months later, a manuscript of more than 200 pages lay on my dining-room table. I wrote it to honor Patrick and as a gift to my husband to say, "Here's your son's life in words. Proof that he lived and is forever immortal."

"You should publish this!" my writing friends said. I asked my husband. He said, "Do it."

I selected a self-publishing company. Then, for an unexplainable reason, I couldn't let go of the manuscript. I wasn't content with the epilogue. So, the manuscript continued to sit on the dining-room table until a day when David brought in mail.

"Here's something from Fort Polk," he said.

He handed me a large manila envelope.

"What's in it?" I asked.

"It's Patrick's briefing notebook. I flipped through the pages, but I don't see anything important."

I placed the envelope and notebook inside a trunk at the foot of our bed. The trunk already held Patrick's wallet, sunglasses, watch, camera, photographs and other items that he had touched, used, and left behind for us to cherish.

I returned to David and gave him a quick kiss. Unsurprisingly, he disappeared again to take one of his "grief drives" in Patrick's car that had been returned to us from Fort Polk months before. I sat down at the dining-room table and stared at the stacked pages of my manuscript. Again, I wondered about my gut feeling that the epilogue wasn't right.

Then I felt something warm touch me, and as if in a trance, I was directed to return to the bedroom and look at that lime-green military-issued notebook again. I stared at the cover inscribed by him in large letters with a black magic marker: SGT PATRICK TAINSH

2/2/ACR EAGLE TROOP. I opened the cover to look through the same pages David had already seen. But why? I had no reason to disbelieve David's earlier observations.

I turned the pages until I reached hand-printed words in red ink. My heart raced as I read what our son had written. Two pages later, I sat on the floor crying. "Thank you, Patrick. Thank you!"

I wiped tears from my face and walked to the living room with the notebook. Shortly afterward, David returned from his drive.

"Honey, I need you to sit down. I found something you need to read." I brought the notebook to him.

"What's this?" he asked.

"It's a message from Patrick. I don't know how you missed it when you flipped through the pages."

David turned his attention to Patrick's note:

> *Hi: I'm writing you this letter because something went wrong. It may or may not have been my fault, but it was time. I just want you to know I tried to do the right thing. I came to help people who couldn't help the situation they were subject to. It was an honor to fight and die with an American flag on my shoulder. Honor. That's a big word and some people don't know what it means. It's not something that happens right away. It's something that builds up inside your soul. Dad, I want you to know I've always wanted to be like you and be successful. It may not have happened on your timeline like you would've liked. I know I made some bad choices in life, but I don't regret it. People have to learn from the mistakes they make. That's part of life. Just know I've always loved you and appreciate all you've done for me. I've always been thankful for you. Just remember me for who I used to be and for who I'm known as now. Someone who lived through some tough times but turned his life around because he wanted a different definition of fun, his job as a U.S. Cavalry Scout. Someone who loved his family and father. Until we meet again, my heart, soul and love are with you. Don't ever forget that.*
>
> *Love, your son, Patrick*

David stood and embraced me. "This is the epilogue to the manuscript," I whispered. "In Patrick's own words, he said everything that needs to be read and heard."

I replaced the epilogue I'd written with Patrick's letter and sent it to the self-publishing house. Within a year, a traditional publisher asked to take the book.

There's no doubt that divine intervention caused me to delay sending in that manuscript. With perfect timing, it provided not only the perfect ending for the book, but our family was provided the perfect gift of greatest comfort during our most difficult time.

— Deborah Tainsh —

A Birthday Blessing

Sometimes, our grandmas and grandpas
are like grand-angels.
~Lexie Saige

It's always a good day when I get my birthday off from work as a paid holiday. I don't usually request my birthday as a day off, but I wasn't about to complain if the new company policy allotted me one extra day of compensation within the calendar year to not be at work. And, to make it even better, my birthday fell on a Friday this year.

To start the three-day weekend right, my husband found a pretty little place called Crystal Lake for us to backpack into and stay the night. It was a great opportunity to get away from it all and clear our heads to refresh for the week to come. We hiked in about four miles with our hound dog and set up camp. We found a beautiful place nestled in a little circular grove of pine trees, with an opening on either side of camp where we had a perfect view of Mt. Crystal and more of the breathtaking Rocky Mountains on the other side.

We hiked around a bit more before settling down for nightfall. We made a fire with the fire starter and hydrated our supper for the evening. I always forget how much my mind, body, and soul relax without the constant background noise of the city and the stimulation from technology and our busy schedules. We cuddled together by the fire, with our hound curled in a ball at our feet, delicately snoring with his paws twitching as he dreamed. He let out a deep, slow bay, abruptly waking himself up. We chuckled and patted him on the head until he laid his head in my husband's lap and quickly went back to sleep.

The flames of our fire danced wildly in front of us, appearing to crash violently into one another as the burning wood snapped, sending embers into the night sky. We took in the smell of burnt pine and smoke from the fire as we gazed up at the stars. The Milky Way was visible without the pollution of light from the city, and it was all perfect, except for one thing, something my heart yearned for that I couldn't have.

"The only thing that could make this day better would be if I could have just one more conversation with my grandma and grandpa," I said as I laid my head on my husband's chest.

"They're here with us always. That piece of your heart will always carry them on our journey, wherever we go." My husband hugged me tightly and kissed the top of my head, trying to comfort me the best way he knew how.

His words provided some solace, but I couldn't help thinking about all my past birthdays and how my grandparents had always been there for me. Even when we couldn't be together, they always called and sang "Happy Birthday" to me, even into my thirties.

With the fire winding down, we made sure it was entirely out and retired to our tent. As we settled down for the evening, I had an urge to check the voicemails on my phone. Oddly, we had service where we were camping, which usually wasn't the case. We hadn't had service for the entire hike, but for some reason in that little circular enclave, we managed to find a sweet spot. I typically did not like to employ the use of technological devices while we were camping, but I just felt the need to check my voicemails that day.

As I listened to my new messages, I heard birthday greetings from friends and family. After listening to the messages, my phone informed me that I had one saved message. I let it play, and the magic of two voices singing in unison overwhelmed me.

"Is everything okay?" my husband inquired when he saw my tears.

I clicked to re-play the message, this time putting it on the speaker. The sweet birthday song sung by my grandparents played in our peaceful campsite. I had no recollection of ever saving this message. It was the best birthday gift I could have asked for, and a reminder that they are always there watching over us and loving us from afar.

— Gwen Cooper —

Leap of Faith

Music gives a soul to the universe, wings to the mind, flight to the imagination and life to everything.
~Plato

As an intensely shy writer who had been sending out manuscripts for years, I wasn't sure which frightened me more: that I might never get published, or that I would get published and have to promote myself at book signings and other engagements. It was a real dilemma. I wasn't just a little timid—I was petrified of speaking to strangers. I'd once attended a small writers' circle and found myself close to tears when it was my turn to introduce myself.

Several friends suggested I join Toastmasters to tackle my fear. After many months of procrastination, I worked up enough courage to attend my first meeting. Just getting through the door was a momentous step, but the members who greeted me were warm and encouraging, so I took the plunge and signed up. The timing was clearly preordained. Less than two months later, a publisher offered me my first contract for a juvenile novel. I was over the moon!

I was still soaring when I ran into my friend Barb, a high-school teacher. "That's wonderful!" she said after I'd shared my news. "You're an author now. You should come speak to my tenth-grade English class."

"Oh, no," I said, feeling my cheeks turn red. "I appreciate the invitation, but I'm nowhere near ready to speak to high-school students. Maybe next year when my book comes out."

Barb was gracious as we said our goodbyes, but I couldn't help kicking myself for my cowardice as I drove home. Wasn't the opportunity Barb offered exactly why I had joined Toastmasters? *Sure,* I agreed silently, *but later, after I've had more time in the program.* Just then, a song came on the Christian radio station that further pricked my conscience. "What if you jump? And just close your eyes?" Nichole Nordeman sang. "What if the arms that catch you, catch you by surprise?" By the end of the song, I knew what I had to do.

I called Barb the minute I walked in the door and asked if I could accept her invitation after all. "Of course," she said. "I'm delighted you changed your mind." Before I could change it again, we set a date for the following week.

Over that next week, anxiety was my constant companion. I lost count of how many times I had to fight the urge to call Barb back and cancel. What had I been thinking? I wasn't ready to speak to a classroom full of teenagers! I couldn't imagine a more intimidating audience. What if my voice cracked, my cheeks flamed, or my knees shook? What if it was so bad that I had to flee the room? How would I ever recover my dignity?

But as frightened as I was, I kept clinging to the challenge and implied promise in the lyrics of Nordeman's song. It was 2005, and I didn't own her CD or have access to streaming music, so whenever "What If" came on the radio, I would immediately stop what I was doing and listen to every word. There were times I even curled up on the floor by the speaker in my living room. "I'm scared, Lord," I whispered. "But I'm jumping, and I trust that you will catch me."

The day finally arrived. The entire morning, I prayed that my song would come on the radio one more time, but I still hadn't heard it as I started the twenty-minute drive to my husband's school. My husband had kindly invited me to speak with his Grade 7 class as a dress rehearsal before the main event at the high school. I knew my husband's students, and they were younger and therefore less intimidating than the high-school students. At least, that was the theory.

"Oh, please," I begged as I drove through the gently falling snow. "I just need to hear my song one more time." But to my disappointment, it still hadn't come on as I pulled into the parking lot.

I managed to get through my presentation to the Grade 7 students with my dignity intact, but I still felt anxious as I said goodbye and returned to my car. "Oh, Lord," I prayed as I sat down. "You really are going to have to catch me. I am terrified." I took a breath and then turned the key.

A song was just starting as the radio came on — the same song I'd been praying to hear all morning. Nordeman's voice kept me company as I drove the few blocks over to the high school. Tears streamed down my face as I held onto every word. "Thank you," I whispered when it was finally over.

As I exited my car, I knew with absolute certainty that I was going to be okay. Somehow, I was not at all surprised when I checked in at the office and recognized the student — a close friend's daughter — who had been chosen to guide me to the right classroom. As we chatted on the way up the stairs, the last trace of anxiety left me.

I didn't just survive my class visit that afternoon — I had a wonderful time. Barb was warm and welcoming as always, and her students were engaged and enthusiastic. I read some excerpts from my work, discussed my creative process, and then invited questions. A lively discussion ensued, and our time together flew by.

In the intervening years, I have continued stepping out in faith, and my trust that I will always be caught has been rewarded in ways I could never have imagined. I've published four books and countless stories and articles since 2005, but my personal transformation has been even more dramatic. Not only am I no longer a timid wallflower, but I now make a significant portion of my income telling stories and speaking to audiences of all ages. I've lost count of how many schools, churches, libraries, retirement homes, theaters and other venues I've presented in over the last decade — and it all began with a single leap.

— Rachel Dunstan Muller —

The Day God Showed Up at the Doctor's Office

A God wise enough to create me and the world I live in is wise enough to watch out for me.
~Philip Yancey

"Dr. J., please come to Room 2. Dr. J., please come to Room 2." There I was, walking on an inclined treadmill for a stress test. I was at my cardiologist's office to get cleared for an upcoming foot surgery to remove a bunion. As I continued to walk, I didn't have any idea that the person they were concerned about was me!

Upon Dr. J.'s entry into the room, he looked at the monitor on the top of the treadmill with great horror in his eyes. He looked at me and asked, "Are you out of breath?" I told him that I was winded but did not feel out of breath. The technician who was monitoring me had also called another technician into the room. They both looked scared. The technician told me to stop. As I sat down, I asked him what was going on. He told me that my heart appeared to be skipping a beat.

I was terrified. Was I going to die? Would my heart give out? Was I going to be just like my mother? I started to cry. And then I was left alone in the room and I began to pray.

The nurse called me into another room to give me some medicine to open my heart up for another screening. This was the next stage in my clearance process. It felt like everyone was looking at me with pity. The tears continued to roll down my cheeks as the nurse asked me to lie back, and the machine began to take more images of my heart.

My doctor's appointment just happened to be near the anniversary of my mom's passing. She had gone to sleep one night and not woken up, a victim of heart failure. Shortly after my mom's passing, I, too, was diagnosed with heart disease. I had been under a doctor's care for approximately ten years, on and off medication, until finally I decided to stick with the medication to see just how much healing would take place. At least I would have my heart health under control.

I made a commitment to myself to speak up about heart disease and the impact on women of color. I participated in a "Couch to 5K" program offered by a local television station in my area, in partnership with the American Heart Association.

My journey was chronicled on live television each week, along with a team of other heart-disease patients. I shared my mom's story on a television commercial that went viral. But now I found myself in that doctor's office deflated, dejected and just about ready to give up.

After the nurse completed the test, I was shuffled into another room for the next stage of the clearance process. A nurse took several vials of blood, but she would not make eye contact with me. I wanted assurance that all was well. I needed to hear someone say that I was going to be fine. However, no one said those words to me. They were not even looking at me.

At this point, my husband had been sitting in the waiting room for about four-and-a-half hours. When I emerged from the back of the office, my husband looked at me with concern. He could tell that I had been crying. Before I could respond, the nurse who had given me the last test came out of the back of the office and asked if I was wearing a necklace. Before I could answer, she was touching my chest. She had a shocked look on her face, and her skin appeared to be drained of color. When I told her that I did not have on a necklace, she repeated her question. She patted my chest again.

She told me that I had to come back to the room because she wanted to show me something. Looking at the screen and the images of my heart, I could not believe my eyes. The nurse used the same office intercom to ask Dr. J. to come immediately to the exam room. Several other people came to the room, too. By this time, I was trying to control my sobbing. I ran out to grab my phone from my husband, who was confused and concerned. I told him that I would tell him more in just a second, but I had to take a picture of what the nurse had shown me.

I returned to the exam room, where several people were looking at the image of my heart on the screen. They could not believe that the image of a cross was displayed prominently on my heart! The nurse showed all of us the first images she took of my heart, and the image of the cross was not there. However, after the scare in the office, and the internal war I clearly felt was brewing inside me and my prayers in response, God showed up in that office to settle the matter. I would walk out the victor!

As I walked out of the exam room, people were looking at me, trying to make sense of what had just happened. When I returned to the waiting area, the receptionist said, "You must be somebody special. That is some Jesus stuff right there." Through my torrential flow of tears, I told her that I am not anyone special, but I know that God responded to my heart and what I felt was a desperate situation in the office. My hope was restored, and my heart was rejoicing before I left the doctor's office that day. I have since been released from the cardiologist, having been given a clean bill of health, and I have the photo documentation to prove it! I am most grateful to have had such an encounter.

—Nicole S. Mason—

Someone to Watch Over Me

Music is well said to be the speech of angels.
~Thomas Carlyle

When I was in my fifties, I was struck down by swine flu. The massive headache that came with it was relentless and almost unbearable, even to a person like me with a high pain threshold. I couldn't eat. I couldn't sleep. I couldn't escape.

After fourteen days and nights of agony, I lay in bed and realized this could be it. This could be the end of me. I didn't have the strength to endure the fire in my brain much longer. It would be a relief to surrender to the red flames and just check out. For the first time in my life, I thought about giving up.

Then the music miracle happened — a miracle tailormade for a person like me.

I have been surrounded by music all my life, ever since I picked up a ukulele and taught myself basic chords, and then progressed to guitar. I would fall asleep at night while my mother played piano downstairs in the living room. When I was a kid, my family played country music together every Saturday night. Though I had a strict bedtime, I would listen to my little transistor radio with its single earphone until the station went off the air at ten o'clock. My sister and I consumed a collection of classical music albums while we wrote stories and cleaned our rooms.

As a teenager, I was introduced to an even wider array of classical composers while taking private clarinet lessons. So, I can safely say that I know a lot of classical music by heart and recognize numerous passages of music. In fact, I enjoy the challenge of trying to identify a composer when I hear a piece of music.

But nothing prepared me for what I was about to experience.

As I lay dying—and I believe to this day that I was very close to letting go—I heard a gorgeous melody, lush with strings. It was stunning. Golden. Celestial. Unlike anything I had ever heard. I tried to identify the composer. I couldn't. Then the pain cascaded over me, taking me back down.

The music changed. I heard something like a Rachmaninoff concerto, but it was no concerto I recognized. It was better than Rachmaninoff. How could that be? I could see horses pulling a sleigh through the snow of a Russian countryside. Bells tinkling. Snowflakes, cool and glittering over my hot face. Minutes later, the pain roared back.

The music changed yet again. The passage was similar to Debussy, tropical and full, wafting a sea breeze over my feverish body. But it was no Debussy work I had ever heard.

What was this music? How could I have missed such spectacular music in my lifetime of exposure to classical composers? Surely the work I was hearing would have been the pinnacle of a composer's career and widely known.

Then the thought occurred to me. This exquisite music was not of my making. I was not recalling passages from memory. My brain was not hallucinating by feeding my favorite songs to me. No. Someone or something had decided to inspire me with music that did not exist on earth.

The revelation shocked me. Suddenly, I was aware of a supernatural force watching over me. Someone loved me enough and knew me well enough to create the exact combination to keep my spirit engaged: music and a puzzle. Someone cared enough to keep me hanging on. Was it my mother's spirit? Was it a guardian angel? Was it the Great One who gave such a gift to me—this gift of pure love? Because that's what it felt like: pure, golden, radiating love.

As the music continued, the theme changed every few minutes, ensuring that my mind would remain captivated. And it was. For the first time in two weeks, I disassociated from the iron clamp around my skull. For the first time in days, I felt my spine relax. What was a mere headache in a body, anyway, compared to the angelic concert inside my head? I lay in a state of rapture.

I don't know how long the concert lasted. I only know that I finally fell asleep. When I woke up, the roaring in my head had abated. I wasn't totally healed, but my will to live had been restored. I was going to be all right. Someone had made sure that I stayed in the land of the living. I couldn't believe that an entity had cared enough to cradle me with love at the lowest point in my life. Someone or something had held my hand when I needed it most.

One might say that the experience was a product of delirium. One might argue that my mind could have conjured all those songs, just as a human brain creates dreams. I've considered the argument many times. But if that were the case, my subconscious brain is the greatest composer of all time. I don't think so.

The musical miracle changed me forever. I was shown that I was not alone — not here on Earth or even beyond Earth. I was shown the presence of something that far surpasses the here and now. Something to look forward to.

The celestial music forged a faith inside me that to this day fills me with joy and makes me smile whenever I think about it. I am sure now that my mortal life is only part of a greater path, and others who care are beside me. I am unwaveringly, gloriously certain of this.

It is difficult to describe how the celestial music transformed my belief structure. I am blessed among people. I am certain. And years after my recovery, I am still smiling about the experience. I now know I have — just like the song says — "someone to watch over me."

— Patricia Simpson —

A Divine Promise

Never lose hope. Just when you think it's over…
God sends you a miracle.
~Author Unknown

School had just let out for the day at the small Christian school where I taught first grade. I sat at my desk preparing for the next day when Mr. Todd, our school custodian, came in as he often did in the afternoons to vacuum the floors. That particular day, he came into my classroom and announced that he needed to talk to me.

Mr. Todd pulled up a chair next to me. "I know this might sound strange coming from a man covered in tattoos, but I believe God wants me to share something with you. My wife and I were praying a few weeks ago, and God laid it on my heart that you've had complications with a pregnancy in the past. God wants you to know that everything will be okay next time."

I was slightly taken aback. I didn't know Mr. Todd very well, but I believed with everything in me that what he was telling me was absolutely from God. You see, what he could never have known, and what I quickly filled him in on, was that I had been dealing with infertility for several years. I had suffered a miscarriage just the year before. I was in the middle of receiving fertility treatments, so what he shared with me gave me hope that a successful pregnancy would soon be coming.

But it wasn't to be anytime soon. It was the fall of 2005, and I continued to struggle through infertility for several more years. In the summer of 2008, my husband, Brian, and I adopted our daughter, Isabella, after giving up on the idea of having a biological child.

We were nearing Isabella's first birthday when we got the biggest surprise of our lives. It was a Friday morning, and I was already several days late. I kept thinking that I couldn't really be pregnant after all these years. It was July 3, 2009. I only remember the date because it was a holiday weekend. I loaded my daughter into the car and drove to the store to buy a test. I came home and took it immediately. My husband called me just as I was walking back into the bathroom to read the test. I answered the phone. "Hey, babe," I said as I looked down to see two pink lines. I had a huge grin on my face, but I couldn't let on to my husband about this surprise.

I don't remember what I said to him, but I knew this wasn't news I could announce over the phone. It had been seven and a half years since we had started trying to have a successful pregnancy.

When Brian came home, I met him at the door and shoved the pregnancy test in his face. I asked him if he knew what it meant. He did, of course. We stood in the kitchen, just looking at each other and laughing. God really does have a sense of humor!

We knew two things right away. This tiny baby, not much bigger than the size of a poppy seed at this point, was a boy, and this pregnancy would continue without complication. We knew it was a boy because, back in 2004, my husband felt like the Lord had given him the name Isaiah for our future child. And we knew the pregnancy would be successful because of the boldness of a simple custodian willing to share what God put on his heart.

We didn't hesitate to tell our families because we wanted their prayers and support. However, I was hesitant at first to tell our friends. Brian wanted to tell the world, and God gently reminded me of that promise he had made almost four years earlier that everything would be okay with the next pregnancy. I decided to trust God to keep His promise, and we told everyone.

I had a very smooth, uncomplicated pregnancy. At our twenty-week ultrasound, our suspicions that it was a boy were confirmed. On March 15, 2010, I gave birth to a healthy baby boy.

— Michelle Armbrust —

Miraculous Strength

It's our faith that activates the power of God.
~Joel Osteen

One chilly December evening, I was preparing dinner. Suddenly, while setting the table, I heard a tremendous crash from the second floor. It was the kind of rare, heart-stopping noise that instantly strikes fear into a mother's heart. Even the dishes in the kitchen cupboard rattled! My seven-year-old son began screaming for help, and I raced up the stairs without even stopping to put down the dinner fork I held in my hand.

Entering my son's room, I found my frightened toddler trapped under a five-drawer wooden dresser. It had been ripped from its wall anchor. I could hear crying as I ran toward him. As I leaned over, I saw his small, bloody face and the terror in his eyes.

I pulled the large dresser off him. At that moment, I felt I could move mountains. I was fearful to look but quickly tried to assess how badly he was hurt. Pleading with him to stay still, I dialed 911 and began to pray. I prayed for the mercy that spared him and the healing he would need, given I wasn't sure of the extent of his injuries. In those minutes before the ambulance arrived, although I was in a chaotic situation with both my sons in tears, an inner calm kept me focused and controlled. I felt a strong presence keeping me steady.

After the paramedics conducted a brief assessment, it was agreed he should have a more extensive examination since this was a possible chest or head injury. A moment of pause forced me to process what had just happened. I recalled dashing up the stairs with a sense of dread as to what I would find. In only a few seconds, a lifetime of tender memories replayed in my mind. I had asked myself, "Is he still breathing?" "Are bones broken?" "How will I explain to his daddy that his small son was terribly hurt?" One moment, I was simply preparing dinner; the next, I was tearfully praying for my son's life.

En route to the emergency room, I tried to keep him calm. His nose was still bleeding, and he was complaining about the bump on the back of his head. I continued to pray for his recovery and the miracle that he survived the impact of that heavy dresser. Arriving at the emergency room, I recounted the accident. The nurses had looks of shock and disbelief as I explained it. One asked curiously, "Are you sure it was a large wooden dresser? His injuries should be much more extensive."

After testing, it was determined that he could return home. The doctor said, "Wow, he sure was lucky!"

I responded, "It wasn't luck, it was God's grace."

Back at the house, my husband straightened up the bedroom and found what we believe to be my son's guardian angel—only this angel had large wooden ears instead of delicate wings. Earlier that year, my husband's brother and his wife were on an African mission trip and had brought my son a small, hand-carved elephant as a special memento.

My husband explained that the elephant had taken the main impact of the dresser when it crashed. The elephant's tail and ear had broken off, and the dresser top had a perfectly angled chip where the elephant's back had held it firmly off the floor. The carved animal was only inches wide, but those few precious inches gave my son the space he needed to avoid terrible injury. I faithfully believe that although it was my family's mission to visit Africa, it was also the mission of that carved elephant to save my son.

Although that wooden elephant was moved from shelf to shelf on occasion, it somehow ended up resting on the dresser top where its true purpose would be served. As we've recounted this story to close friends and family, many are in shock and deeply moved by its message. Even some who claim to be non-believers have admitted openly to the fact that a higher power had a hand in protecting my son's precious life.

—Jamie J. Wilson—

Chickens from Heaven

Be an angel to someone else whenever you can,
as a way of thanking God for the help
your angel has given you.
~Eileen Elias Freeman,
The Angels' Little Instruction Book

Our granddaughter, an EMT, is living with us during COVID-19. One sunny morning, she wished us a happy day and headed to work. Shortly after she left, we received a call from her.

"Well, I hit a chicken on the way to work! Why do people in the country let their chickens wander wherever they want?"

"They're free range," I explained. "They don't cage them in at all."

"Well, I tried knocking on their door, but no one appears to be home."

Lisa described the house nearby where the chickens were and then rang off.

After breakfast, John and I headed to Tractor Supply and purchased a couple of chickens. We released them in the yard with the other chickens, hoping it was the right house.

The following week, Lisa was so busy with emergencies that we didn't see anything but the clothes she left in the washer. She was being very careful about taking off her uniform immediately when she arrived home, tossing it in the washing machine before taking a shower and going to bed.

We were awakened one foggy morning, sometime later, with another panicky call from Lisa.

"You won't believe what just happened! I just hit another chicken… and at the same house! The people never seem to be there… that, or they just don't answer the door. I don't have time for this! There are people dying out there who need me more, although I'm really sad about the chickens."

After breakfast, John and I headed to Tractor Supply. Luckily, they still had plenty of healthy chickens available. This time, we bought three, releasing them in the yard we thought they belonged in. True to Lisa's word, the people didn't ever seem to be home. Perhaps they were also essential workers.

Finally, Lisa had a weekend off. She slept through most of it and certainly deserved the rest.

That evening, she awakened bright and bushy-tailed, chattering like a magpie about all her calls at work. Listening was the least we could do.

Over steak salads and comforting music, we tactfully shared with Lisa how we had replaced the chickens, hoping we'd found the right house nearby.

Suddenly, Lisa burst out laughing.

"What's so funny?" we asked.

"Those people are going to think they've witnessed a miracle! I replaced the chickens, too!"

"How could you? When would you find time?" John asked.

"I felt so guilty. We went during our lunch break one afternoon. My co-workers thought it was a fun adventure."

Later that day, we headed out to run errands, masks in place. As we passed the "chicken house," we noticed a new sign, bold, big and beautiful.

"Get your eggs here! Heaven-sent!"

We decided not to tell the people why they had such a surplus of chickens.

After all, the world needs a few miracles right now.

— Mary Whitney —

Coincidences & Synchronicities

Inspiration from Afar

When you live your life with an appreciation of coincidences and their meanings, you connect with the underlying field of infinite possibilities.
~Deepak Chopra

The mail was late on this spring day, and it was raining. I ran between the raindrops to fetch the good or bad news of the day. Once inside and at my desk, I discovered only bills and advertisements. One of the envelopes contained a thick notice from my go-to credit-card company. As a self-published author, I depend on this particular card to purchase physical books for reselling at book events. With headlines about COVID-19 appearing all over the news media, I wasn't even sure if I could sell any books. Everything might be closed in the near future.

I began to wade through thirteen pages of the credit-card company's new policy. I wasn't sure how it was going to affect me personally. I dreaded calling for more information, but I went ahead and did it anyway.

As I waited to be connected to a customer service rep, I contemplated whether I should even write the fifth novel in my *Old Cape House* series. Did my readers really enjoy the mysterious historical stories I told? Should I take on more debt to buy my paperback books? I thought about all the author events, book signings, and book fairs that might be canceled because of the virus. When would normal life return?

"Hello, Ms. Struna, this is Thomas. May I have your account information?" "Thomas" sounded like he was in India based on his accent.

I turned down the music and repeated the information he needed.

"Thank you, Ms. Struna. How may I help you today?"

I explained my dilemma in trying to understand the new policy and asked how it would affect my future purchases.

"Please, do not worry. You will have no change."

"Are you sure? I am an author and travel frequently. I need to have access to my card at all times for big or small purchases." I laughed to myself, thinking I wasn't going anywhere for a while, at least until there was a vaccine.

"Let me reassure you. There will be no change to your card."

"Well, thank you. You've answered all my questions."

"Is there anything else I can help you with?"

"No. I'm good."

"That's wonderful. Ms. Struna, may I ask you one more question?"

I immediately assumed he was going to try to sell me a promotion or something. He was nice and had answered all my questions, so I decided to listen. "Of course."

"Are you the author of *The Old Cape House*?"

My jaw dropped. He was talking about my first novel of suspenseful historical fiction, *The Old Cape House*, published in 2013. I was stunned and I stammered, "Why, yes I am." I was still skeptical about what he wanted from me.

Thomas kept talking. "I thought it was you. I recognized your name, and when you told me you were an author, I knew it was you."

"Oh, my goodness." My heart started to beat faster with delight at the connection I was making with an unknown foreign reader.

"I really enjoyed the story so much. You changed my life."

His last comment didn't sink in right away, and I asked where he'd found the book, still trying to trip him up and find out his real reason for continuing the conversation.

"There is a wonderful used bookstore here in New Delhi, and

your cover caught my eye right away."

"You know, that's actually my house on the cover."

"No. I can't believe it. Do you really live in that house?"

"Yes, I do."

"Did you find the red bricks on top of the old root cellar behind your house, too?"

When he mentioned the bricks, I knew he was for real. He had actually read the book and was genuinely interested. I felt more at ease. "Yes, I did find the bricks but did not find treasure like my character did. As you know, treasure means different things to people and comes into our lives in many unusual ways."

"Ms. Struna, your book changed me. It changed how I look at the world. It showed me ways to be more adventuresome and to be open to new things. Thank you so very much."

I was flabbergasted at the idea I had made a difference in someone's life. I wanted to talk more, but I knew Thomas might get into trouble if he stayed on too long talking about things other than credit-card policy. "Well, Thomas, it's been a pleasure speaking with you. I hope you'll find the other books in the series so you can enjoy the continuing adventures of my curious modern-day character."

"I most certainly will. I'm looking forward to reading more."

I hung up and raced to tell my husband. Then I called all my kids living in other states about my once-in-a-lifetime phone call and its coincidental connection to a fan reader in a faraway place. Feelings of pride sprouted inside me, knowing I had made someone happy with my tales.

I calmed and had a chance to collect my thoughts. What are the odds of a person connecting with another voice on a random phone call to a customer-service call center thousands of miles away? It was truly amazing that an unexpected notice from a credit-card company had led me to an unwanted phone call, which led me to feeling inspired enough to devote the next few years to writing another 80,000-word novel.

I'd always written about and lived with the mantras of "It could happen…" and "What if…?" I knew everything appears in life for a reason, and this unanticipated encounter was a prime example. Meeting Thomas had served me well and made me eager to write another volume in *The Old Cape House* series.

In my heart, I knew the search for fulfillment and purpose was universal as we all travel different paths. And if I could have a positive influence on someone with my novels, as I had on Thomas, I was content.

His words stayed with me. "Ms. Struna, your book changed me."

Just remembering this happenstance made me giddy again. I will never forget it.

— Barbara Eppich Struna —

Drugstore Dreams

Angels love to create synchronicities because each synchronicity produces an illumination point for a soul to connect the dots on life experiences.
~Molly Friedenfeld

We are an Army family, which means we move very frequently. Once, as I arrived at a new post, two things occurred that also happened frequently: My husband was away, and the movers did not appear. Since the day was half over, I chose to drive around and acquaint myself with the new town.

At one small shopping area, I entered a gift-kitchen-housewares store and stopped dead in my tracks. Against the wall in front of me stood a huge old-fashioned apothecary cabinet, the kind one sees in old movies such as *It's a Wonderful Life*. The cabinet was about sixteen feet by eight feet; the upper section had shelves covered by glass doors, and the lower section had something like a hundred small drawers.

A feeling came over me like none ever before or since. *Déjà vu* does not remotely describe the sensation. I asked the clerk whether the cabinet was for sale. She looked at me as though I had gone mad. Frankly, I felt I had. She assured me it was not for sale. The bulk of the store's inventory was housed in it.

I left the store and spent the night in my empty house. The movers delivered our furniture and household goods the following day.

End of story, right? Not so much. I began regularly dreaming of the cabinet. Other old cabinets held no charm for me, although I am a frequenter of every antique show, sale, and thrift shop I can find. Nothing moved me like that cabinet. Somehow, I knew it was mine.

I returned to the store often over the next six years. Each time I went, I could feel the staff eyeing me, thinking, *Here we go again.* I made sure everyone had my address, e-mail address, and phone number should it ever go up for sale. They dutifully took my cards, but I was certain these went in the wastebasket.

The dreams continued, and each time the cabinet grew bigger, and I grew smaller. The quality of the dreams was hazy, as though I were viewing something through a gauze curtain.

I grew up in a small town in West Virginia. My father was a country lawyer. In a manner similar to old-fashioned, circuit-riding preachers, he visited little backwoods places on a regular basis. His clients were those who needed small claims, certificates of all sorts, wills, and bail. He did this while listening to their stories, and he heard many. Dad's law partner was a Jewish man who had escaped Europe between the world wars. He was like an uncle to me.

I frequently accompanied Dad on his rounds. He would leave me at different places in small towns while he conducted his business for the day. The good people who watched me would let me play with their kids and pets and often gave me lunch. I loved going around with him, and it gave my mother a much-appreciated break.

I had a fine childhood. I was happy, well fed, and surrounded by good people with funny accents. What I did not realize or appreciate was that my father and his partner helped several families leave Germany as World War II loomed. Small West Virginia towns were quiet and safe. My dad and his law partner helped them start businesses and make new lives.

And now, about those dreams…

One day, I received an e-mail—more than six years after my "apothecary apotheosis." The cabinet was for sale. The owner was revamping his store. If I wanted the apothecary, it was now or never.

I rushed over to seal the deal—and this is the final act.

The owner (whom I had never met before—probably avoiding me

at the behest of his staff) told me he had only scant information about the cabinet except that it had come from a German-owned drugstore in a small town in West Virginia, several hundred miles and a couple of states away. It had been in this present location for many years.

The owner told me he wanted to point out one issue. There was a handle missing from one drawer.

Suddenly, I knew! The gauze curtain lifted.

I said, "I know. If you open that drawer over there and look way in the back, you will find the handle. I broke it off accidentally when I was four years old and I hid it in there more than fifty years ago."

—Anne Oliver—

Namesake

There is always another layer of awareness,
understanding, and delight to be discovered
through synchronistic and serendipitous events.
~Hannelie Venucia

In March 2014, I joined a foreign-language-learning class. The students were from all walks of life and belonged to various age groups. On the first day of the class, during the introduction round, we learned that there were three pairs of similar names. The teacher suggested that one person from each pair use a pet name or a surname. Thus, the two Sanjays of the first pair and two Nehas of the second pair were identified.

Now, it was time for the third pair, of which I was a part. I looked at my namesake and waited for her to come up with her pet name. "Manu," she said.

This amused me and I surprised the rest of the class when I told them that I'm also called Manu at home. The teacher then suggested the surname. We were even more astonished when it turned out the girl's last name was the same as mine, as I had changed my surname when I got married. By this time, the class thought that we were making this up, and some of them asked to see our IDs!

The teacher was in a fix. The idea suggested by her, in our case, was not working, and it was getting late to begin the lessons. Sensing her dilemma, I suggested addressing us by our birth months. I told the class I was born in April. The other Manoshi announced that she too was born in April!

We finally zeroed in on numbers 1 and 2 as name suffixes.

Both of us belonged to the same culture and ethnicity, so matching names and surnames were not unusual, but having the same nickname and birth month was quite baffling.

Classes went on, and so did life. I had only enrolled for a certificate course. My session was over after two semesters, and I stopped going to the institute.

Some years passed, and then, in the spring of 2017, I got a call on my cellphone from an unknown number. Usually, I ignore such calls, but that day something compelled me to take it.

"Hi! Remember me?" the voice on the other side asked.

I instantly recognized the caller. It was my namesake. Her voice was feeble, barely audible. She handed over the phone to someone. The person told me that she had met with an accident and needed platelets. They'd tried many donors, but none was a match. She had remembered our synchronicities and wanted to check if we were synchronous in this situation, too.

When my blood was tested, it was a perfect match. Though I was happy and agreed to donate my platelets, a strange anxiety started bothering me.

After the blood transfusion, she recovered fast. Her family, especially her mother, thanked me repeatedly. She held my hand and said that had it not been for me, her daughter would have died. I was happy to have a clear benefit emerge from our synchronicities, but I thought to myself, *I want this chain to break now*.

One day when I visited her in the hospital, she introduced me to her husband.

"I wonder if his name is the same as your husband's," she said.

"No, it's different," I replied with a big smile.

"Oh, thank God for that!" She heaved a sigh of relief. "I'm using his surname now, so our names are different, too. I was hoping for this chain to break. It was getting spooky."

Did it break? I thought. She had just echoed the exact sentiment, using the same words, that I had expressed a couple of days before.

— Manoshi Roy —

Connected by Kindness

Remember there's no such thing as a small act of kindness.
Every act creates a ripple with no logical end.
~Scott Adams

"There's our guide," I said to the bus driver, pointing at a woman I'd never seen before. The guides were easy to spot. They stood near the entrance gate of Arlington National Cemetery, waiting and watching for the arrival of our big red tour buses. The driver stopped and opened the door for me to step off.

"You must be Becky," she said. "My name is Anne."

As tour director for the group of forty-three, I quickly confirmed with Anne the sites we would like to see during the next four hours: the Kennedy graves, Lincoln Memorial, Korean War Memorial, Vietnam Veterans Memorial, U.S. Capitol, and White House. Most importantly, we discussed when and where to provide a restroom break, not a simple undertaking with so many people. Then we climbed aboard to begin our tour of Washington, D.C.

After introducing Anne to the busload of waiting tourists, I handed the microphone to her and made my way toward the last seat. Conversation with a guide usually ended there since she stayed busy engaging guests, and I counted and recounted heads at every stop to ensure nobody got lost. But on that day, we managed a brief chat in the shade of an elm tree along the National Mall.

"Where are you from?" Anne asked.

"Alabama. Are you from D.C.?"

"Well, I've lived in California and Europe, but I live here now," she said. "I was born in Ohio, though."

"I was born in Ohio, too."

"Where?" she asked.

"Middletown," I answered.

"Me, too!"

"I was a Selby," I said.

"I knew some Selbys. I was a Kiefhaber."

"My doctor's name was Kiefhaber," I said.

"That's my dad!" Anne exclaimed.

My parents had told me the story all my life. I was born without a left arm, and my left leg turned inward. Right away, an orthopedic doctor placed a cast from my hip to my tiny toes. He monitored my progress closely and was able to exchange the massive cast six weeks later for a shorter, below-the-knee one. Mom said I enjoyed the freedom of the lighter cast and wore out the foot of it while bouncing in a baby swing on the front porch. That new cast also became a helpful tool for rolling from my back to my stomach. I'd fling it across my right leg, and the weight would flip me over.

Thankfully, my leg straightened out and grew strong. By ten months, I was cast-free and taking my first steps. Amidst the joy, however, my parents dreaded the final bill for the months of orthopedic care. They already struggled to make ends meet on a steel-mill worker's salary. How would they ever afford the specialist's charges for that length of treatment? When the envelope arrived, Dad took a deep breath, opened it, and stared at the amount due. Surely, it was a mistake. The bill said they owed only twenty dollars.

The doctor who showed such great kindness to my family was Anne's dad.

The chances that Anne and I would meet and discover our connection were almost zero. She was one of hundreds of guides in D.C., and I was one of hundreds of tour directors who escorted groups through the city. I don't believe those few surprising moments under the elm tree were just a coincidence. Anne needed to hear the wonderful story about her dad, and I needed to see the tale from my childhood come to life.

Anne and I are now friends, with a connection that goes beyond our hometown. We are connected by kindness—Kiefhaber kindness—which touched my family long ago and inspires me yet today.

—Becky Alexander—

Dream on My Doorstep

Life is magical, and the synchronicities continue
to fill me with wonder every day!
~Anita Moorjani

As a young, single mom raising three little boys on a preschool teacher's salary, I was always short on cash. I did manage to meet our needs, but there was never any money for extras.

But then there was my dining room. It was a drab beige from the carpet to the walls — perfectly serviceable, yet my soul dreamed of something more. This was where we celebrated birthdays and other milestones, and I longed for the room to be filled with color, reflecting the vibrancy of life and love we shared there. I started dreaming of redecorating after I fell in love with a lovely fabric at the sewing store. It featured hunter-green ribbons on a cream-colored background with a profusion of burgundy roses.

I saved up for a long time, and finally I had enough for a gallon of pale green paint, a few on-sale yards of solid hunter-green fabric for the chair seats, and a lovely pair of framed rose botanical prints from my local thrift store.

One summer Saturday when my boys were at their dad's house, I rolled up my sleeves and got busy. As I rolled paint on the walls, my dining room was transformed.

Almost.

The old beige valance hanging over my sliding glass doors looked forlorn amidst the new colors, but the fabric I had seen was just too expensive for my limited budget. I made myself a cup of tea, stood back to admire my hard work, and admonished myself to be thankful.

As I contemplated who would be my first dinner guest in this "new" room, my doorbell rang. It was my young neighbor next door bearing a leaf and lawn bag. He was often sent on delivery errands by his grandmother, a crafty old gal, who gifted me with various leftover supplies from her finished projects.

Past donations had included balls of yarn, pompoms, felt squares, fabric scraps, shiny sequins, plastic coffee-can lids, a collection of glass jars, Styrofoam forms, wooden Popsicle sticks and old crafting magazines. I wondered what her goody bag held this time.

"My grandmother said she found this in the back of her closet, but she never got to use it so she hopes you can."

"Well, tell your grandma thank you. It's very sweet of her to always think of me."

I watched him retrace his steps and then closed the door. I hoisted the bag onto my dining-room table, pulled open the drawstring and peered inside.

My breath caught in my chest, and my skin seemed to tingle.

I carefully unpacked the contents of what seemed like a treasure chest to me. Instead of gold, it contained yard upon yard of cream-colored fabric emblazoned with hunter green ribbons and cascading burgundy roses.

For a moment, all I could do was stare at the fabric. It was nearly identical to what I had seen at the sewing store. There was enough yardage for a lush valance, a table runner and several coordinating pillows for the sofas in the adjacent living room.

Hugging the fabric to my heart and feeling richly blessed, I looked up teary-eyed, filled with gratitude for a dream come true, delivered right to my doorstep.

— Sheila Petnuch Fields —

Remembering Carol Harrison

Sweet is the memory of distant friends!
Like the mellow rays of the departing sun,
it falls tenderly, yet sadly, on the heart.
~Washington Irving

Finally, I had a job I could tolerate. Thanks to my mother, I had an entry-level position working for her employer, a national defense contractor. After eight miserable years in the blue-collar world, I was working in an air-conditioned office every day, doing physically undemanding work for much friendlier managers.

But the money was no better, and it was clear that to move up I would have to go back to school. So, I took night classes at the local community college.

After a year in the data control department—and growing discouraged at the mountain ahead of me—I was promoted to the operations department, a small step up.

Most days in operations, we sat around with little to do, waiting for requests in a drab, windowless computer room. When tasks did come in, newbies like me learned them. Whenever I needed help, I usually asked Carol Harrison.

You probably know someone like Carol. She was easygoing and friendly, but clearly unhappy and discouraged with life. Despite being overqualified for this type of work, she seemed stuck. I think she supported her husband, and she was raising a son who called her at work multiple times a day.

Sometimes, I answered the phone when her son called. He always sounded sick, like a child trying to persuade his mother to let him stay home from school. His voice would moan weakly, "Carol Harrison?" And I would hand the phone to Carol. To her, it was just something she dealt with on a daily basis.

Carol and I were never close, but I took a liking to her. Despite her plight, she never caused anyone any trouble. I felt great sympathy for this good-natured person whose employer, husband and son took advantage of her.

One day, I started to pray for her to land a position for which she was qualified. Every day, I'd see Carol and say a silent little prayer, asking God to give her a better job.

Soon after I started praying, curious things began happening. For the first time since I'd known her, Carol began caring about her appearance. She wore nicer clothes, had her hair done, and got contact lenses to replace her glasses. I never told her I was praying for her, but Carol seemed to transform into a different, more attractive person. It was as if something had lit a fire inside her.

One day, I heard her on the phone angrily berating her son. I had never seen her lose her patience with him before. She'd clearly had enough of something. I remember thinking, *I hope she's okay.* But maybe her son needed it. From the stories she told me, I certainly thought so.

Soon, my prayer was answered. She landed a better position in the company, in an office with carpeting and windows, with actual work to do and more money to go with it.

We went in different directions and lost touch, but I still occasionally saw her and was happy for her.

In October 2012, Carol passed away. She was only sixty years old. I wrote in her guestbook on Legacy.com, sharing my experiences with her and how she was such a kind and decent person.

The years passed. After finally finishing school and landing a worthwhile position, I became disgusted at never getting promoted, despite taking on as much responsibility as several people who outranked me. I began applying for other positions, but for two years was rejected in multiple interviews.

One reason I was turned down was my lack of a Security+ certification. Security+ is extremely difficult to obtain. You had to take a ninety-question test about a wide range of cybersecurity subjects. With a full-time job, a part-time job writing webpages, and two young kids, I didn't think I could make time to study for this test.

Yet something kept nudging me to try.

I ordered a 500-page study guide and read the first two chapters. I started the third chapter and quit. It just seemed too overwhelming.

But I couldn't ignore the urge to get back into it. When work became slow, I tried again. I studied a chapter a day, took endless notes, and passed the practice tests. I had my wife and daughter quiz me on the hundreds of acronyms and definitions. I watched dozens of online videos to better understand the complex concepts.

For three months. Then test day came.

The test was nothing like the practice tests. It might as well have been a completely different exam. During the test, I was not only certain I would fail, but I couldn't even imagine how I'd prepare to take it again. I even almost ran out of time… rare for me. Depressed and discouraged, I finally finished the test, wondering what I was going to do next.

Then the words appeared on the screen: I passed.

It made me happy, but I felt so much like I had just been lucky that I couldn't even bring myself to celebrate.

Still, lucky or not, a barrier was gone, and I started applying for new positions. I had one interview that I thought went well, but I didn't hear back. When I e-mailed the manager asking why, he said he'd recommended me to another manager named Kelly. Kelly set up an interview with me, and she and I hit it off.

As I was driving to work on October 10, 2019, my phone rang. It was human resources informing me about an offer, with a raise and union representation. Finally, I was moving up.

Ecstatic, I arrived at work and opened my e-mails. Among them was a message from Legacy.com. The subject line read: “Remembering Carol Harrison.”

I stared at the words, my face breaking into a huge smile. After fifteen-plus years, Carol had returned the favor of a better job for me from the next world.

— Kurt Smith —

Tucker's Flowers

Grandmother. The true power behind the power.
~Lisa Birnbach

Maybe we should've known when Grandmom heard opera music playing in-flight on her trip to Italy. But I brushed it aside when my cousin told me how Grandmom had driven her crazy asking if she knew the name of the song playing that no one else seemed to be able to hear. Maybe someone next to her had the music turned up really loud. It didn't mean she was hearing things.

I ignored Grandmom's questions about what day it was. As a busy almost-adult, I barely knew myself. I figured she didn't have a job to report to, so why did it matter if she was asking if Easter had passed even though it was already August?

There was no reason to worry about Grandmom… until there was. Hearing opera music is funny; leaving the burners on for hours with nothing on the stove is not. Our large extended family was forced into the conversation none of us wanted to have. What should we do? Where would she live?

My mother and aunt agreed to split time with her as my uncles shuttled her back and forth. That way, Grandmom could stay with people she knew and still recognized. She could stay where she was loved.

In the beginning, she kept busy with little projects that were second nature for this hard-working woman. She darned socks and hemmed clothes. She knitted, watched TV, and enjoyed watching the hustle and bustle of her family.

My mother noticed that Grandmom was getting worse, but didn't mention it. I figured it out one day when I saw the blanket she was working on. It was made with leftover yarn in every non-complimentary color of the rainbow—green next to mustard yellow, coral next to red, brown next to purple. It was the kind of blanket you'd have to pay someone to hang on to, except that it would be the last of her knitting masterpieces. Despite its ugliness, it is still in my possession thirty years later because she completed it when her faculties were failing her and all she had left was the muscle memory in her arthritic fingers.

When I picked up the blanket, looking past the awful colors, I noticed nearly an entire line that she hadn't fastened on. There was a big gaping hole as if this atrocious thing had been designed as a poncho and not a blanket. That's when I knew we didn't have much longer with her.

One day, she was sitting on the front deck enjoying the first hint of autumn, a day just slightly cooler than the one before it. My mom's potted mums were radiant in the late afternoon light.

I didn't have a lot of time for Grandmom then. I was always in a rush, and she was at a point in her dementia when she didn't do much talking.

I waved as I walked by her, not intending to stop, but she reached out and grabbed my hand. I cringed a little, not sure what would come out of her mouth. Sometimes, she yelled at me for laughing too much. Sometimes, she wanted to know who that "pale girl is who's always running around."

Instead, she said, "Aww. That's nice."

She seemed like she was in a good mood, so I sat next to her on the bench. When someone you love has dementia, you must take hold of the good moods with both hands because you don't know when the next one will occur. My grandmother could sometimes be antagonistic and angry.

But Grandmom's face that day radiated a calm I hadn't seen in a long time. Her eyes shone in a far-off way like she was remembering a lost love.

"I hope you appreciate that," she said.

"What, Grandmom?" I asked, immediately regretting it because I was afraid of what she might say next.

It was such a peaceful moment, and I wanted to enjoy it without the guilt I would feel after she spouted nonsense and I got angry. I knew she couldn't help it, but how can you not take it personally when the woman you loved your entire life tells you to leave the room like she's banishing you from her kingdom?

"Tucker brought you flowers. Such a nice boy."

I followed her gaze. No one was there. I placed an arm around my grandmother's shoulders and kissed the side of her head. Her once sturdy build felt fragile under my squeeze. I didn't know any Tucker, and I could only assume she was looking at the mums and thinking she saw someone standing there.

We lost my grandmother the year I graduated from college. I dated several men over the next several years, none of them named Tucker. I wrote it off as another one of her confusions.

I went on to marry (not a Tucker), divorce, and date several others — none of them named Tucker.

Nearly twenty-five years later, I reconnected with the guy I had dated at the time my grandmother passed away. When Barton proposed and I said yes, I finally let go of the idea that I'd ever get flowers from "Tucker."

Later that week, when my fiancé came over for dinner, he brought me a bouquet of sunflowers. I was busy trying to concoct my grandmother's secret meatball recipe, and my hands were covered in goo. I asked that he get a vase out of my cupboard, and when he turned to do so, I saw the name on his football jersey.

"Tucker" had finally brought me flowers.

— Christina Metcalf —

Tidbit of Joy

Dogs are miracles with paws.
~Susan Kennedy

The exhilaration of publishing my first novel was incredible. There would be no more rewriting my opening paragraph, no more shifting scenes forward and backward in time, and no more wondering if my novel would be printed for the world to see.

Writing my first book was a tremendous journey, and I learned so much along the way. Because I chose to write a series, I would continue to spend time with my characters and get to know more about them. I found that the better I understood my characters, the more real they became on the pages, even the four-legged ones.

One of the characters I created was a Bichon Frise, the pet of one of my human characters. Because I have several dogs, I know that not all dogs are alike. Not owning a Bichon Frise, I was unsure of their behaviors. I turned to the Internet to uncover what it was Bichon Frises are like, and it helped to read and watch videos of the dogs in action. The research made my Bichon Frise appear more realistic.

My book wasn't quite finished when my family received a call from a neighbor. They had found a dog, dirty and matted, and were not having any luck finding her owner. Because we had multiple dogs in our family, our neighbors knew we understood how to take care of them and asked if we could keep her until the owner was located. When we went to pick her up, we came face-to-face with the cutest, fluffiest, albeit matted, white Bichon Frise!

We never did find her owner, so we named her Tidbit, and she became a part of our family. I had no idea I would have the opportunity to get to know a Bichon Frise close-up. Watching her antics in real life allowed me to weave bits and pieces of her personality into my character, which brought the pet Bichon Frise in my book alive. Tidbit makes me laugh and brings joy to our home every day.

I am excited that the universe brought her into my life. I am also extremely happy that I did not give my human character a pet python!

— Kelly Cochran —

A Chance Encounter

Take a small step in the direction of a dream
and watch the synchronous doors flying open.
~Julia Cameron, The Artist's Way

My diary entry from 1981, when I was eleven years old, reads: *Dear Diary, I just found out my favorite singer Jon Anderson is going to be at Madison Square Garden and I can't go to concerts until I'm 16!! DARN!!*

I still remember writing in my diary that day, sitting on my bed and listening to one of his records. Anderson is the lead singer of the band Yes, and he was to me what Elvis or The Beatles were to others. My older sister, Betsy, first introduced me to his music, which captured my imagination immediately. Jon has a unique voice; on many occasions people have compared his voice to that of an angel. I've personally never heard an angel, but there is a mystical quality to his sound that spoke to me even at that young age. That day, while I was writing in my diary, my heart was broken. I felt like I'd lost my only opportunity to ever see him.

Of course, that turned out not to be the case, and I was fortunate as an adult to go to many of his concerts.

Last spring, I got an e-mail announcing that Jon was going on tour, and one of the stops was going to be at Levon Helm Studios in Woodstock, New York. One of the ticket options was "The Ultimate

Fan Experience." Over the course of three days, ticketholders would get to sit in on the rehearsals and even have lunch with Jon. It sounded absolutely amazing, but with a $1,500 price tag, it wasn't feasible for me. I'm a big believer in fate, though, and I figured if I was meant to go, I'd somehow find the extra money to do it. I held out to the last minute, hoping for a winning lottery ticket or unexpected windfall, but they never materialized. Betsy and I purchased the regular tickets, and we made reservations at a hotel to stay overnight.

One week before the concert, the hotel called to say they were doing construction, and we'd have to find a new place to stay. "We have two options," Betsy said. "The creepy, haunted-house B&B or the cabins in the woods." I don't do creepy, so cabin it was.

The day of the concert was spectacular. The sun was shining and the sky was bright blue. I'd never been to Woodstock before, and as soon as we hit the main drag, I felt right at home with my people — tie dyes and crystals, coffee bars and restaurants, all tucked into the Catskill Mountains.

The GPS told us to turn left, then right, then left. We kept following the directions but realized we were going in circles. "Where the heck is this place?" I said. "It looks like it should be right here."

We were driving through tight, tiny streets filled with adorable cottages and lush foliage by the stream. We could see the cabins but had no idea where the reception area was.

"Okay, I'm just going to turn around in that driveway up there, and we can call the front desk," Betsy said. She pulled in while I was busy searching on my cellphone for the hotel's number.

Then, suddenly, she grabbed my leg. "There he is," she said. She said it so calmly. I looked up, and she was right. There, straight in front of us, was Jon Anderson — my ultimate musical idol — looking out a kitchen window.

"Are you kidding me?" I screamed.

He looked at me. I waved. He waved back.

"What do we do?" I said.

"We're getting out!" Betsy replied.

I screamed again.

"Don't scare him!" she admonished.

As I opened the car door, Jon came out the side door into the yard.

"Are you looking for someone?" he asked.

"Yes, YOU!" my sister and I both said.

The rush of adrenaline was so intense that it's difficult for me to even remember what was said. We explained to him that we were there for the concert and had gotten lost.

"I just switched to this house," he said. "We were down by the waterfall before, but the lights kept flickering, so we moved over here."

I was on the brink of hyperventilating, but thankfully Betsy holds up well during times of extreme emotion. She engaged him in conversation while I struggled to keep my head from exploding. He hugged both of us, and we talked about rehearsals and the plan for the evening. My sister asked if we could take a picture, and he graciously obliged.

"Okay, we won't bother you anymore," she said.

"Can you tell us how to check in?" I asked, laughing.

He gave us directions. "Go around the block and take a right. You'll see the signs."

And, of course, he was absolutely right.

— Patti Woods —

Divine Sisterhood

Family is like branches on a tree;
we all grow in different directions,
yet our roots remain as one.
~Author Unknown

I was laid off from my job and was muddling through the unemployment process and sending out resumes. I was spending lots of time on the computer, looking for a new job but also getting sidetracked. I figured that I would do something productive with my time on the computer and research my genealogy. The first website I visited was offering a free trial—two weeks at no charge. I could have fun with that.

I began delving into my family history. I reached out to some family members for help with names, and began piecing people, places and faces together. Soon, I was hooked.

There was so much information and it was so easy to do the research, so I wondered what else I could research during my free trial. I thought of my friends Diane and Donna, two sisters who were separated from their family when they were very young and eventually adopted after years in foster care. Their adoptions had not worked out well, and I always hoped they could one day find their original family.

Donna came to live with my family for a while after high school, and even my grandparents made sure to make her feel part of our group. Diane moved in initially with a boyfriend and his family, later getting a place of her own with friends.

Diane and Donna had clung to the precious memories of their early years, looking at a photo album of themselves and their biological family. Tragically, a burst pipe ruined their album.

Over the years, Diane spent thousands of dollars hiring private investigators and writing to every talk-show host imaginable asking for help. The information that trickled in over the years seemed to be all dead ends, but neither of them stopped hoping.

I didn't want to give them any false hope with my own search, but still I messaged Diane asking for their surname and city of birth to see what I could find.

With those details, the search began.

It took only twenty-four hours. Little did I know that divine intervention was going to play a part, waiting in the wings, possibly a keystroke or two away. I felt like I was on a mission, reviewing multiple files and cross-referencing information with the power of Google. Entering in some names for a search, a photograph of an elderly woman popped up on my screen. It was attached to an obituary. The woman in the photo could have been an age-progressed photo of Diane. I realized this was most likely her biological grandmother, who had just passed away two months prior. In the notice, there was a list of all her children's names and cities of residence.

I felt like I had hit the lottery.

Typing furiously, I continued to search for addresses or phone numbers to reach any of the surviving family members. And I got one! A listing with an address *and* a landline phone number.

With shaking hands, I dialed the number, and a gentleman answered. *WAIT! What do I say? Why didn't I give myself a moment to think?* And so, I began, "Hello, my name is Jean, and you do not know me, but…." Biggest clichéd sentence ever. "I believe you may be related to some friends of mine. They're sisters."

His reply made me lose whatever bit of composure I had. "Do you mean Gail?" Gail had been Donna's original name. He then proceeded to tell me that he never lost hope and always prayed he would find his girls. Not only that, their brother was living nearby. After profusely apologizing to the man for crying and blubbering my way through our conversation, I asked for his permission to give Diane and Donna his number. "Of course!" he said. Ending the call, I opened a new box of tissues to finish crying tears of joy.

The next dilemma: Diane and Donna. *Should I call them now? Can I wait until tomorrow? Maybe meet them somewhere? Am I able to contain myself any longer?*

Now. Do it now. Donna answered on the first ring. "Hi there, sweetheart. I am heading home after working a long day." I told her that, before she went anywhere, she should just sit in the car. Bracing myself, I said, "I spoke to your father."

"Bill?" she replied.

"No, your real father."

"Wow, are you sure?"

I went over my research, the steps I had taken, and how I spoke to him and had him confirm it all by providing me with a name without me asking.

Two months later, the sisters were on the road to reunite with their father and brother. Now they have aunts, uncles, and cousins, too. Plus, photos! Family photos from their childhood and new photos of everyone back together.

I was invited along, but I got a new job and I couldn't make the trip.

When we talk about how the search for their lost family ended, Diane and Donna mention my great sleuthing skills, my tenacity and that soft spot in my heart that wished for a miracle.

However, to me, most of the credit goes to their grandmother, who passed away before they could all meet again. Her photograph caught my attention and created an extremely happy ending to a long-time mystery.

—Jean Flood—

As Luck Would Have It

Learn to recognize good luck when it's waving at you, hoping to get your attention.
~Sally Koslow

Have you ever felt lucky? I have. It feels as if your choices are scripted, like confidence on steroids. I understand the skepticism because it's possible there's no such thing as luck. But one autumn afternoon I had a gut feeling that I should take a chance.

At the time, I was a stay-at-home mom, and my husband had been laid off unexpectedly. The amount of unemployment he would get was about one quarter of what his paycheck would have been. We felt anxious and unsteady.

While we plotted our next course, I was faced with the task of budgeting the few hundred dollars that remained in our checking account. That early fall night, I went to the Kroger near our house to get something for dinner. A University of Tennessee pep rally was just getting started. Kroger and UT were giving away all sorts of prizes. The cheerleaders were performing, and the local pizza shop beside Kroger had a great deal on a large pizza with two sodas for ten bucks.

I called my husband. I had registered us to win $100 in free groceries, but we had to be present to win. I told him I felt lucky. He thought I was crazy, but I was convinced that since we truly needed free groceries until one or both of us could find work, we would win them. He reminded me that not everything works out like we hope or expect.

I laughed. "Come on!" I said. "I can't cook a meal for less than ten dollars, and it's a perfect night out here. I know our little gal will enjoy the cheerleaders."

I could virtually hear the eye-rolling on the other end of the line that went along with his excuses for not driving all the way there. (We lived five minutes away from the store.)

Then I heard our daughter say, "I wanna see the cheerleaders, Daddy! Please?"

That was it. I knew I had won.

Soon, we were enjoying our pizza at an outdoor table, watching the pep rally, and listening as the various first-round prizes like twenty-dollar gift cards to restaurants and UT sports paraphernalia were given away between dance and cheer routines. When the gift table was mostly emptied of prizes, my husband looked at me in that I-told-you-so way because he was convinced that, if we did win anything, it would have been one of the lesser-value prizes.

It was nearly dark, and the pizza was gone; my husband was ready to go. Many others were also leaving as the parking-lot lights came on.

"Oh, come on," I said, "let's wait for the big prizes. I feel lucky."

My husband sighed, giving in, and finally the moment we'd been waiting for arrived. The grocery-card winner was announced and… It was not me.

I couldn't believe it. I'd been so sure. I'd felt like we would win while I was putting my name in the box.

My husband gave me an oh-well shrug, his folded lips curled upward in a sympathetic smile. I think he hoped my enthusiasm and confidence were going to be rewarded. He gathered the pizza trash to dispose of.

He looked toward the car. Before we could argue about staying until the event was completely finished, we heard my name being called over the loudspeakers. I had won the drawing for a pair of UT football tickets! My husband just about fell over. I cracked up (and may have "woo-hooed," but that could have been someone else).

"See? I told you I was going to win," I said.

The very minute I had the tickets in hand, a couple approached me. They offered me $100 cash for the tickets because they'd come to the pep rally hoping to win tickets to a home game since the games usually sold out. We all left the parking lot happy.

I had stayed, hoping to get $100 for groceries, and I did, even though it didn't happen in the way I thought it would. My husband found a job soon after that. But the money I was offered for those tickets was just enough to get us through the extra week until he got paid from his new job. It also gave us a little boost to know that things were going to be okay, even when they felt uncertain.

That was years ago, but still whenever I say that I feel lucky, my husband says, "So, do you think we should play the lottery?"

— Lorraine Furtner —

Messages from Heaven

Love Letter from Dad

While we are sleeping, angels have conversations with our souls.
~Author Unknown

Mark was the epitome of a big brother. He taught me to ride a two-wheeler he borrowed from his best friend. He showed me the best self-defense techniques for my young, scrawny frame. And he always beat me at chess and Monopoly but let me win at Hūsker Dū.

He left for the Marines as soon as he turned eighteen. I was so proud of him. I was in seventh-grade History, learning about the valiant Marcus Aurelius, and wondered if we were descendants of a Roman warrior. Would Mark succeed as a Marine and leader? He certainly had the strength of character to do so.

A few months later, our father unexpectedly passed away from a massive heart attack. Mark came home on emergency leave. I watched him solemnly step into place as a pallbearer. The weight of our father was on his shoulders.

Every so often, Dad would visit me in my dreams with a fatherly hug when I needed it or a word of encouragement. And Mark often sensed when I was having a bad day, and he would call when he knew I would be home from school to pick up.

Years later, I was away from my nuclear family, having moved to the Midwest for college. My brother was ten years into his service, and he was sent to fight in Desert Storm. Smart with logistics, he was one of the guys who could get the necessary equipment where it needed to be, when it needed to be there. My mother was the one who called to tell me about Mark's deployment. It was possible I wouldn't hear from him for months or, if tragedy happened, ever. After we hung up, I sat on the floor against my bed and cried into my knees.

I fashioned a small yellow ribbon onto a safety pin and placed it under my sheets. The tiny bump reminded me to pray for him before falling asleep each night.

I don't remember how long the war had been going on. Each day, I called home to Mom. Most days, she said she hadn't heard from him. A short note mailed weeks earlier. Never anything of depth.

Days passed. Weeks. Perhaps months.

One night, I had a dream. We were back in our old country church: Mom, my other brother, and myself. The absence of both Mark and Dad was palpable. It was one of those sensory moments that felt so tangible, so real. I can still smell the old wood benches in that hundred-year-old building. Still see the stained-glass windows sheltered by protective bars. Still hear the choir bells ringing gently from the loft.

I remember getting up from the pew. Turning into the aisle. And there stood my father, arms outstretched. Hesitant at first, I moved into his comforting arms. He held me tenderly, and in a flash of contact, I knew all his questions, and he knew all my answers.

How is college? I hate one of my instructors, and I'm not good at the math.

What's your favorite course? Phonetic Speaking and Writing Mysteries.

Are you being good to yourself? I try to, but sometimes I think I fail.

Do you know how much I love you? Yes. Hug me tighter, Daddy. Don't let me go. This feels so real. I miss you so much.

He did squeeze me tighter and planted a kiss on the top of my head before pulling away. "I have a message for Mark."

I tried to step closer, but he stopped me. "This is important. You must write to him. Tell him I love him. I'm proud of him. And this is the worst that will happen to him."

"I don't understand." I licked the salty tears from my cheeks.

"That's okay." Dad smiled with parental love. "He will." He pulled me back to him before saying goodbye.

I didn't want to let him go. Didn't want to wake up. But this was more than a dream, and I knew I had to obey it.

I lay in bed as the dawn began. My pillow was damp and my chest heavy with sobs. The nub of the yellow ribbon under my hand begged for my attention.

If my brother had strength to fight a war, I could at least muster the strength to get out of bed.

I wrote the letter, stuck it in the white envelope trimmed with blue and red edges, and mailed it off. I knew it would take a while for stateside mail to catch up to the troops, and I didn't expect an answer for perhaps two months.

I was surprised when Mark called a few weeks later. "I have a story to tell you," he said.

I loved his stories. When we were younger, he would tell me the same ones over and over. His voice, his mannerisms. My love of storytelling comes from his example.

"Yesterday, our troops were getting ready to move out, and I had to help load heavy equipment onto the transporters. We were chaining down a tank onto a truck, and to do so, because of the tracks they use, we roll them about one inch per second."

"What happened?"

"My hand was on the deck as we were securing it, and it shifted."

"Oh, my gosh!" I hollered into the phone, surprised at my intensity. "Are you okay?"

"Yeah, I'm fine." I could sort of hear him smile. "That's not the part I want you to know."

"What then?"

"It shifted onto my hand, and I couldn't get my finger out of the way. It took them a moment to move the tank and free me, and when they did, I passed out. They took me to the infirmary."

"I thought you said you were okay."

"I am." He went on to explain that he underwent emergency surgery but still lost the tip of his finger. In recovery, as the anesthesia wore off, he had a dream. "A very tangible dream. I dreamt Dad was standing at the side of my bed. All he kept saying was, 'I love you. I'm proud of you. And this is the worst that's going to happen to you.'"

"Mark," I tried to speak. "I wrote — "

"Wait." He interrupted me. "A few hours after I came out of anesthesia, they delivered the mail. And I got my letter."

I knew but needed confirmation. "My letter?"

"Your letter. From Dad."

In both our dreams, Dad was wearing the same fat tie he loved. The same creamy-yellow shirt. His hair was styled the same.

In both our dreams, we knew it was so much more than a dream.

It was our dad, bringing his family together from halfway around the world — and farther.

— Molly Jo Realy —

Sally

The tie which links mother and child is of such pure and immaculate strength as to be never violated.
~Washington Irving

We knew the end was coming; we just didn't know when it would arrive. Mom had been in an assisted-living home for almost two years, and over the past six months her health had deteriorated. We visited over our sons' spring break, and even though I knew Mom wasn't doing well, my hopes rose when I saw her. She was pale, and her once brown hair was now snow-white, but her spark, her essence, was still there.

"Come sit next to me," she ordered. "I want to tell you about Sally."

Sitting next to her bed, I reached for her hand. "Who's Sally?"

"She comes to see me once in a while. She's a little girl with blond hair. She wears a blue sweater and a red baseball cap."

I exchanged glances with my husband, who was sitting across the room. We didn't know anyone named Sally. "How little?" I asked.

"I'm not sure. About five or six. Maybe seven."

"Does she talk to you?"

"No, not really. She comes in and plays with her baseball and keeps me company."

I held my mother's hand tightly. I'd heard that when people are close to the end of their lives, occasionally they see loved ones who'd already passed, but I'd never heard of anyone seeing someone they didn't know.

"Is she nice?" I asked. I might not know this Sally, but it was suddenly incredibly important to me that this little girl be nice to my mother.

"Oh, yes, she's a nice little girl. I can tell. I had three girls myself, you know, and you were all nice little girls."

I raised an eyebrow. Mom was talking about my older sisters and myself. While I loved my sisters, none of us was what I'd call "nice." We all tended to be more on the naughty side.

Mom changed the topic to her grandsons and never brought up Sally again. We had to return to our home in Minnesota a few days later, but we made plans to come back in June as soon as school was out for the summer. In the meantime, Mom and I promised each other we'd talk daily.

"I've been thinking," Mom said one day toward the end of May. "I wasn't always there for you. I'm sorry. I owe you an apology for that."

I couldn't believe what I was hearing. "What are you talking about? You were always there for me when I needed you. What made you think that?"

"All I can do is think these days. I can't read and I'm tired of TV, so I think. And I think how I wish I'd done more for you. There wasn't enough left of me to give to you after taking care of your older sisters. I'm sorry."

"Mom, you have nothing to apologize for. Nothing. You're a wonderful mother."

"Thank you, darling," said Mom, "but I still wish I'd done more. I tell you what: When I go, I'll send you a special goodbye."

"Don't talk about it."

"I won't, but I mean it," she said. "You're getting something special."

We talked a little longer, but I could hear Mom's voice growing tired.

"I'll talk to you tomorrow," I promised, "and we'll be there next week."

"I love you," Mom said.

Around 2:00 the following morning, I was awakened by a bright stream of blue-white light coming through the bedroom window, a light I'd never seen before. It shone brightly for several seconds before evaporating. I stared at where the light had been and knew even before the telephone rang that my mother was gone. This was her special goodbye to me.

My husband got up to answer the phone. He returned to the bedroom a few minutes later. "It's your sister," he began. I stopped him, my voice thick with tears.

"I know. She just said goodbye to me. Do you think Sally came to get her?"

"I hope so."

I did, too. I hoped a nice little girl with blond hair, a blue sweater and a red baseball cap took her hand as she left this world and showed her the way to the next, pausing a moment to send me that wonderful goodbye. And I hoped Sally told her she was wrong about owing me an apology because she didn't. She didn't owe me a thing. How could she? She'd already given me the only thing that matters: her love.

—Nell Musolf—

The Language of LEGOs

Sons are the anchors of a mother's life.
~Sophocles

Our son Nick struggled with anxiety from an early age, and that struggle increased during his teen years. We pursued every form of help we could get for him, including counseling and medication, and we showered him with love and encouragement. But on June 16, 2018, only two months after his eighteenth birthday, anxiety and depression took him from us.

Over the following months, I slowly went through Nick's belongings, finding special places to display items that held the most meaning, locking away things meant to be kept private, and donating what could help someone else. There were some belongings, though, I wasn't sure what to do with, including the stack of bins filled with LEGOs. I didn't want to dump them off as a donation somewhere. They needed to go to someone who would appreciate how special they were because they'd belonged to Nick.

As I stood in Nick's room about six months after his death, I stared once again at the stack of bins. This time, a name popped into my head: Connor. A ten-year-old boy from our homeschool group, Connor had already connected with our family when his family took in our neighbor's dog. She'd become a valuable companion for Connor, who has autism and other special needs.

I wrote an e-mail to Connor's mom, Molly, asking if she thought Connor would like Nick's LEGOs. She answered with a resounding "Yes!" We made plans for me to bring them to the park where our homeschool group met. Connor thanked us sweetly at the time and then surprised us later with a more touching thank-you.

"Connor told his dad he's the luckiest boy in the world," Molly said in a message that evening. "When asked why, Connor said that it was because your family had given him Nick's LEGOs, and that must have been very hard." She went on to tell me how Connor had asked to see a photo of Nick so that he could say "thank you" to him as well. Yes, this was touching, but nothing compared to what would happen over the next year.

Molly and I met for coffee the Friday before what would have been Nick's nineteenth birthday. Unaware of the significant day, she arrived with a plastic container, which she set on the table in front of me.

"These are from Connor. This is going to sound strange, but he insisted Nick wanted him to build them for you."

I opened the container to find two LEGO creations. They were new sets, not from the stash we had given him, but my mind was blown nonetheless. The set meant for me was a boy dressed in a dragon costume for Chinese New Year. Nick's Chinese zodiac sign was the dragon. The set meant for my daughter, Anna, was a white bear holding a red heart. When Anna was turning one, Nick had picked out a stuffed white bear, and inside was tucked a little red heart. He named the bear "Birthday Bear" for her, and it has been one of her most valued possessions ever since.

None of this really sank in at the time, however, and I mentioned nothing about Nick's upcoming birthday. When I got home, Molly sent me a message with a picture of a third set Connor had wanted to build for my husband after making the other two. She could not understand his reasoning for the third set, which was a clown holding balloons and a sign that said: "Happy Birthday."

Realization came crashing in. All three sets pointed right to Nick's upcoming birthday. I told Molly everything.

She and Connor had no idea Nick's birthday was coming up. Yet, how could it be purely coincidence that Connor had picked those three sets, especially because he'd insisted they were sets Nick wanted him to build?

Over the next few months, Molly sent me e-mails with photos attached. One message said: "Look at Connor's newest creation! He said that Nick helped him with it." Even after the birthday LEGOs, I would have brushed off the comment had it not been for the nature of what he'd made: a tractor. Maybe it was something any ten-year-old boy would choose to build, but Nick's job for the last year of his life involved driving a tractor much like the one Connor had constructed. Tractors like that had become inextricably connected to Nick in my family.

Another creation was even more specific: a vacuum cleaner. This was not at all typical for a ten-year-old boy to build. So why would Connor choose that? Part of Nick's fears had included germs, and he was the only teen boy I knew who had three different kinds of vacuum cleaners in his room. If a vacuum cleaner didn't scream "Nick," I don't know what would.

But it was more than just what Connor built with the LEGOs at Nick's urging—it was the fact that he was using blocks to send messages. When Nick was only four years old, I got the news that I would need major surgery to remove a benign tumor. The placement of the tumor was a concern, and I was quite scared. One day, I sat on the couch silently praying for a sign that everything would be okay. Specifically, I asked for a rainbow. (I'd had an amniocentesis while pregnant with Nick and saw a double rainbow when I left the doctor's office, which I felt was a sign. Sure enough, the amniocentesis results were completely normal.) Nick had no idea what my prayer was even if I hadn't been praying silently, as he was in his room playing with a set of building blocks that snapped together with bristles. But the moment I opened my eyes, Nick walked into the room and held out his hand.

"Mommy," he said, "I made you a rainbow to make you happy."

With my prayer answered so quickly and clearly, my fears completely disappeared.

For years, I recounted that story to Nick. I told him over and over how he'd reassured me with that little multi-colored arch of blocks. I shared the story in an anthology several years later. For the rest of Nick's time here, it remained one of the most vivid moments of my life. Nick knew how much it had meant to me, and it was a connection I would make that pointed directly to him and no one else. So, there is no doubt in my mind that Connor's creations really were messages from Nick, speaking a language he knew only I would recognize.

—Kat Heckenbach—

Our Feathered Messenger

Remember that although bodies may pass away, the energy that connects you to a loved one is everlasting and can always be felt when you're open to receiving it.
~Doreen Virtue, Signs from Above

I was never much of a believer in messages from beyond—not until the summer of 1986. A few years earlier, my husband and I had visited my father-in-law in England. His wife had recently passed away, and he seemed anxious to talk about his own mortality. As we gazed at the flowers in the garden, he explained, "You know when I pass, within a couple of days after my death or sooner, you will be visited by a little bird. He will come into your home, and you will wonder how it could possibly happen."

My husband and I looked at each other, not saying a word and not wanting to discredit my father-in-law. "I know you both think that I am daft, but this visit will come to pass. Until it happened to my good friend, I did not believe it either. I told him that he was crazy. I thought that he had had one too many at the pub. But I swear it is true that it really happened!"

We continued visiting with Dad, and he brought up the subject periodically. Each time, he delivered his message with the same amount of urgency. Even as we were leaving to go home, his parting words were, "Don't forget the wee bird. It is a sign, and it will happen to you." We returned home and forgot about his words for the time being.

One morning a few years later, my husband was greeted by the chirping of a tiny bird in our kitchen. "Gail, come quickly. You aren't going to believe what I have just found!" Strutting around the floor was this little creature. It seemed somewhat bewildered as to where it was, but it did not appear scared. "Could this be the bird your dad spoke about? Was this the sign he predicted would happen?"

We had no idea how this small bird had managed to enter our home. This little fellow should have been very intimidated coming into our house as we lived with four cats. It was extremely fortunate for our visitor that none of the cats appeared. "How did it ever manage to get inside?" I marveled. All the windows and doors were closed. Yet there it was!

My husband and I spent the next several minutes trying to coax our feathered friend to come closer. It was small, brown and looked like a finch or a sparrow. For some time, it continued to chirp and strut back and forth on the kitchen floor.

I watched as my husband Tony gently spoke to it. "It's alright, little guy. I will help you get outside." Eventually, my husband was able to pick it up and cradle it in his open hands. Tony continued to gently stroke the bird while I unlatched the doors leading outside to our garden.

Carefully, my husband raised his hands, allowing our visitor to fly to its freedom. We were in awe at the experience that had just unfolded before us. I could not help thinking that what we had witnessed was indeed the sign that Dad prophesied.

The shrill ringing of the telephone jolted us back to reality. It was my husband's sister from England. "I have bad news: Dad died early this morning. I found him when I went to take him his tea." We were in shock. He had not been ill.

From that moment on, I became convinced that Dad had visited us on that warm summer day. He was letting us know that he was okay and we were loved. I will always be grateful for our feathered messenger and the wonderful lesson he taught me.

— Gail Sellers —

The Purple Bunny

Deeply, I know this, that love triumphs over death.
My father continues to be loved, and therefore
he remains by my side.
~Jennifer Williamson

Deep inside the toybox at my mother's home was a raggedy purple bunny. It had been well-loved by many children before it became part of the collection of toys that my mother kept handy for my nephew.

Once a talkative chap, the poor bunny only spoke now when one removed and then reinserted its battery. Then and only then would it chirp a heartfelt, "I love you." My parents had tried to fix it, but to no avail.

This particular afternoon, I sat at my mother's table. Both of us were putting on a brave face for the other. The unthinkable had happened only a couple of weeks prior: My dad had suffered an aneurism. He hadn't survived.

Losing my dad had been the most difficult thing I had ever faced. At almost thirty-nine, I was still every bit the daddy's-little-girl I'd always been. And my mother had lost her soulmate. Her grief was palpable, and I was grieving not only the loss of my dad but the loss of part of my mother as I watched her pain, helpless to ease it in any way.

So, there we sat, coffee before us, each attempting to comfort the other, when it rang out.

"I love you."

Tears filled my mother's eyes. "There's yours!" Her exclamation was gleeful. "There's yours!"

Confused, I stared at her. As she talked, my eyes filled with my own tears.

She'd been alone, just a day or two after I'd finally moved back into my own home and left her in the house she'd shared with Dad for decades. She'd been thinking of him, she told me, when the rabbit spoke to her from somewhere beneath the other toys.

"I love you."

No one had touched it. No one had reinserted its battery to activate some fractured electrical connection. It simply called out to her.

A few days later, my brother had stopped in to visit. He'd barely arrived and was settling in at the table with Mom when the rabbit sang out.

"I love you."

And now, on this day, as my mother and I sat together, the rabbit had made its final proclamation.

"I love you," it told me.

Had Dad found a way, before his spirit fully flittered away from its earthly home, to tell us all one last time how much he cared?

I have no proof other than this: Three individual "I love yous" gave comfort to each of us. But especially to Mom, who received not only the reminder that he loved her beyond measure, but that he loved the children that she had borne him. Her grieving heart received an unexplainable balm from that raggedy stuffed bunny.

And in the twenty-plus years since, no matter the circumstances, it has never uttered another word.

— Tammie Rue Elliott —

The Christmas Code

And, when you want something, all the universe conspires in helping you to achieve it.
~*Paulo Coelho,* The Alchemist

For what would be her final Christmas, my mother-in-law, Pam, bought me some T-shirts. I was disappointed to discover they didn't fit and had to be returned, which I did, receiving store credit. I decided to use the store credit to purchase the Blu-ray of a film I'd been wanting; that would be my present from Pam.

Sadly, finances were not great with it being just after Christmas, and when I got to the checkout, I found I had to put things back as I didn't have enough money to pay for everything. The Blu-ray was a high-value item amongst all the little groceries, so it had to be sacrificed.

Shortly afterward, Pam passed away from liver disease. The item I'd wanted to buy was forgotten amid funeral preparations and the like.

Toward the end of February, I went shopping again and remembered how I still hadn't picked up the movie. It had been on sale for more than two months at this point and was nowhere to be found, replaced by newer releases. I searched the other part of the store that had movies — nothing there either.

I started searching through all the shelves. I was about to give up when I wondered if maybe it had been misplaced. Sure enough, in entirely the wrong section, I found what appeared to be the final copy in the store, complete with the code for a digital version, which was the main reason I wanted this specific release.

Pleased that my diligence had yielded results, I placed the item in my cart and headed for the checkout. I finally had what was the last present I'd ever receive from Pam. This made me tear up a little. While we didn't always see eye-to-eye, I missed her a lot and hoped she knew I was sad she was gone.

I returned home and grabbed my movie from the bag. I tore open the packaging, eager to use the download code before it got lost in a pile of papers.

I took the slip of paper from the case, followed the instructions and started typing in the code. As I got to the final four characters, I felt chills, not quite believing what I was seeing. I recalled the struggle I'd had to find the movie, arguably my last chance to find a copy with the code. It had seemed to be the final copy in the store, placed in completely the wrong section. I held the code in my hand, and there it was, plain as day. The final four characters read: PAM0.

I finished entering the code and just stared at the slip of paper. I showed my wife and kids, and their eyes grew wide. A math check at the time estimated that the odds of those characters appearing in that sequence were astronomical — in the millions, at the very least.

Thank you for the final present, Pam!

— Steve Coe —

Dad's Promise

Goodbyes are only for those who love with their eyes.
Because for those who love with heart and soul
there is no such thing as separation.
~Rumi

I watched Dad attempt to cut the ribeye, his wrinkled hands struggling. Two months earlier, we had celebrated his ninety-eighth birthday.

He took a break, fumbling for a tissue to blow his nose. I looked at the painting of cowboys on the restaurant wall and back at Dad, so old, so frail. The contrast between the vigorous cowboys and Dad struck me.

I swallowed hard. "Dad, someday, after you pass, I'm going to want you to keep in touch, you know?"

Dad took my mention of his death in stride and set down his fork. "How did you girls say your mother came back?"

"As a great blue heron. Whenever we were stressed or needed guidance, we would see a heron. She also usually shows up when we all manage to get together."

He nodded, a slow, solemn confirmation. "That's what I'll do, too."

Later that week, Dad's minor sniffles became pneumonia, kicking his congestive heart disease into high gear.

Three weeks into his battle to recover, he roused. "Is my brother...?" He labored to breathe. "Is Phil still alive?"

"He's fine," I replied. My body tensed. I realized I didn't know for sure. Dad and Phil hadn't been in touch since Phil grew hard of hearing. Worried I'd inadvertently misled Dad, I texted my cousin, who replied with somber news. Phil had entered hospice care. I updated Dad. "Phil is sick and trying to get better, just like you are."

The look of stoicism in Dad's tired eyes told me he knew about his younger brother. My gut clenched. How had he known?

Odd, impossible and inexplicable. I interpreted it as an important communication, reassuring me that my father's passing was not happening in a vacuum. My burden to help Dad cross over with a sense of peace and love somehow felt a bit lighter.

At home that night, I slept soundly until a sense of urgency jolted me awake at dawn. Heart racing, I felt called to go to Dad. Avoiding the sign-in desk at the front, I sneaked in the back door of the assisted-living center and sped to his room.

Dad, attended by a hospice nurse, lay motionless. The nurse stepped out, leaving me alone with him. Holding Dad's unresponsive hand, I felt alone and sensed his spirit was readying itself for the journey or perhaps was already gone.

A few moments later, his breath stopped, and my world, the space my father and I had inhabited together, turned still. All my senses heightened as my soul searched for the essence of Dad's, trying to feel his life energy. I found only a void and sat holding his hand until my sisters arrived.

Phil, who had emulated his big brother all his life, passed away in an eerily similar manner a week later. That same week, my sister Trish and I were driving to a writing workshop.

"It's comforting to think Dad is with his brother," I said. She nodded.

"Look." She pointed to a pond. A blue heron stood like a stately sentinel beside two ducklings paddling nearby.

I let out a small gasp. The back of my neck tingled, and I understood. Dad was glad my sister and I were together, as were he and his brother.

A few days later, I was dumbfounded to learn more about the strength of Dad's abiding connection from beyond. At family gatherings, Dad had loved that his great-grandsons and their cousins all called him simply "Grampa." One of them, a two-and-a-half-year-old, had rarely spoken an intelligible word, but on the morning when Dad died, he had stopped playing and said clearly, "Bye-bye, Grampa."

A month later, the scheduled date for my summer trip to the Appalachian Mountains arrived. It didn't feel right to have fun while missing my father. I felt guilty that I was now free to travel without worrying about Dad's care. No longer "on duty," I could leave my cellphone turned off. Dad wouldn't be needing me.

After driving nine glum hours, my husband Dale and I arrived. Our cabin was nestled deep in the woods, normally a place of peace and joy, my spiritual sanctuary. This time, all I wanted was to plop onto the couch and do nothing.

My husband carried in the last bag and looked at me planted on the couch. He insisted we go outside, maybe to walk around the nearby lake.

We walked side by side. He showed me a deer track in the mud. I didn't care. He pointed out where the beavers had gnawed down a tree. Usually, I would join him, eagerly searching the water in hopes of seeing a beaver or two. Instead, I trudged on next to him, apathetic and focused only on my grief.

A huge splash shattered the quiet. I turned toward the lake in time to catch a long-legged blue heron lift off from his noisy touch-and-go maneuver and soar across the water. As if my brain couldn't comprehend what my eyes had seen, I asked Dale, "Was that a…?"

He nodded. "A blue heron. You know, it's been over ten years, and we've never seen one up here."

I hugged my husband and held tight. The iron clamp around my heart released, freeing me of sorrow and guilt.

Our return walk, steeped in tranquility under a sun-dappled canopy of green oak leaves, overwhelmed me. In gratitude, I stopped and gazed up to the majestic sky, silently thanking my father.

Months later, I still had a tough time not turning into the parking lot when I drove by his assisted-living center. I had been Dad's go-to person for twenty-five years, ever since Mom's death. The habit of helping him deal with every aspect of life — replacing his old easy chair, doing his taxes, buying family gifts for him to give, and handling myriad other concerns—was not easy for me to discontinue. My life was not back to normal because my normal had always included Dad.

Thinking of Dad was so ingrained that I picked up the phone to remind him to watch his favorite football team. My throat tightened when I remembered he was gone. Fatigued by an unexpected wave of sadness, I fell onto my bed.

My husband's voice interrupted my wandering thoughts. "Hey, let's take a walk."

After a mile or so, we settled onto the riverbank. With my head in his lap, we listened to the water rushing over rocks. The cooling shade of the towering, moss-draped cypress trees soothed me.

A loud squawking drew our eyes upward. Above us flew a blue heron, his elegance unmistakable. Dad's message could not have been clearer. This time, I accepted that my father was gone from this earth but happy, and he wanted me to be happy, too. The bird's widespread wings angled gracefully, and he coasted across the blue sky, lifting my soul.

I gave my husband a knowing smile. Dad always did keep his promises.

—Wendy Keppley—

The Visit

Mother, the ribbons of your love
are woven around my heart.
~Author Unknown

My mother-in-law lay in a coma, hospitalized after a massive heart attack. Her doctor said even if she did wake up, there was only a small chance she would not have brain damage. The family considered taking her off life support, but no one wanted to make the call. I didn't blame them.

As I stood by her bed, I rubbed her arm lightly and thought back to when we first met. I was only sixteen years old. Her son and I met in church, were friends for a time, and later dated and got married. From the beginning of my marriage, it was easy to call her Mom. My own mother had moved across the country, and I welcomed another mom to spend time with. Whenever I heard a friend complain about her mother-in-law, I considered myself lucky. I not only loved my mother-in-law; I liked her.

Mom was gentle and kind and had an easy laugh. We could talk about anything and everything. She was creative and talented. Her home looked like something from a magazine. Her yard and garden caused drivers to slow down as they passed. Her home-sewn clothes looked as if they were made by a tailor.

Only one thing about Mom was a bit odd—she had a doll collection. I don't mean two or three dolls; I'm talking about so many dolls on her sofa and chairs that no one could sit down. In her hobby room, doll heads, arms, and legs lined the shelves. She would put them together, buy wigs, and sew beautiful outfits. I couldn't understand why a grown woman would have so many dolls in her house, but Mom loved showing me her latest creation. She named each doll and would hold it up proudly, beaming like a small girl.

Mom and I loved musicals, and when she asked me to see *Annie*, I eagerly agreed. The girl who played Little Orphan Annie was very good, and I especially enjoyed the music. When it was over, I clapped enthusiastically and turned to Mom. I was surprised to see her crying. The musical didn't seem sad enough to prompt tears. Over lunch, she told me the play reminded her of when she was little.

"My mother put me in an orphanage when I was six years old," she said.

I was shocked. "Why would she do that?"

"She was single and had lost her clerical job. The only job she could find was a live-in nanny and housekeeper. But they wouldn't consider someone with children. She thought an orphanage was the answer."

"How long were you there?"

"It was supposed to be for a few months until Mother could find another job, but it stretched into two years. I hated being there. Kids made fun of me and said I shouldn't be there because I had a mother. They taunted me, saying my mother didn't want me."

She went on to tell me that a Christmas present arrived for her one day. She was so excited that she forgot to do one of her assigned chores. A matron — Miss Jane — made her open it right then.

"It was a sweet little doll," Mom said. "I held it up. Miss Jane grabbed it, and it slipped from her arms, falling onto the floor, the head cracking."

"I'm so sorry you had to go through that, Mom," I said, tears in my eyes. "Is that why you have so many dolls?"

She nodded. "I guess."

I never questioned her hobby after that and finally understood how much dolls meant to her.

Years later, when her son and I divorced, I thought maybe Mom wouldn't want to see me anymore. I was wrong. We still got together, either just the two of us or with my daughter. I bought a house and invited her over to give me decorating advice.

As we did a walk-through, she offered tips, and I wrote them down. Then she went to her car and came back with a box. "A housewarming present," she said.

Inside was a doll dressed in a white satin gown with a gold headband that looked like a halo.

"I named her Angel," Mom said. She sat her in a chair in my bedroom. "She'll watch over you in your new home."

I gave Mom a hug. "Angel is perfect."

So many memories floated before me now as I sat in her hospital room. Visiting hours were ending, so I left.

My daughter was with her dad that night, and I was alone in my house. I tried to sleep but was having trouble. I read and drank a cup of tea. Finally, I drifted off. In the middle of the night, something woke me. My bedroom was glowing, especially Angel. I stood up and looked out the French doors. Silvery moonlight bathed the garden. I felt something that's hard to describe — a feeling I had never experienced before. Abundant joy. Intense euphoria. Overwhelming love. I knew it was Mom. I knew she was happy.

In the morning, my ex-husband called to tell me what I already knew. Mom had passed during the night. No one had to make a decision about taking her off life support. She left this world on her own.

I looked at Angel. "Thank you for your present, Mom, and thank you for visiting me."

— Wendy Hairfield —

Voice-Over

To her, the name of father was another name for love.
~Fanny Fern

My father, a soldier in World War II and a gifted writer, wrote my mother every day while he was in the Army. She kept his letters and transcribed them. They tell of his day-to-day life as a soldier and show two people in love, separated by the war in Europe. After he came home and as we grew up, he communicated his concerns about my sister's and my behavior through her.

"Your father is troubled," my mother would begin and then point out our transgressions. When I was four or five, she related his complaint about my babyish behavior when guests were visiting. Later, as a teenager, I arrived home from a friend's party at 12:15 a.m. and, in the dark of the hallway, my mother let me know, "It's too late. Your father is going to be very upset. He'll talk to you in the morning."

When I woke up, morning had arrived, and he was out playing his Sunday game of tennis. All morning, while he played, I worried about his coming home to talk to me. What would he have to say? He arrived around noon, stopped at the doorway to my room and, his tennis endorphins having kicked in, said, "Oh, Rosanne, when did you get home?"

Years later, when I first thought about getting his Army letters published, he was working at a Madison Avenue advertising agency, a "Mad Man" in today's terms. I asked him to write what he left out, what he hadn't written about during the war, to fill in the gaps. He started, but his old nightmares returned, and he couldn't continue. He died a year or so later at the age of seventy-three.

Six or seven years after that, I picked up his letters when I was "on hiatus," common downtime between film shoots in Los Angeles. While I was waiting to go back to work, I started to think about turning the letters into film form—a documentary.

In the next weeks, I began to lay it out, using the letters to follow his journey and getting footage of places he'd been and things he'd seen from the National Archives. By now, out of work, I was paying for things on my credit card but stayed focused on the documentary. I arranged a shoot in New York to film my mother, now eighty-three, talking about her reactions to his letters. In putting it together for a rough cut, I got the idea of having my twenty-six-year-old son narrate, to be my father's voice, the voice-over for the film. My father was twenty-six when he wrote those letters.

We recorded my son reading the letters, but it didn't sound right. He wasn't an actor. Did I have to tell my sweet son he was fired and feel guilty, or did I ignore it and confront my doubts every time I heard the narration? But the voice had to be right.

I flew back East and visited my mother at her nursing home. She knew I was making a documentary about the letters, but she didn't know anything more.

My mother believed in reality. "Things are what they are," she would say. She and I were talking in her room when she paused, looked at me and said, "You know, I had a psychic experience."

She's never used those words before, I thought.

"Your father is unhappy about a part of the documentary. You are very undecided about it, too."

I flew back to Los Angeles and hired an actor for the voice-overs.

When it was finished, the documentary was shown in thirteen film festivals and on PBS. It won several awards.

Thanks, Dad.

—Rosanne Ehrlich—

Dad's Okay

Pay attention to your dreams — God's angels
often speak directly to our hearts when we are asleep.
~Eileen Elias Freeman,
The Angels' Little Instruction Book

My dad battled cancer for nearly seven years. I can't remember what my life was like before his diagnosis. What I do remember is the repeated heartbreak. Over those years, the news got worse and worse. I heard phrases like, "Your dad needs to go through chemo and radiation before he can have surgery." "Your dad's lung was punctured during surgery. We don't know if he will make it." "Your dad's cancer came back."

And then, when he couldn't face the pain and sickness of chemo, "I can't go through treatment again."

My dad passed away in the fall of 2019, two years after they gave him six months to live. He made it to my wedding, walked me down the aisle, and danced with me at the reception. He was that strong — he pushed through to see me get married.

I stayed at my parents' house during his final days. He went through hospice at home. One day, I was sitting with him, and I could tell he saw someone. He then raised his hand and waved at the empty room. He pointed and told me he was "saying goodbye to him."

There was no one else in the room. I know there is a scientific explanation for this, and it is considered normal when people will soon pass away, but I don't believe that my dad was just having a hallucination. It was too peaceful and appropriate to be an illusion. He knew that I was there, but someone else was in the room.

During the next couple of days, I saw him acknowledging and smiling at someone I could not see. I choose to believe that his deceased family and friends were helping him prepare for his journey.

I was not there when he finally passed. The days afterward were a blur. I did not know what to do. I would frequently collapse on the floor in tears. I was only thirty and it seemed so unfair that we had so little time together. He would never get to meet his grandchildren, and he was such a kind person that it didn't seem fair that his time on earth was so short. I was angry.

A couple of weeks later, I saw my dad in a dream. He was on a crowded street, wearing his trucking jacket and baseball hat. He smiled at me and waved. It was only a small moment, but it was enough. I knew that he would never be completely absent from my life. It's hard to describe the experience, but it wasn't a normal dream. My memory of the dream is crystal clear. It has never faded. I vividly remember his smile and the warmth in his eyes.

Ever since I had that dream, I've felt at peace with my dad's passing. Even though he isn't physically with me, he is always with me. And he was telling me he was okay.

— Monica McClure —

How Did That Happen?

Last Words

Angels descending, bring from above,
Echoes of mercy, whispers of love.
~Fanny J. Crosby

I have been a firefighter and paramedic for many years, and I know we take chances every time we respond to a call. We all understand we are testing fate every single day as we work to snatch people back from the jaws of death or disaster.

One particular day while working in Louisville, Kentucky we responded to an elderly woman who was having a heart attack. She was in her upper eighties and terribly ill. While working on her, I was talking with her, as I do with all my patients, about what I was doing as well as all kinds of subjects, whatever came to my mind at the time. I was down in the space between the bench seat—the long seat on the side of the ambulance—and the stretcher. This was a small opening not meant for people of larger sizes; luckily, I could still fit there.

As we were driving with lights and siren to the hospital, and I was busy working on the lady, a horrific booming noise came out of nowhere at the same time that I felt a huge pain in my side. Suddenly, our ambulance was on its side, and I was stuck in that small space, basically lying on top of my patient from the waist up. All this, I learned later, was the result of an elderly lady running through an intersection with her old Buick and T-boning our ambulance.

As we lay there, my partner, though injured, asked, "Are you okay?"

I said, "Yes, do what you have to do." He exited the unit and started to care for the patient who hit us. While this was going on, I asked our primary patient if she was okay. She stated, "I'm fine, honey. Are you okay?"

I replied, "Yes," as I continued to work on her.

I couldn't move much because I was still trapped by the bench seat, but I continued to talk to my patient, reassuring her that we would have her at the hospital as soon as possible. This sweet lady said that she understood and urged me to make sure that I was okay. I advised her that I was and continued to work.

When responding ambulances and the fire department arrived, my colleagues began to extricate us. Due to the way our ambulance was positioned and how it had collapsed, it took a long time for them to cut us out. All the while, I was talking to my patient and working on her. As she was finally being removed from the unit, I apologized for this happening and told her that she would be at the hospital momentarily. She smiled and said, "Honey, it's not your fault."

I wished her well and told her I would pray for her fast recovery. She smiled and said, "Please make sure you are okay. I'm heading home. I'll be okay."

I was then taken for evaluation at the hospital. I was released with a clean bill of health—just bumps, bruises, and soreness. When I got back to the office, I was advised that my patient had passed away. I asked, "When did she pass? Did she make it to the hospital?"

My supervisor asked worriedly, "Bill, are you sure you are okay?"

I answered, "Yes. Why?"

He said, "Just make sure you put everything in your report. The coroner will need it as soon as you finish it."

While I was finishing my report, the coroner arrived at our station headquarters. We talked as I finished my report. He said, "She passed on impact."

I said, "I spoke with her through the entire event until she went with the other ambulance."

He asked, looking at me with concern, "Bill, are you sure you are okay?"

Getting agitated, I answered, "Yes. Why does everyone keep asking me that?"

He responded, "Bill, the other crew members, including your partner, confirmed that she passed on impact. When your partner asked if you were okay, he said it took a little bit for you to respond. Also, when he exited the ambulance, he checked you out, then checked out your patient, and then went to work on the patient in the Buick."

Again, I stated, "You all are crazy. She was talking to me, encouraging me, asking me if I was going to be okay."

Her autopsy confirmed that she did pass on impact. So, who was talking with me all that time?

I believe my patient told God, "Hold on, I'll be there in a minute. This boy who was watching over me now needs me to watch over him."

I was so blessed to have this sweet angel by my side who kept talking to me. Godspeed, you truly were my angel.

— Bill Hess —

The Angels Always Come

In their eyes shine stars of wisdom and courage
to guide men to the heavens.
~Jodie Mitchell

For many years, I worked in the marketing department of a continuing care retirement community (CCRC). A CCRC provides five levels of care to the senior population: independent living, assisted living, memory care, sub-acute rehabilitation, and skilled nursing. Not surprisingly, the hospice area of the skilled nursing unit is usually quite busy, and I have the utmost respect for the direct caregivers who work in that challenging environment.

It's no wonder that many of these "angels," as I referred to them, needed to take a break after two to three years of caring for patients at the end of life. Many of them would transfer to the assisted-living area or memory care for a few months and then return to working with hospice patients. Though most of our Certified Nursing Assistants looked upon their work as a calling, not a job, the work in the hospice unit could be quite draining, psychologically, physically and emotionally.

Overall, however, our community was a good one, 5-star rated from Medicare, newly renovated, and located in a wealthy suburb. The unit was fully staffed, the employees were paid well, and the residents had private health insurance.

A good friend and colleague of mine worked in a similar senior facility, rendering direct care to hospice patients. Like ours, hers provided end-of-life care, but it was located nearly forty miles away in a rural area, surrounded by farms. There were even horses grazing in the neighboring field.

Like ours, the community was 5-star rated, and while the facility was clean and well-maintained, it was nearly fifty years old. In addition to needing an aesthetic face-lift, it required a technology overhaul. While the employees were dedicated, the staffing could have increased as well as the salaries.

When my community had a job opening in the hospice area, I immediately called my colleague and encouraged her to apply for the position. To me at that time, working in a modern facility closer to home for more money was a no-brainer. I thought she would jump at the chance. That's before I realized there were more important things than high-tech, an easier commute, and a fatter paycheck.

My colleague was extremely gracious, thanking me for thinking of her, but told me in no uncertain terms that she had no desire to leave her current position. When I pressed her for an explanation, she just smiled, and invited me to visit her on the job at my earliest convenience. A month later, I had an opportunity to do just that.

Her community was an hour away, and I must admit it was a beautiful ride. When I pulled into the parking lot, I marveled at the countryside and noticed that the horses from the farm next door were standing, not grazing, at the fence separating them from the nursing facility. My colleague was waiting for me outside the visitor's entrance.

I asked her about the horses next door. Why are they standing so still and in a perfect line? Why did they seem to be almost motionless, like statues standing at attention? Why were they so calm?

My colleague offered me what I referred to long ago as her "Mona Lisa smile." Then she asked me if I had any idea why she would never consider another job, why she never seemed to suffer from "burn-out," and why she never needed a sabbatical or a transfer to another department after working with hospice patients for nearly twenty years. I had no answer.

Then she glanced over at the horses. "Because of the horses," she said.

I exclaimed, "What do they have to do with you and the hospice patients?"

Then she walked me inside the hospice unit. "One of our patients passed away an hour ago," she said. "Several hours before he died, the horses, who had been grazing in a distant field, started making their way over here to the common fence. Before he died, all seven were lined up, quietly keeping a vigil.

"The funeral director will be here soon," she continued, "and the horses will keep watch until the body is safely removed. It happens every time someone makes their final journey."

Her words stunned me. I returned to the window, and the seven horses were quietly waiting by the fence. The undertaker arrived several minutes later, and the body was removed through the back entrance. The horses continued to stand guard. It wasn't until the car disappeared that the horses silently dispersed to the neighboring field.

"They do that every time someone passes away," my friend reported. "It's like they have a sixth sense. As I said, they actually assemble at the fence before the person passes away. It's like they see the angels coming for another soul. It's not a scary thing. It's actually quite comforting."

At that point, the horses seemed almost mythical to me, and I recalled a school day in my distant past learning about Greek mythology. I said, "I remember reading how the ancient civilizations used to think that horses pulled the chariot of Apollo, the sun god, across the night sky every morning. The chariot was followed by the sunrise every morning, beginning a new day."

Again, that Mona Lisa smile from my friend. "Is this really all that different?" she asked. "These same horses of today are doing the same task as their ancient ancestors. For those souls ready to leave this world, it is like the night sky. Then the horses come. They stand still and wait. Instead of waiting to pull the chariot across the night sky, they wait for the angels. The angels always come; there is always a new light, a new day."

— Barbara Davey —

When Change Blew In

Each day offers us the gift of being a special occasion
if we can simply learn that as well as giving,
it is blessed to receive with grace and a grateful heart.
~Sarah Ban Breathnach

It was not a good year. In 1999, I was newly divorced and trying to keep up with a mountain of bills. In the past, weekly trips to the grocery store involved a bulging cart and a credit card. Now, forty dollars in cash, a calculator, and crossed fingers were the new normal. My two children, ages six and nine, received birthday-party invitations by the dozens, but the required gifts were proving to be such a strain on the budget that I had to RSVP "no" to all except the closest of their friends.

Lots of people helped in small but much-appreciated ways. After hearing of my difficulties, my church graciously waived the fee for the kids' religious education, a neighbor fixed our lawnmower, and a friend dropped off a box of gently used clothes, all in my children's sizes. Still, despite my salary and the child support I received, the bills piled up: mortgage, car payment, insurance, legal fees, daycare, and on and on.

When summer came, my kids naturally wanted to go on vacation. They saw their friends jetting off to exciting places—the Caribbean, the Grand Canyon, and even to a castle in Austria—and they wondered why we couldn't do the same. Not wanting to burden them with our financial problems, I made up one excuse after another.

Aware of my situation, my two good friends, Bonnie and Carol, called and told me about a plan they had cooked up. "How would you like to go on a 'Women and Children Only' camping trip?" they asked. Our destination would be the Yogi Bear Jellystone Park campground in Amboy, Illinois.

Perfect! It wasn't too expensive or too far away, and we'd save money by bringing our own food. There were tons of activities included for the kids, like mini-golf, swimming, crafts, and fishing. They were sure to have a blast.

"We have all the camping gear we need," Bonnie said, "except we're short a tent." Between us, there would be three adults and seven kids, so we decided that three tents would be needed: one for the grown-ups, one for the girls, and one for the boys. My assignment was to find a tent. The date was set, the site reserved, and the sleeping bags aired out. We'd be off to Jellystone Park in two weeks.

I called everyone I could think of, but no one—not friends, relatives, or co-workers—had a tent to lend when we needed it. Since money was so tight, I couldn't part with the close to one-hundred-dollar price of a small, three-man tent. I knew either Bonnie or Carol would most likely be able to locate one, but since the divorce I felt like I was always asking people for favors. They had asked me to do this, and I was determined to find us a tent one way or another. But how?

My fortunes took an amazing and unbelievable turn a few days later. One windy evening I opened the garage door to bring the trash cans to the curb, and something in the front yard caught my eye. There was a large, dark object in the low branches of the linden tree next to the driveway. It was big. And it was shaped like a tent! Daylight was fading fast, and I couldn't quite make out all the details, but as I cautiously approached the tree, the image became clear. It was a tent, a small three-person tent, fully intact, gently swaying back and forth in the breeze.

My mouth flew open, and I quickly looked around, sure that someone was playing a weird trick on me. There was no one around. Not knowing what else to do, I got a ladder, untangled the tent from the branches and wrestled it into the garage.

The zippered entrance flap was open, and inside I found a lone sweat sock, dirty and damp, so I knew the tent had recently been used. Our house is located about two miles from a Boy Scout campground, and I figured that it must have somehow blown over the trees and into my neighborhood after it had been emptied and the stakes removed. I imagined how surprised and helpless those boys must have felt as they watched their tent take flight and disappear!

The next morning, I drove over to the campground, found the caretaker, and told him my bizarre story. He laughed and said no one had reported a lost tent; that was a new one on him. He promised he'd make some calls and get back to me if he heard anything. I went back home and walked up and down the block, ringing doorbells, telling and retelling my story, looking for the owner to no avail.

My kids had spent the night at their dad's house and, upon their return home, were delighted to see a tent set up in the garage. I told them the whole unbelievable story but warned that we might have to give it back if the owner was located. Then my son, the six-year-old, said matter-of-factly, "It's probably from heaven."

Stunned, all I could say was, "Yeah, that's got to be it."

After they ran off to tell their friends, I sat down, bewildered, and finally had a long cry. I knew my son was right. For the first time since the divorce, I could feel the weight of the world lifting from my shoulders. Money problems or not, I knew we'd be okay. Someone was looking out for us.

The camping trip was everything I had hoped it would be. We didn't need a Caribbean cruise; we had giant inner tubes on the lake. We didn't need to fly off to the Grand Canyon to hike perfect trails. And accommodations? We didn't need a castle with luxurious king-sized beds; we were happy with air mattresses and the little gray tent that had blown into our lives like a tumbleweed.

Over the years, we used our tent for several more camping trips and backyard adventures. Eventually, because of rips and leaks, I replaced it with a larger five-person model. Today, it lives in a box in the basement, and whenever I come across it, I smile and remember how this precious gift from heaven showed up one windy summer night long ago.

Maybe 1999 wasn't such a bad year after all.

— Loretta Morris —

Command Performance

There's no other love like the love for a brother.
There's no other love like the love from a brother.
~Author Unknown

Any avid traveler knows that the lure of the open road has little to do with the destination. At least half of the reason for a journey is the mental freedom of movement. The vehicle is also irrelevant. A fast horse or bicycle can be as liberating to the human spirit as an Italian sports car or supersonic jet.

I discovered this phenomenon early in life. Bullies, upcoming math tests, and other childhood worries vanished when I was careening down the sidewalk on a skateboard. Because motion clears the mind so well, the most dedicated wanderers are often the most troubled.

Such was the case one Saturday morning when I threw some supplies into a duffle bag and headed for the desert. But not just any desert—Death Valley, California—the most foreboding and deadly stretch of land in America. It probably would have been wiser if I had gone somewhere cheerful because I had just experienced the worst loss of my life—the death of my older brother, Paul.

I had lost all my grandparents except one, but they all lived overseas in Northern Ireland and I hadn't seen them since I was a child, so I was saddened but not devastated by their deaths. This was different. Paul was my only sibling. No friend made later in life can match the person who knows us our entire lives. He was thirty-seven when he died, three years my senior. It crushed me so much. I wasn't just depressed; I stopped noticing beauty in the world, and I resented happiness in others. On days when my grief was the worst, I would get in the car and just drive, as if trying to run away from it. I probably chose Death Valley on this particular day because it was as barren as I felt.

When we were kids, our parents took my brother and me on a lot of trips that required driving through Death Valley. We would beg them to pull over so we could search for snakes and lizards. One of our other favorite stops back then was Calico Ghost Town. In its heyday, it was a silver boomtown. When there was no more silver, it was abandoned for decades until someone restored it. There's no denying that it's touristy, but it's so authentic and the shopkeepers are so friendly that it makes it a worthwhile destination. My brother and I would raid the mercantile store for candy and then chase each other around with cap guns, pretending to be cowboys. It was heaven for boys.

I arrived at Calico in the late afternoon. The front gate was locked. A security guard in a maintenance cart said, "Sorry, we're closed."

"Darn," I replied. "I haven't been here since I was a boy."

He thought about it and said, "I'm not supposed to do this, but go on in. The shops are closed, but you're welcome to walk around."

I thanked him profusely and went inside.

Walking the dirt road, I imagined my brother and me there as children, but all I could hear was the wind whistling through the cracked wood facades of the shops. I had hoped returning to a place so full of memories would alleviate my depression, but it only made it worse. The old saying, "You can't go home again," came to mind, undoubtedly written by someone who had returned to some sacred place from their childhood hoping to capture that feeling again, only to find that their sense of loss was deepened.

I sat down and looked out over the empty street. A tumbleweed rolled by, as if on cue. I couldn't help but feel a certain kinship with it, having been blown around aimlessly that day, too. The sun was setting.

I spent some time talking to Paul as tears fell into the dirt at my feet. I wondered how I would ever shake this deeply rooted sadness. The whole world felt empty, and I resented it for continuing to revolve after his death. I even lost my faith. Still, out of sheer desperation, I prayed with the smidgen of belief I had left for a sign that my brother was okay, hoping that the prayer of a desolate man might receive some priority over prayers from those with blessed lives and untested faith. I waited ten minutes for anything out of the ordinary to happen, but again all I heard was the relentless wind.

It figures, I thought. *Don't be a fool. Life isn't a movie where something magical happens when you're broken. You're alone. Get used to it.*

I stood up and walked toward the exit, feeling pretty dumb for thinking that grief could be alleviated by going to DEATH Valley and a GHOST town. When I reached the front gate, a peacock walked across my path, stopped, and stared at me. I was surprised because I hadn't seen any other living thing there that day. It walked back into town and then looked back at me. I turned to leave, but it let out an ear-piercing screech. When I turned around, it started walking up the street again, and then stopped a second time as if to see if I was coming. It screeched again, which I interpreted to mean, "Well? What do you want? An engraved invitation?" Amused and having nothing else to do, I followed it.

We walked right up Main Street, and then the peacock crossed a bridge at the top of town and strutted into the outdoor theater. Growing even more intrigued, I sat in the front row and watched in amazement as it walked up the stairs by the stage, crossed proudly to dead center, faced me, fanned open its tail (or "train feathers," as they're called), and started to shake them and do a little dance. It was the first time I had ever seen this natural wonder in person, and this show was apparently just for me. It was as if the peacock were a reincarnated actor who had performed on that stage and wanted an audience again.

After a minute or so, it folded up its feathers and stared at me quietly, even meditatively, and then walked offstage. The show was clearly over. I sat there stunned, certain that something mysterious had just happened. I even yelled, "Encore!"

My faith fluctuated wildly in those days and only became strong in recent years, so I'm not qualified to be a preacher. I'll only say that the comment I made to myself—that "nothing magical happens when you're broken"—has been proven wrong over and over again, especially since my father died five years ago. At times when my pain was deepest, I found that incredible and unexplainable events would occur, events I could write off as imagination or interpret as a sign or message.

In this case, at a time when unbearable sorrow had blinded me to beauty, I was given a private "performance" by arguably the most beautiful creature on earth. It reminded me that life is full of beauty, even in the most barren places, if I only keep my heart open and follow where it leads me.

— Mark Rickerby —

Just Another Rainbow

Be thou the rainbow in the storms of life.
The evening beam that smiles the clouds away,
and tints tomorrow with prophetic ray.
~Lord Byron

I live in Sedona, Arizona, one of the most beautiful places on earth. The back yard of my home faces a golf course. Far across the golf course are more homes. Sedona's famous "red rocks" are part of our view, which makes most days at sunset feel like a miracle.

Sedona attracts many creative types: artists, authors, etc. I'm one of them — a photographer and author. My favorite camera these days is my iPhone. We have every kind of weather, from beautiful sunny days to rainy days and even snow days. I take photos of our back yard in all different types of weather with my handy iPhone. I'm always ready to capture the beauty of our neighborhood and my partner and sweetheart, Ken, is very patient during those times. I cannot count how many images of rainbows I have captured digitally on my phone and posted on Facebook. My family, scattered all over the country, just smile and usually ignore them. At least they know I am alive.

But one late afternoon, as Ken and I were sitting inside and having supper, there were rain showers, and I saw a magnificent rainbow outside — so close. As I excused myself and ran outside, he said it was "just another rainbow." I smiled and continued snapping images. One of the images seemed to show the rainbow going from our home directly into a home across the golf course. That was the one I immediately posted on Facebook.

A message popped up. "When did you take that photo, Beverly?"

I replied, "Just now."

Another message: "Oh, my heavens, can you send me that one privately, Bev? I am inside the house where the rainbow 'ends' and my good friend has just passed away here. I have to make copies of that photo to send to her family members. It just feels like it was heaven welcoming her. I've never seen anything like it."

After I told the story to Ken, he never again made a comment about my constant photography. In fact, he loves telling this story to anyone who will listen. Yes, it was "just another rainbow" — but with a miracle attached.

— Beverly Kievman Copen —

A Wedding Day Miracle

There are no miracles for those that have no faith in them.
~French Proverb

The DJ announced that the next song would be the last one. I smiled as I watched my friend Chrissie dance with her new husband, Dave. Her wedding had been so much fun, and she was a beautiful bride.

When the song was over, Chrissie asked me if I would grab her keys from her purse and get her overnight bag from her car. I agreed, but when I searched her purse, her keys were not inside.

"They have to be in there," she said. But after she'd emptied her entire purse onto the table, the keys were still nowhere to be found.

"My dad drove my car here to the wedding venue," she said. "He must have accidentally kept my keys."

Her parents had left the wedding nearly an hour earlier. "I hate to call them and make them drive back, but I have to get into my car." She dialed her dad's phone, but there was no answer. Same with her mom's.

"They must be asleep already," I said.

Chrissie looked at Dave. "What are we going to do now? Our flight takes off at 6 a.m., and we were going to drive my car to the airport."

Several people immediately offered to give them a ride in the morning, but Chrissie shook her head. "My suitcase is in the car. If I can't get my keys, the only outfit I'll have to wear on our honeymoon is my wedding dress."

Frantically, she dialed her parents again with the same results.

Bill, one of the groomsmen, offered to drive to her parents' house to retrieve the keys, but Chrissie shook her head again. "They booked a hotel for tonight so they wouldn't have to drive all the way home. And I didn't even think to ask which hotel. If they don't answer their phones, I have no way to get my keys before our flight takes off in the morning."

Dave patted her hand. "I'll call a locksmith. We'll get your suitcase, honey."

But none of the locksmiths he called answered their phones at 1 a.m. on a Saturday night.

Bill found a coat hanger and headed outside to Chrissie's car to try to get the door open. He came back inside, defeated.

Tears filled Chrissie's eyes. "We have only two choices," she said. "To postpone our flight to later in the day, or to just go without my suitcase." She looked down at her dress. "And as much as I love my wedding dress, I really don't want to wear it all week on our honeymoon in Maui."

Dave tried to call her parents one more time. When there was still no answer, he sighed and said, "I'll call the airline and see if there's a later flight. That will give us time tomorrow to reach your parents."

I felt so bad for my friends. They'd had the perfect day, and now it was ending badly. I could tell that neither of them wanted to delay their honeymoon, but they didn't see another option.

Bill pulled me aside. "Where are your keys?" he asked me quietly.

"My keys? In my bag. Why?"

"It's a long shot, but I read somewhere that there are only so many codes programmed into those key fobs. And since you and Chrissie drive the same model car, there's a chance that your key fob could work on her car."

"It's definitely worth a try," I said. We headed outside with my keys. I pointed the fob at her car, held my breath, and pushed the button. I heard the locks click open.

Bill and I cheered, grabbed her suitcase out of the car, and hurried back inside. "Don't call the airline," he said, holding the luggage victoriously.

Chrissie's mouth dropped open. "Did you break my window?"

"No, my key fob opened your locks," I said. "Can you believe it?"

"That's crazy but wonderful," she said. She hugged Dave. "We can catch our flight as planned, and I'll have clothes to wear!"

The happy couple still needed a ride to the airport since my key fob wouldn't actually start the motor on her car. One guest offered to drive them in the morning, and someone else made plans to get her keys from her parents and drive her car back to her house.

Everything had worked out. Dave and Chrissie flew out in the morning and had a great time in Hawaii.

When they got home, Chrissie and I met for coffee at our favorite place. When it was time to leave, I jokingly said, "Let me get your door for you." I pointed my key fob at her car and pushed the button. Nothing happened. I tried again. Nothing.

"The battery must be low," I said. I pointed it at my car and pushed the button. The locks clicked open.

Chrissie and I owned those cars for several more years, and every time I saw her, I tried my key fob on her car. In literally hundreds of tries, it never worked again.

Chrissie calls it her wedding day miracle, thanks to General Motors and our friend, Bill.

— Diane Stark —

No Fear

I realized that I don't have to be perfect.
All I have to do is show up and enjoy the messy,
imperfect, and beautiful journey of my life.
~Kerry Washington

Newly married, I said goodbye to my Lilliputian-sized apartment and hello to a house in a cozy neighborhood near a cul-de-sac. My husband literally rescued me from one of the higher-up rungs of the corporate ladder and offered me the opportunity to be a stay-at-home wife. This was a blessing and a dream come true. I could finally put stress behind me and take advantage of the latitude afforded me to pursue my hobbies and interests full-time, preferably for profit.

It should've been the best season in my life, yet something was missing. By the fourth month, I was well-acclimated into my new role and routine — and bored to pieces.

I still hadn't dived into my passions wholeheartedly. Perhaps I was in over my head. I'd convinced myself it would be impossible for me to pursue artistic ventures for a living at that stage in my life. Truth be told, I feared I didn't have what it took to do what I loved on a professional level. Fear had stolen my drive and confidence.

One day, I dipped my Filbert brush in a container of water while listening to a prophetic minister online. She claimed her audience would each receive a divine visitation that day. This was nothing new. I'd heard promises like that before.

The Hubby called from work requesting to take me shopping—and I assume to get me out from behind the four walls. Eager to upgrade the floral-sundress component of my wardrobe—and tired of staring down a bare-naked canvas—I accepted his invitation.

I laid down the paintbrush and dragged my supplies to the guest bedroom, passing by my in-home recording studio that I'd neglected. My condenser microphone had surely collected a family of dust mites by then.

I scurried to the bathroom to get ready, deciding on the fly to listen to a song that the minister had played in the background. I hopped in the shower and sang along at the top of my lungs as it blasted from my cellphone.

I hadn't learned the whole song but came in on cue when the catchiest part of the chorus repeated, "I'm no longer a slave to fear. I am a child of God."

Lukewarm water escorted most of my worries down the drain. The atmosphere shifted in some way. I couldn't quite put my finger on it. Nevertheless, I still wanted to know how my dreams would ever come to fruition in this lifetime if I couldn't get them off the ground—if I couldn't believe.

I left the shower humming the infectious melody and walked straight into a much larger than normal cloud of steam. The giant mirror above the his-and-hers sinks caught my attention. I stopped mid-hum and squinted. There were letters on the mirror, forming as if to spell something out, almost shapeshifting in the glass.

My heart sped up, not sure if someone had quietly broken in while I was in the shower or if something paranormal was going on. I looked over my shoulder and whispered my husband's name. Maybe he'd arrived early and pranked me or something.

There was no answer.

Just as I was about to run for the hills, I recalled the song that had been playing moments before. I was no longer a "slave to fear," right?

Immediately, it dawned on me: The minister had said I would have a divine encounter. I took a deep breath and moved closer to the mirror, wrapping my towel around my body, which was covered with goosebumps.

I looked intently as the letters continued forming, becoming more legible. I tried to make out what they said. And then, finally, I could read it: PUSH YOURSELF.

My jaws—and my towel—dropped.

I stumbled around looking for my phone to take a photo, eventually remembering in the living room that the phone was already in the bathroom.

I went back in there to capture the phenomenon, but the letters vanished as I struggled to put my camera on the proper setting. "No!" There went my viral moment.

My husband pulled in the driveway.

No sooner had he come in the house than I told him about my eventful day. He insisted I really needed to get some fresh air. I read between the lines and obliged.

Days passed, and I couldn't help but harp on what had happened in that mirror.

I'd taken at least 100 unimaginative showers in the same bathroom. The incident at hand was certainly no coincidence.

Subsequently, I took longer, steamier baths, singing the song at the top of my lungs, intending to prove it. I needed The Hubby to know that I was not a nutcase and had experienced the supernatural.

The more we discussed it, the more he side-eyed me and shook his head. "I'll believe it when I see it."

I couldn't take it anymore. I asked, "Lord, in the name of Jesus, if that was You, please put those letters back up there, so I will know—and so my husband will realize I'm not a nutcase. Thank You. Amen."

Almost two weeks later, instead of singing, I meditated on the mirror situation during a swift and not-so-steamy shower, and the letters returned.

I grabbed my phone and screamed for The Hubby to come to the bathroom.

I took snapshot after snapshot of the letters in the meantime. He was not going to be able to dismiss it.

To his shock, the phrase was there in plain sight: PUSH YOURSELF.

The Hubby just slinked out of the room. I followed him, and we debated it for the umpteenth time.

He said, "Babe, you wrote that."

I put my hand on my hip. "What? I thought you said you'd believe it when you saw it."

"Be real. You wrote it. Admit it."

"How? With what?"

He stroked his goatee. "Your finger?... I don't know, but you did that. Either you or... or... I don't know."

I couldn't help but smirk. "Unbelievable, isn't it?"

For months on end—and likely to this day—my husband couldn't accept the truth about the mind-blowing encounter, so he requested we not speak about it. He couldn't process such a wonder. I understood, and I still do.

I didn't write those words, but the message was loud and clear. No more running, no more hiding, no more doubting.

The Creator believed in me, so it was only right for me to believe in the gifts and talents He put in me. It was time for me to "push myself."

And so I did, picking up my mic and Filbert brush once again, without fear.

—Latonya Johnson—

The Inheritance

Out of difficulties grow miracles.
~Jean de La Bruyère

My grandmother and I were always close. When I was seven, I stayed with her while my parents were on vacation. After I graduated from high school, I lived with her for a couple of months while I figured out what I wanted to do with my life. She was there when I got married to my husband Mike and when my son Jake was born. Through happy and tough times, she always supported me, making me feel safe and protected.

When she passed away, I was heartbroken; it felt like we had lost the matriarch of our family. As part of my inheritance, I received enough money to buy some much-needed furniture, which included a china cabinet for my dining room. It consisted of five beautiful pieces in red oak and glass that stood side by side in a mission-style design. I absolutely loved it! At that time, we were living in Illinois, but when Jake turned five, my songwriting career moved us to Nashville, Tennessee.

We found a cute rental home just northeast of the city, where all five pieces of the china cabinet were able to line up on the living-room wall. Satisfied for the moment but longing to buy a home, my husband and I set out on a search to find a permanent place. We soon learned it was easier said than done.

We couldn't find a house with a wall long enough to accommodate my china cabinet. Mike was growing increasingly frustrated by my insistence that any new home had to accommodate that cabinet. At one point, he stood in front of a house shouting that if I didn't want to buy this one, he wouldn't buy me anything ever again!

In the meantime, he had to go back to Illinois for his job, but on weekends he would come to Tennessee to continue house-hunting with me. Then we got the devastating news that he had stage IV lung cancer. When he died six months later, we were still in the rental house.

Less than a year later, I found a new subdivision where I could build the perfect house — one that would work for fourteen-year-old Jake and me, and also have a wall long enough for the china cabinet. I was so excited. At 2 p.m. on a sunny spring day, I returned from signing the contract to build the new house. I was in the mood to celebrate with Jake, but as I walked through the door of our rental house, Jake called to say that he was staying at school where they were in a lockdown. A tornado was heading straight toward his school and our neighborhood.

I turned on the TV to see a map on the screen with our town circled in bright red. Five seconds later, the screen went black. Thirty seconds later, the electricity went out. I ran to the kitchen and dragged my dog's crate, with her inside it, to an interior hallway. Then I ran back to the kitchen to get my purse.

Then I heard what sounded like a jet about to land on our house. I ran into the bathroom, shut the door and jumped in the bathtub. I crouched down and put my hands over my head, hoping I was in the right position. There was no time to cover myself with a blanket or pillows.

I could hear things hitting the outside walls amidst the roaring of the wind. The atmospheric pressure caused my ears to pop. My heart was pounding, and I could barely breathe.

I started to pray, begging to survive. Jake was an only child and had just lost his dad. I couldn't bear the thought of him losing me, too. After a few minutes that felt like hours, the winds moved on, and an eerie silence settled over the house, except for the person screaming. Shocked, I realized that person was me.

I climbed out of the tub and checked the dog and then the inside of the house. I walked into the kitchen and saw that the curtains were still hanging on the sliding glass door and nothing seemed broken. There was no glass on the floor; nothing had fallen off the counters or tabletop. Our pictures were still hanging on the wall. There was a small hole in the roof over my son's bedroom, and in my bedroom one of the double-pane windows had broken on the outside but not the inside. There on my nightstand, completely unmoved, lay a gift from a close friend: my Bible. But what was on the wall next to that nightstand held the biggest surprise. The storm had cracked that interior wall in the shape of a cross three feet tall and two feet wide. I took it as a precious sign that my prayers had been answered.

As I slowly moved through the house, I thought I had totally overreacted until I opened the front door. I will never forget the overwhelming shock I felt as I looked down the street. There were giant piles of rubble where my neighbors' homes had been.

Our yard was littered with items from other people's homes. I saw pieces of silverware, a package of hotdogs and a woman's shoe. Insulation was wrapped around tree branches, and the lawn was covered in shards of glass. My next-door neighbors had a big hole in the wall of their kitchen.

On the next street over, three homes were moved off their foundations, and the end of our block was totally destroyed. Two houses had been picked up and thrown across the street, landing on two other houses. One was a house my husband and I had considered buying but didn't because the china cabinet would not fit. Another house we had considered buying had lost its roof and half of its second floor. We had declined to buy that one, too, because of the china cabinet.

It turned out that every house that Mike and I had passed on because of the china cabinet had been seriously damaged. And that house he stood shouting in front of? Well, it was gone, demolished by the tornado! That china cabinet I bought with my inheritance from my grandmother was our saving grace in the storm.

My son was able to make it home safely from school hours later. We camped out on the living-room floor with the dog for the next few nights until they were able to get the electricity and water turned back on. The roof was tarped and eventually repaired. The National Guard protected our area from looters, and the Salvation Army brought hot coffee and sandwiches every morning for the next two weeks.

I learned the tornado had 206-mile-per-hour wind speeds and was on the ground for twenty-three miles, creating sixty-nine million dollars' worth of damage. Many people were killed or injured. I don't know why we were spared, but others weren't. But I do know that our five-piece china cabinet, as frustrating as it was to fit in a house, was the reason why we were still living in that rental house where we escaped the worst of the storm. I wish my husband and my grandmother were here to see how everything fell into place, but I know that somehow, somewhere, they both know.

— Debra Zemke —

Unexplainable

The guardian angels of life fly so high as to be beyond our sight, but they are always looking down upon us.
~Jean Paul Richter

Very early one Friday morning, I left southern Washington for the long trek home. I was pacing myself to miss rush-hour traffic in Seattle but stopped for breakfast around 8 a.m. I called my husband and never imagined it could have been the last time we spoke.

Interstate 5 is a five-lane highway with a speed limit of seventy miles per hour. I was in the center lane when suddenly a car was edging very close to the right side of my car, traveling at the same speed. I was shocked that it was so close without hitting my car.

There was no time to check my side-view mirrors. I moved to the next lane on my left, and she followed just as closely. I held down my horn, but she didn't respond. She continued moving along with me. I let up on the accelerator to slow down, and what happened next is not understandable.

Just as I started to slow down enough for her to pass me, I realized I was now in the far-left lane. As she passed, I noticed her brake lights were not on, and I imagined she was in a hurry and would proceed in the left lane in front of me. But she was not stopping or slowing down or even moving into the lane ahead of me. Instead, she kept heading left and hit the cement barrier head-on with her driver's door directly in front of my car. On impact, her car spun sideways, and my SUV was approaching the driver's door dead on.

I did not have time to react. I did not have time to apply the brakes. But all the laws of physics were defied. My truck stopped within inches of her door. I had not applied the brakes and the engine was still running. I stopped so smoothly that it was as if I had been traveling at ten miles per hour. My purse didn't even tip over from its upright position on the front seat.

As her airbag deployed, I saw her cellphone in her right hand. Was she texting at that speed? Was she trying to kill herself?

By now, a couple of cars pulled up to see if we were okay. The front of the girl's car had disappeared, completely disintegrated, gone.

A man asked me to back up my truck so he could open her door and pull her out. Then he said, "What's this?"

I stepped out of my vehicle. There was a mound of sand as high as my front bumper right in front of my car. Where did that sand come from on an interstate highway in the left lane? That sand had stopped my truck.

I looked at him and said, "My angels must have put it there!" A weird smile came across his face, not sure how to explain any of it.

There is only one explanation as to what happened to me and my truck. It was divine intervention. There is no doubt nor any other clarification other than it was a miracle.

—Carol Graham—

The Cuckoo Clock

The probability of a certain set of circumstances coming together in a meaningful (or tragic) way is so low that it simply cannot be considered mere coincidence.
~V.C. King

We used to visit my father's aunt and uncle, Clyde and Vern, in Cincinnati, Ohio. They were very much the quintessential loving couple, two peas in a pod. When we were children, they gave my father a very old German cuckoo. Although it became a bit annoying to hear the old cuckoo clock "cuckooing" every hour on the hour, we eventually got used to it.

One evening as we all sat down to have dinner promptly at five o'clock, my father noticed that the cuckoo didn't come out of the clock to announce it was dinner time. The clock had never malfunctioned before. As soon as my dad said he would look at it, the phone rang. It was a family member informing Dad that Uncle Clyde had passed away. We all thought it was odd that the clock had stopped and he had passed away on the same day, but no one really said anything. Dad said he would fix the clock, and within a week or so, he did.

Life in our household went on as usual. About a year later when we sat down at dinner, my mother remarked that the cuckoo clock had stopped again. No sooner had she said it than the phone rang. We all looked at each other. Dad reluctantly answered the phone. Sure enough, it was a family member calling to say Aunt Vern had passed away. I think we already knew that.

From that day on, the cuckoo clock did not function, although my dad tried to fix it many times. It stayed on the wall in honor of Clyde and Vern until my father eventually stored it. When he passed away, we found the box with the cuckoo clock inside. My older brother Donnie and I just looked at each other. Our little brother Jeff took the clock to keep it in the family, but chances are it will remain in the box — and we're all okay with that!

— Lacy Gray —

Angels Among Us

Mikayla's Angel

Make yourself familiar with the angels and behold them frequently in spirit; for, without being seen, they are present with you.
~Saint Francis de Sales

The photograph I had been awaiting for years was finally in the palm of my hand. The man gazing at me from the black-and-white snapshot was holding a baby. His lanky frame sported a baggy, button-down shirt tucked into high-waisted black trousers. He had a half-smile, a full head of jet-black curls, and deep-set eyes.

My hands were shaking so much that it took me several attempts to snap a clear shot with my iPhone. I sent the photo to Mikayla. Text was not needed. If this were the man, she would recognize him.

It was one of only two photos my mother-in-law had uncovered of her father, a man she never knew. Before Mom was born, her father was killed by a truck while crossing at East 86th and 3rd Avenue in New York City in 1927. We assume the baby in the photo is Mom's brother Jack, now ninety-four, who still has eyes as blue and bright as polished sapphires.

I started asking for a picture of my husband's grandfather just weeks after an accident that potentially could have killed my youngest child, Mikayla. She was twelve years old and was begging to drive the ATV that she had only been in as a passenger. Following several driving lessons, Mikayla was allowed to drive it herself. She was cautious by nature, and her slow and deliberate circles around the back yard gave me false confidence. "One more loop," I motioned as I started up the deck stairs.

It happened in a flash. I heard a blood-curdling scream rivaling any heard in any horror movie ever seen, followed by an ear-deafening and sickening whack, and then silence. I scanned the back yard. Where was she?

More screams followed, but they were my own. Her dad, who had been raking the front yard, joined me and I ran to her where she was sobbing in the woods.

She was lying on a bed of leaves just a few feet from the ATV, which was wedged into a mature oak, crumpled and smoldering. I fell beside my daughter, expecting to see the same kind of damage that I saw on that oak tree, which was stripped of bark where the ATV had crashed into it.

There was not a scratch on her, not a bruise, no blood, just a face reddened from embarrassment and tears.

Mikayla said she was sorry. She had held the handlebar grip tight, thinking it was the brake. She wanted to know where the man went, the one who lifted her off the ATV before it crashed. After setting her on the ground, he stepped onto a nearby rock and silently watched her. At first, I tried to convince Mikayla there was no man in the woods, but her hysterical insistence intertwined with an honest and vivid accounting of his rescue had me scanning the landscape.

When she asked me why the guy was dressed in a long white dress and wasn't wearing shoes, I began to consider that my daughter was saved by a being not of this world. More questions led to further details. The man was tall and thin; he had curly black hair; and he had the bluest eyes she had ever seen. Not a word was spoken as he lowered her to the leaf carpet just after the ATV catapulted over a stack of stones at the edge of the lawn, and just before it crashed into the tree.

We referred to the man in the woods as Mikayla's Angel from that day on. I had many one-sided conversations with her angel as my daughter matured from teenager to young adult. I requested he be with Mikayla during her spinal-fusion surgery the following year. I imagined him watching over her as she lay on the cold operating table for ten long hours. I continued to pray to Mikayla's Angel too many times to count as she healed, relapsed, and healed again over the next three years. I asked him to go with her to college to keep her safe.

Whenever she was feeling scared or anxious, or when faced with a new challenge, I reminded Mikayla to bring her angel along for support. And just in case she forgot, I prayed to him as well. I continued to thank Mikayla's Angel for being with her through college and until she landed her first teaching job.

A few years ago, when Mikayla was home on a college break, I surprised her with a gift—a class called "Connecting with Your Angels" at a local spiritual center. The instructor professed that if we were open to meeting our angels, we could do so through guided meditation. Lying on feather-soft pillows with our eyes closed, we listened to her silky voice tell us to allow our angels to approach.

Mikayla slipped into a relaxed, meditative state, and when it was over, she whispered, "I didn't see him, but I felt him. He was right behind me, and I felt so safe. His name starts with an M."

That was the last time we spoke at length about angels, yet the encounter motivated me to identify Mikayla's protector. I considered all our departed relatives and friends, surveying many photographs while searching for a man who matched her angel's description. After dismissing all of them, I tried harder to get my mother-in-law to search for a photo of her father. I knew that striking blue eyes were predominant in his family.

When I finally saw that photo of Mikayla's great-grandfather, even though I couldn't tell his eye color from a black and white photo, I had a feeling this was it. At first she texted back, "Who is this?" I typed back, "Take a closer look." Her second response came within seconds. "OMG, it's him, the guy in the woods."

I picked up on the first ring. At first, we just laughed and shrieked and cried. But then I was finally able to say, "Mikayla, meet your angel. His name is Michael."

—Holly DiBella-McCarthy—

The Orange Pinto

Angels represent God's personal care
for each one of us.
~Andrew Greeley

My family and I were headed to a lake cottage for a week. As a teenager, a whole week away from my friends sounded like solitary confinement. I was dreading it. This was back in the days before cellphones, so I had no distractions for the two-hour drive except to squabble with my siblings or watch the boring Indiana countryside fly by. How would I survive this week?

Along the way, I convinced my younger brother, George, that the stalks of corn, standing in rows along the highway, were asparagus. The tassels that stick out at the top kind of look like asparagus. As it turned out, he continued to believe corn was asparagus for the next two years before my mother corrected him. He tells me he hasn't trusted anyone since.

We arrived at the lake and got out to stretch our legs. I looked at my older brother, Guy, and noticed he was wearing a purple tank top with red, white and blue shorts. I was mortified. I was glad no one I knew was going to see me with him.

That first night, while I was trying to go to sleep, I could hear the traffic from the nearby highway. At that moment, an idea was born. I got out of bed and went over to the window. I unlatched it and opened it.

Stealthily, I got dressed and stuffed my pillows under the blankets to make it look like I was still in bed in case anyone checked on me.

I climbed out the window and headed for the highway. I knew some of my male friends hitchhiked all the time. So, at about 10 p.m., I boldly stepped out on the shoulder of the road and stuck out my thumb. Looking back, I don't even know whether I was on the right side of the road for heading home.

A couple of cars whizzed by, and then one slowed down and pulled over to the side. Wow! This was even easier than I thought! I ran up to the old orange Pinto and looked in the passenger window at the driver. I was sure I could spot a bad guy when I saw one.

As the window rolled down, I made eye contact with a twenty-something man who looked clean-cut. I figured him for a college student, and he looked safe and friendly enough.

He asked me where I was going.

I replied, "Muncie."

He responded, "Okay, I'm going that way. Get in."

I opened the door and slid into the passenger seat, excited about my new adventure.

"What is your name?" he asked.

"Laurelyn. What's yours?" I replied.

"David. Why are you going to Muncie so late at night?" He pulled out onto the highway and accelerated.

"I want to go home to be with my friends. I don't want to stay in some stupid lake house with my family."

"Won't they wonder where you went when they wake up? Did you leave them a note?"

"No, I didn't think of that. They knew I didn't want to come here. I'm fourteen and old enough to stay home by myself."

The car slowed, and he turned off the highway onto a dirt road that led into the woods. I didn't remember this turn from the trip up here. The lights from the highway diminished as he drove farther into the woods. At this point, my excitement was starting to dim. I began wondering what I had gotten myself into.

The road came to a dead end at the lake's edge. He stopped the car and turned off the engine and the lights. I started to panic and tried not to show it. What was he going to do?

He looked at me for a long minute without saying anything. I looked down at my hands in my lap. How was I going to get myself out of this? No one knew where I was. He could strangle me and throw me into the lake, and no one would know.

Finally, he broke the silence.

"Do you know what I could do to you right now?"

I nodded, still looking down. My hands were clenched in my lap, and I was holding my breath.

"You are lucky I am the one who picked you up and not someone else. I am a nice guy and am not going to hurt you. I will either drive you to Muncie and make sure you are safe with a friend, or I will take you back to the cabin. Which would you prefer?"

"The cabin," I managed to squeak.

"Okay. I hope you have learned a lesson from this and will never hitchhike again. It can be very dangerous. There are some really bad people out there, and you could have gotten hurt or killed tonight."

I gazed up at him with tears in my eyes.

"Thank you. You have helped me learn my lesson. Thank you."

With that, he drove me back to the cabin, and I climbed back in my window with my heart racing. I hopped back in bed and approached the week with new enthusiasm. I'm sure my parents wondered what caused my attitude adjustment when I joined in every activity without complaint.

For years after that night, whenever I babysat, I told the preteens in my care the story about the orange Pinto. I hoped they also learned from my lesson. I'm glad my guardian angel was awake and on duty that night.

—Laurelyn E. Irving—

Rust

Hope fuels the engine of determination.
~Amy Newmark

When I became pregnant with my son, it was a disaster. No one wanted him except me, although I had no clue what I was getting into. Back then, a Caucasian girl having a biracial baby was not well accepted.

After I got kicked out of my parents' castle of a home, I moved into the cheapest apartment I could find. I struggled through my pregnancy because I had no furniture, few clothes, and no funds left in my birthday account. Fortunately, I found a job, so I was able to pay rent and utilities. I slept on the floor by myself, walked the gang-infested neighborhood by myself, and ate a solitary bowl of oatmeal for every dinner because that's what I had to do to survive. I'm not the most religious person in the world, but the only thing that kept me sane throughout the ordeal was prayer.

And then he was born, but the joyous occasion of his birth was marred. Something was wrong. My son—my beautiful, beautiful son—was born with a defect. He had misshapen feet.

"It's not as bad as it looks," Dr. Rust tried to console me when he saw my concern. "It doesn't hurt." Dr. Rust—a hospital physician who assisted with the delivery—was an elderly gentleman with a smattering of white, cotton candy-like hair and grandfatherly eyes.

As I viewed my son's malformed feet, I was overcome with worry. "But they're shaped funny, and they're crooked. Will he be able to walk on them?"

"Not like that." Dr. Rust frowned. "Tomorrow, a pediatrician will come and see little Joey. The pediatrician will tell you that having clubfoot is rather common, and they have methods to correct deformities like this. It just takes time."

"How much time?"

A nurse came over and took my baby to have his blood drawn.

"You should probably ask the pediatrician."

"What are the methods? Will my insurance cover them?"

"To tell you the truth, some of these methods are rather brutal. One involves waiting until Joey is three or four and breaking his bones and resetting them in casts. They repeat the process until his deformity isn't as bad."

"That's horrible!" I gasped.

"And painful," Dr. Rust agreed. "The other method involves cutting your son's feet open and inserting tiny metal rods along his phalanges (foot bones) to stretch them out. Unfortunately, this method is also painful, and in most cases, the patient finds it unbearable to walk for extended periods. I'm told running with the rods can be difficult, if not impossible."

"Those are terrible. Is there anything I can do to help my son?"

"Well, if you are serious, I can recommend a method. Something that's not in any medical book or taught in any class."

"What?" I needed to know.

"It's simple." Dr. Rust shrugged. "Massage them straight."

"Excuse me?"

"Baby bones—particularly fresh out of the womb—are pliable; they're almost like putty. Take little Joey's feet and ever so gently massage them. Don't hurt him. Simply guide your thumb along the sides of his feet until they align straight. I think you'll find this unorthodox method quite effective."

"Can I have my baby now? I'd like to get started."

Two hours later, Dr. Rust checked on me in my room. "You're still at it, I see. Very good."

"Dr. Rust, it works!" I exclaimed as I showed him my son's slightly improved feet. "He likes it! I can even do it while I'm breastfeeding."

That night, I massaged my baby's feet for a minute or two of every hour, gently straightening them.

The next day when Dr. Rust came to the room, he was amazed at Joey's progress. "They look good," he observed with a nod. Dr. Rust never mentioned anything about my baby's ethnicity, the fact I was alone, or the situation with the absentee father. Instead, he said something amazing. "I'm gonna go now, but I wanted to tell you that you're doing a remarkable job. Keep up the good work. I think you'll make an excellent mother."

And from the way he said it, I believed him. All my hopes, fears, and insecurities evaporated. I knew I could handle my son being biracial. I could handle every part of being his mother.

"By the way," Dr. Rust added before he strode through the threshold, "little Joey is going to be my last delivery; I'm officially retiring. After forty-seven years, he's the last little guy I'm going to help bring into the world." He smiled at my son. "He's a special one."

When the pediatrician walked into the room at 9:45 that night, he took one look at my son and scoffed, "That's not an emergency! The paperwork Dr. Meyers (my OB/GYN) submitted indicates this baby has severe clubfoot in both feet." He inspected my son's feet. "This baby's fine," he snapped, perturbed. "Nothing but a slight curve. He'll probably grow out of it in a week or two. This baby's big and healthy and fine." He shook his head. "I don't know why I had to stop by tonight when it could have waited until tomorrow."

Even though the hospital pediatrician was grouchy and dismissive, he gave me the best news I ever heard. My baby was fine!

Two weeks later, I brought Joey to see a pediatrician on my medical plan. During that appointment, the doctor remarked how strong my baby was and how he had little evidence of clubfoot. Later that day, I called Sharp Hospital to thank Dr. Rust for his kindness and advice.

"I'm sorry… Who?" the receptionist said.

"Dr. Rust. I believe he's in gynecology."

"Oh, dear. We had a Dr. Rust, but he died last year. He's the only Dr. Rust I know of. He was a really nice guy."

"Are you sure?"

"Of course, I'm sure. Everyone here misses him."

I hung up, feeling baffled and deflated.

My son is thirty-seven now. He's enjoyed a life filled with walking, running, bicycling, swimming, dancing, jumping out of helicopters, riding motorcycles, scuba diving in oceans throughout the world, and carrying all four of his children on his shoulders. Over the years, I've wondered if the receptionist was mistaken. Maybe that doctor borrowed Dr. Rust's old lab coat. Or maybe some weird, unexplained phenomenon really did happen. I guess I could have gone down there or written a letter. Perhaps I should have asked Dr. Meyers. But for me — at a time when the odds were stacked against me — that mystery and the possibility of divine intervention was just what I needed. Just like rust spreads and grows, so did a new layer of hope spread itself over my life and help me move forward.

— January Joyce —

Angel in the City

When we are touched by something, it's as if we're being brushed by an angel's wings.
~Rita Dove

The sweat beaded on my neck as my husband, mother, and I drove the ninety minutes from our farm to the hospital in the city. Despite the fall chill, I was hot and anxious. Dad had come through his surgery with flying colors the day before, yet now something felt wrong. I had a gut feeling that he was in danger.

When we arrived, we hurried into the hospital, and found it surprisingly peaceful, almost eerily empty. A woman quickly appeared beside us. She was fair, with bright red hair — quite striking and she seemed to exude serenity and comfort. She had an Irish brogue. She led us down a corridor to an elevator that required the use of a key. As she turned it, she faced us and told us not to worry. Bob (my dad) would be okay. We entered the elevator and ascended rapidly. When we reached the right floor, she squeezed my shoulder and, with reassurance, stated that we should go to him. She did not follow us out of the elevator. The doors closed with a soft clank.

We entered my father's room to find a maze of tubes and wires across his body. I almost fainted. What had happened? He was fine the night before.

Doctors stood around the bed, tall and imposing like columns on a building. They said that Dad had given them quite the scare and was lucky to still be with us. He had experienced an unexpected bleed while sleeping. As they began to explain what had happened, Dad stirred from his sleep and awoke with a smile. The largest of the doctors, a monolith of a man with a square jaw and warm eyes, said: "I'll let Bob tell you what happened. It truly is a miracle."

Illuminated by the overhead lighting, Dad had an unusual glow about him as he shared his story. He said, "I went to sleep last night and was woken up by a beautiful, red-haired woman with an Irish accent. I felt so safe and peaceful with her in the room. She held my hand and told me that I was a touch blue but not to worry because she would get help. I saw a bright light, and a moment later the nurses and doctors came in to bring me back… They had lost me for a few minutes."

The doctor cleared his throat and wiped his eyes with his handkerchief. He had seen the red-haired woman when she came to get help. Bashfully, the doctor looked to the floor and said that although he was a man of science, what happened that night was unexplainable. There were no personnel who met that description (the pale skin, red hair, and Irish accent) in the building.

We let him know that the same woman had just brought us up in the rear elevator. His face went pale. He said that the rear elevator hadn't been in service for years.

The hospital now stands abandoned. But every single time we drive past it, I recall the cool comfort of that woman's hand on my shoulder, and I say a prayer of thanks for our angel in the city.

—Robyn Milliken—

We Want a Ride

The most glorious moment you will ever experience in your life is when you look back and see how God was protecting you all this time.
~Shannon L. Alder

We moved to Florida just before I entered high school. My new best friend, Donna, lived at one end of town, and I lived at the other end where the Everglades started. We would meet at a halfway point and then walk around all day gossiping and hanging out.

One hot afternoon, we had been walking all day and were three-quarters of the way to my side of town. Donna started chanting and banging in time on her Coke can, "We want a ride! We want a ride!" We hadn't seen many vehicles that day. There were no cars on the road going our direction at that moment. The lone car we could see was heading toward us. It was a white panel van, one side kind of banged up. It made a wide U-turn and stopped in front of us. The driver leaned over and asked if we wanted a ride. I don't know what possessed Donna, but she said, "Yes," and opened the sliding door and jumped in. I was standing on the side of the road, asking her what she was doing. She just shrugged and sat down. I couldn't let her go off by herself, so I climbed in, feeling very uneasy.

The passenger seats had been removed, so we had to sit on the floor. The only seat was the driver's. There was a dark green carpet on the floor, with dark brown stains and a dirty toolbox without a lid sitting near the back doors. Lying next to the toolbox was a length of rope, a roll of duct tape, a hacksaw with what looked like rust on the blade, a screwdriver, and a dirty-looking hammer.

The driver didn't say anything, just put the van in gear and started down the road. We hadn't gone far when he looked in the rearview mirror and swore under his breath. He said, "This is the third time this week they've stopped me." He pulled over to the flashing lights of a patrol car.

A police officer came to the door, asked us to get out, and introduced himself to the driver. The driver handed him his license and stayed behind the wheel. The officer looked at us and asked if we knew hitchhiking was dangerous. We nodded. He then asked us what our parents would say if they knew we were hitchhiking. I'm not sure what caused me to say what I did, other than I would be in deep trouble if the officer took us home. I stared at his badge and said, "It's okay. He's a friend of my brother." My brother was nine.

I remember the hair on the back of my neck raised when I saw the driver squinting at me. I was relieved to be out of the vehicle and thought my lie would get us away from both the driver and the officer. The officer looked at me for a moment and then said, "Okay, just don't be getting into cars with people you don't know." Then he walked back to his patrol car. I was ready to start walking when Donna got back in the van. I didn't know what else to do, so I climbed in next to her. The van started down the road less than half a mile to the subdivision entrance. I told him, "Thank you, we're here." The van stopped, and we got out. I noticed the patrol car had followed us and made a U-turn when we crossed the road.

Two days later, a boy was reported missing. His mother worked at a business off the main road, close to where we had been picked up. When his mother got home and he wasn't there, she called his friends and the school. Friends said he rode the bus home. The bus driver said she had let him off near where the mother worked, as she had done in the past. Several people said they saw a boy who fit the description talking to a man in a white panel van that had one side banged up. Two weeks later, they found the boy's body, tied with a rope, mouth covered in duct tape, his hands cut off and left at the end of the road near the Everglades.

A few days later, I was working at a restaurant when a group of four police officers came in at lunchtime. The restaurant had a policy of giving uniformed fire, police, and EMT workers their meals at half price. I wanted to thank the officer for stopping, confess my lie, and ask if he remembered the van. I asked if they could get a message to him. They said, "No, there's no one on the force by that name." I gave them his badge number. They said, "No, that's not one of our badge numbers." I gave them the patrol car number and received the same reply, "No, we don't have a vehicle with that number. You must be mistaken." I am positive I had the name, badge, and vehicle number correct. I was left with a sense of confusion, relief and a resolve to never get in a vehicle with someone I don't know again.

—TG Gilliam—

A Mysterious Angel

I believe that prayer is our powerful contact
with the greatest force in the universe.
~Loretta Young

It was nearing Christmas in 1987. I was a single mother of a teenager. I was on sick leave from a motor-vehicle accident, and no benefits had come in. There was very little food in the house, and I didn't know which way to turn. I had prayed for divine intervention but so far our situation had not changed.

One morning, I shed a few tears and then said, "Let go and let God." I knew that He could help me in this situation.

A few hours later, I heard a loud rap on the door. I opened it to find an old man with rheumy eyes and huge hands standing there. His beard was scraggly and unkempt. It was frigid out, and I wondered what he could want.

"Can I help you, sir?" I asked.

In a crackly voice, he answered, "Missus, do you happen to have a hot cup of tea and something to eat for a hungry old soul?"

"Well, sir, there isn't much food in the house, but I can offer you some tea and toast with peanut butter or jam."

"That would be most appreciated," he said as the water from his eyes ran down his cheeks.

I was leery about letting this man in the house, so I asked him if he minded waiting on the steps. He assured me he didn't.

I went into the house, prepared a cup of hot tea and four slices of toast with peanut butter, and took them to him. We sat on the porch as he ate and chatted a little about life and how hard it could be.

When he finished, I asked if he would like more, and he assured me he would. While the teakettle was boiling, I looked around for a pair of gloves and a scarf that had been my late husband's. With the items in hand, I took them to him, and he tried on the gloves.

"A perfect fit," he said. Tears rolled down his rosy, cracked cheeks.

We chatted a bit more as he ate, and then he politely thanked me and turned to go. When I went back into the house, I remembered a pair of boots that had been my husband's. I grabbed them out of the closet and ran outside, but there was no sign of the elderly man. I ran to the end of the block and looked up and down… nothing. I ran to the other end of the block… nothing. I jumped in my car and drove around the neighborhood. Again… nothing. Where had he gone?

Christmas Eve was just a couple of days away, and as those hours passed, the situation continued to be desperate. About 6:00 that evening, a rap came at the door. When I opened it, a man stood there with a huge box of groceries. Behind him, I saw a taxi.

"Delivery," he stated.

"From who?" I asked.

"I have no idea," he answered. "It was sent anonymously. I can tell you, I picked this up at the grocery store, and the man was old, scruffy-looking, and had huge hands."

I was stunned. The man he was describing sounded like the old man who had come to my door and whom I had fed.

With a wave and a "Merry Christmas," we parted. I took the box into the house. There was a small turkey and all the fixings for stuffing, as well as a bag of potatoes, vegetables and an apple pie.

We had a wonderful Christmas with lots to eat and gave thanks for the man, whom to this day I refer to as my mysterious angel.

— Mary M. Alward —

The Janitor

All God's angels come to us disguised.
~James Russell Lowell

I glanced at my watch. I'd been gone for half an hour. My family would soon come looking for me. It was wrong to disappear, but I couldn't stay. I couldn't feel their touch, couldn't listen to their words, couldn't bear that look in their eyes.

I intended to run a lot farther than the waiting room. Knowing that my parents were hurting as much as I was stopped me in my tracks. Losing one daughter was enough. It would be too much to have another disappear into the night.

But it was my fault she was gone. My fault my family was in so much pain. If they had read my thoughts that night as we gathered in the waiting room, they'd blame me, too. I had sat there praying she wouldn't be in any more pain. And then she wasn't.

At the time, I thought I was being selfless, but as I sat in front of that window, all I wanted to be was selfish. I wanted her back. Pain or not, I wanted her back. Tears cascaded down my cheeks, causing the Christmas lights to blur into a kaleidoscope. I fought the urge to rip them off the tree and declare all things festive cancelled.

I looked at my watch again and pictured my mother asking if anyone had seen me, while my father checked out the chapel and other places he believed I'd go for comfort. I knew they wouldn't find me, wouldn't even think to look there. I was partly comforted by this thought, but mostly terrified I was hurting them more.

I lifted my heavy body, weary with emotion, off the waiting-room chair and shuffled to the Christmas tree. My distorted face stared back at me from a silver globe. It felt fitting. Now that she was gone, nothing would be as it was supposed to be.

"You can't be here, miss."

I turned and faced an old man with a mop and wheeled bucket. I didn't hear him approach or the squeaky wheels of his mop bucket and wondered where he had come from. It didn't matter. I wiped the tears off my cheeks. "I just need someplace quiet."

"This is the waiting room for day surgery. It's closed now," he said, leaning on his mop. "Wouldn't you feel more comfortable in the chapel?" He started to mop the area across from me. "That's where I like to go when I need quiet."

I let out a loud, "Ha!"

The man stopped mopping and stared at me. "Even if you ain't religious, it's a quiet place, nothing funny 'bout that."

He went back to his mopping.

"They'll find me there," I whispered, honestly thinking there was no way he could hear me.

"Who will find you? Are you running from someone?" He scratched his head. "You don't look like a patient."

"I'm not a patient." I swallowed hard. "My sister was."

The man gave a knowing nod. "Was, huh?"

"She died."

The janitor set his mop in his bucket and walked over to me. "Don't you have someone to talk to?"

I gave him a smirk. "I have plenty of people to talk to. I don't really want to talk to anyone." I gestured around the empty room. "That's why I'm here and not up there."

"Are you sure you don't want to go to the chapel? I can call the clergy on staff."

I laughed again. "I'm pretty sure I just yelled at the clergy on staff."

"Why on earth would you do that?" he asked.

"Because that pastor said God has a reason for the death of my sister, and I think that is a load of crap said to people to make them feel better." I hugged myself. "There is no good reason for my sister to have died at the age of twenty-four. There is no good reason for her to die after we were told she beat the leukemia last week. There is no good reason for Him to take my sister." My voice faded. "My best friend."

The tears wouldn't stay put but dripped from my eyes like a leaky faucet begging to be fixed. As I buried my face in my hands, I felt a loving pat on the back of my shoulder.

"You know that ain't Father Bloom's fault, right?" asked the janitor. "He's taught that God has a reason for everything, so because of his faith he truly believes there was a reason. But you couldn't possibly understand that now because you're mad."

"Of course, I'm mad," I snapped. "She shouldn't have died! Not yet, not like this. She had so much to give, so much to experience, and He took all that from her, from us."

"It's okay to be mad at God," said the man with a firm nod. "He can take it. In fact, lay it all on Him. Your anger, your grief, your pain. He will gladly carry it all."

I rolled my eyes at him, getting a laugh.

He gave me another loving pat on the shoulder. "You don't have to believe me now, but one day you will. And when you're ready, He will take it all for you. But right now, you need to let others help you carry it. You said you had people to talk to… your parents?"

I nodded.

"They're probably worried about you."

I turned and looked in the direction I had come, the direction back to the waiting room where my family grieved. He was right, and I didn't want to worry them any longer. I turned to thank him for listening to me, but he was gone, no footsteps to be heard, no squeaky bucket wheels.

My eyes filled again with what I knew would be endless tears as I looked back into the ornamental ball. A white figure began to form behind me. I blinked the tears away, trying to focus on the reflection in the sphere, too frightened to turn around and face it. Was it an angel or a combination of grief and blizzard?

The figure came into focus. My beautiful sister stood behind me.

Her smile radiated warmth as a sense of peace came over me. The lights on the Christmas tree grew brighter as I turned to embrace her.

She wasn't there.

The lights faded back to their normal brilliance. My sister was indeed gone, but the peace remained.

Even now, all these years later, I have no explanation for what I saw in the Christmas tree ornament or why the janitor came and went so silently. But I have always believed he was an angel helping me through the toughest night of my life, and I will forever be thankful.

—Jennifer McMurrain—

Miracle on Mott Street

A guardian angel walks with us, sent from up above,
their loving wings surround us and enfold us with love.
~Author Unknown

There are certain places on the planet where you can feel a connection with the spirit realm or a loved one. That's the way my mother, Terry, and I felt about Little Italy in New York City. The very streets brought us back to our roots that were planted before either of us was born. It's the spot where, on a hot July night in 1906, my grandfather Tony was born to immigrant parents. "I was born on the corner of Hester and Mott," he often said. Save for the clothes and cars, little had changed since that time period, making Little Italy almost a living museum.

Grandpa Tony loved to tell me stories about when he was a little boy running the streets of the neighborhood. As it turns out, he and my Uncle Dom were running a little too wildly for my great-grandfather's liking, and he soon moved his family to a then very rural town in New Jersey. Occasionally, Grandpa took us to New York for pastries and cappuccino and to walk around the streets, which sadly didn't span the vast neighborhood they once did. Little Italy was whittled down to one main drag, Mulberry Street, and two cross streets, Hester and Grand. The rest had become Chinatown.

Now it's important to note that New York City in the 1970s was nothing like the theme park it's become today. In fact, most parts were downright dangerous. All the trendy neighborhoods, such as Soho (South of Houston) and Nolita (North of Little Italy), were nothing but sweatshops and factories back then. Since those businesses were closed in the evenings and on weekends, the streets were dark and deserted. While it made for easy parking, it was still scary for two women walking them alone. Moreover, it had been reported in the news that gangs were running the streets of Chinatown mugging tourists. While it didn't stop us, we were on our guard when we ventured to Little Italy on Sundays for Italian food and shopping.

One Sunday, I felt lucky to find a parking spot on Mott Street, which was one block over from Mulberry. It was a busy street filled with sidewalk stands selling Chinese vegetables, fish, and fowl. We only had to walk down the street and around the corner to reach our restaurant. After a few steps, though, we saw people scattering. A gang of young men was coming down the sidewalk armed with baseball bats and who knows what else.

Panic set in. There was no time to return to the car. Besides, it really wouldn't offer any protection. Yet if we walked forward, my mother and I would come face-to-face with them.

"Come on." My mother grabbed my arm and pulled me into the vestibule of an old tenement house, which was, surprisingly, unlocked. With our hearts pounding, we hid in the stairwell until we heard them pass. When we walked back out, something struck my mother and she said, "Do you think this could be the building where Grandpa lived?" She took out a pen and wrote down the number.

It's odd, but neither of us remembered Grandpa showing us the house where he lived. It couldn't have been that he was ashamed, because the entire area was terribly poor even to this day. There's a wonderful old photo that's been made into a poster called "Mott Street 1906." It shows the pushcarts and peddlers and the clotheslines overhead covered with the residents' laundry. More importantly, after their precarious start running with gangs in the early 1900s, my grandfather and his brother went on to become very successful men. Grandpa became the first Italian-American man to join the local police force, solving the

Case of the Missing Corpse (the husband was buried under the new patio), and eventually becoming captain.

A few days later, my mother handed me a piece of paper. "Take a look at this." It was my grandfather's birth certificate. "Look at the address." She also had her planner where she wrote down the number of the tenement building we ran into on Mott Street. It was the same building. "Grandpa was looking out for us that day," she said. A chill ran through me as we stared wide-eyed at each other.

Was it a miracle or a coincidence? But isn't a miracle really just a glorious coincidence? We tend to think of miracles as great biblical events, but I believe that we should appreciate those tiny gifts that come our way. Seek simple miracles, and you will always catch a glimpse of heaven.

In any event, Grandpa Tony always loved a good time. If he decided to join us in spirit on our Sunday adventures, he would certainly do anything in his power to keep my mother and me safe, especially from the type of gang he used to run with. Maybe he was working off some old karma.

I'd like to believe he was there with us, and that it was a miracle—the Miracle on Mott Street.

— Lynn Maddalena Menna —

The Key Man

Alone is impossible in a world inhabited by angels.
~Author Unknown

It was a sunny Sunday morning and I wanted to try a friend's Sunday school by walking to her church about a mile and a half away. Her church promised to be "more fun." (I also had not read the Bible passages assigned for the week, so I needed an excuse to skip class.) Surprisingly, my mom agreed that I could go, saying "I'll pick you up at Aunt Ginger's after the service." She and my brother went into our church, and I set off from the parking lot on my adventure.

It was incredibly quiet as I walked. I had not realized this stretch of road through an industrial area was so desolate. I jumped when I heard the swoosh of tires as a lone car drove past me. The driver lifted his hand, and I waved back—then nothing again but the still silence of the factory walls and a weird growing sense of unease. I began walking faster, a thin thirteen-year-old in a bright turquoise coat and "good shoes" with one-inch heels.

The second car that passed me was a shiny black sedan. The car slowed, and the passenger window slid down a bit. "Want a ride, honey?"

I shook my head, looked straight ahead, and almost ran along the side of the road. The car rolled away and eventually disappeared as the first one had. My heart was pounding now.

It couldn't have been more than five or six minutes when that black car cruised up again, rolling slowly alongside me, keeping pace as I walked. The window was down, and this time the driver's voice was not so friendly: "Get in."

My heart lurched, and at that same instant I heard the high-pitched squeal of a machine grinding close by. I saw a small white shack leaning against the factory wall. The door was just a bit ajar, and I turned away from the car. By this time, the driver had pushed the passenger door open. I ran to the shack, hit the door at a dead run, shoved it open, and slammed my right shin into something metal that hurt. A man behind the worktable was grinding a key.

He looked up as the engine whine died down. "Hello. Are you lost?" Apparently, a girl barging into his jumbled workshop had not surprised him.

"There… is a man…" I could hardly speak because my mouth was so dry. I pointed, and the man came out from behind the worktable, jerked the door open and stepped out into the sunlight. Metal shavings that clung to his work clothes reflected the sunlight.

He walked out into the road, hands on his hips, and the black sedan took off like the devil was after it. The man gestured for me to come out of the shack. As I walked to him, I realized my knee was bleeding.

"Looks like you've made a mess of yourself." His smile was kind. "Should you be walking here today like this?" I burst into tears and shook my head.

"Okay—okay—you're all right now." He smiled again. "You go ahead and start walking. I'll stand here and watch you."

Watch me? I wanted to go home!

"Go on… I'll stand right here until you get where you're going. You're safe now."

I took a few tentative steps, felt the blood running down my shin and glanced back over my shoulder. The man was still standing in the road.

"You're safe now," he said again, gesturing that I should keep going. And, so I did—walked a few yards, looked back—the man was still there. Walked a few more yards, looked back—still there. Funnily, he didn't seem to grow smaller the farther away I went.

I completed that walk as fast as I could, weak with relief when the first house finally appeared and I realized I had reached a safer neighborhood. I didn't head for that church. I made a beeline for my aunt's house instead, stumbling into her kitchen sobbing. Uncle Joe looked up from his morning paper in surprise, and then I was the center of attention.

My uncle was a policeman, and while my aunt cleaned my knee, he peppered me with questions. What kind of car was it? What did the driver look like? Did I get the license number?

Mom got to the house almost two hours later, and I sat ashamed while my uncle scolded her for letting me walk that route at all.

"You have to make better decisions," he railed. "You're a woman alone now. You have to be more aware!"

Mom nodded, eyes damp, but then she was all business. "We have to go thank the man who helped her."

"Yeah," Uncle Joe agreed, grabbing his car keys. "I want to talk to him, too."

Mom sat in the front seat, and the look she shot me over her shoulder told me I was in for it when we got home.

We drove down the quiet road, and I pointed to the ramshackle shed. The man had obviously closed the door tightly when he returned to work.

Uncle Joe went to the door, knocked, and then jiggled it and gave a small shove. A portion of the roof caved into the shed.

"Are you sure this is the place?"

"Yes." I nodded, glancing down the deserted road. "It's the only one."

"No way." Uncle Joe shook his head. "No one has been in this dump in years."

"He was here… He was making a key!" I insisted. I would never forget what happened.

My uncle put his shoulder against the jammed door. It opened about two inches but refused to budge more than that.

"It's wedged against something metal on the floor." Mom was looking through the crack in the door.

"It's a cash register," I said. "A big brown cash register — that's what I cut my knee on."

My uncle peered in when Mom gestured to him to see for himself.

"I'll be darned — it is a cash register." He shared a puzzled look with Mom.

We spoke of that day often over the years. It could not have happened, but it did.

— Judy Sutton —

Divine Timing

Miracles Are Real

Personally, I'm always ready to learn,
although I do not always like being taught.
~Winston Churchill

I was fortunate to be brought up in a loving, close-knit family with parents who taught us at a very early age to say our prayers, attend church, and try to live our lives as God ordained. Needless to say, as my brother Derrick and I became teenagers. we often failed to observe the latter as closely as we should have. But on the whole, our parents did a commendable job of instilling good values into our lives. My father was a physician, but he was also a priest in the Anglican church with a deep faith in miracles and divine intervention. To his dismay, I was more skeptical, suggesting that logical explanations could be found for most miracles.

As for divine intervention, like most people, I just didn't know.

My brother was twenty-five years old when World War II broke out. He had already graduated from medical school and finished his internship, so he immediately volunteered for the Royal Army Medical Corps. He was assigned to a regiment bound for India. From there, they would proceed to the Middle East to engage Rommel's desert troops in Libya. The last letter my parents had from my brother was sent from India, telling them he was well and to try not to worry. The next communication they received was a brief telegram from the War Office informing them that their son was missing, believed killed in action.

I had always been especially close to my brother and, like my parents, I was inconsolable. We all prayed for his safe return, but when a large trunk marked "Deceased Officer's Kit" arrived at the house, I accepted the inevitable. My parents, however, continued to pray for him, day and night, hoping for a miracle.

Six months passed.

On a day that none of us will ever forget, a postcard arrived from the Red Cross stating that my brother was alive and was being held in a prison camp in Germany.

After three years, Derrick came home. At first, like so many servicemen who had survived the horrors of war, he was reluctant to talk about his traumatic experiences. It was only later, through several different sources, including an ex–fellow prisoner, the Red Cross, and the memoirs Derrick eventually wrote, that we learned something of the missing three years and the close encounters with death that he had experienced.

Obviously, it is impossible to know whether the following near-death experience coincided with some special prayers the family was offering up at that very moment, but as my parents' intercessions were constant, one can only believe that some Super Being was paying attention. The more I learned of Derrick's close encounters, the more my faith in miracles soared until I was a firm believer in the inexplicable mysteries of divine intervention.

It began in the Libyan desert when Rommel's Army overpowered the Allied troops, and those who were not killed were scattered into the desert. After three days without food or water, Derrick was found, half-dead, by a band of nomad Black Tent Arabs, who took him in and saved his life. He lived with them until he was strong enough to start walking south, hoping to meet the British troops who had landed at Calabria. However, after a few weeks, he was captured by a German patrol and sent to an Italian prison camp.

As the Germans advanced through Italy, they surrounded the prison camp where Derrick was being held. The Italian guards, not knowing what to do, threw open the gates of the compound, and the prisoners poured out in a bid for freedom. Derrick ran with the rest of them, side-by-side with a fellow doctor. German soldiers with machine guns and rifles opened fire on the escapees, and Derrick's friend was shot dead at his side. Miraculously unscathed, with bullets flying all around him, Derrick kept running until he reached a small, wooded area.

As he exited the trees on the other side of the woods, he found himself beside a railroad track. On the other side of the track stood two German soldiers, evidently searching for the escaped Allied prisoners. My brother came to an abrupt halt, facing them on the opposite side of the railway line. As he stood there, transfixed, the soldiers raised their rifles and, at the very moment of his pending execution, like a scene from a B-movie, an express train came roaring down the track between him and the two Germans. By the time the train had rumbled past, Derrick had already doubled back into the woods and vanished.

What followed his incredibly close encounter with death was a series of experiences that can only be described as miracles. On two occasions, in the six months that he spent avoiding capture as an escaped prisoner of war, another companion was shot and killed at his side, and a Red Cross convoy he was escorting with food for starving prisoners was machine-gunned by planes, leaving Derrick's driver and their German guard dead beside him. Were these the times when my parents were on their knees praying for a miracle?

Why was Derrick spared so many times when other good men lost their lives?

This is the question I asked myself countless times. I now believe that my brother was miraculously saved only through the grace of God and His divine intervention.

After the war, Derrick became a specialist in chest diseases and joined the World Health Organization. For the rest of his life, he worked for humanity, using his specialized skills to serve and save others. Not long before he died at the age of ninety-three, we were talking about our own lives, and he said very simply, "I only did the best I knew how."

Was it divine intervention that the train came along just at the moment he was about to be shot? Was it a miracle? I will never know, but let me say that I would never again question the existence of God's miracles and the power of divine intervention.

—Monica Agnew-Kinnaman—

Precious Sleep

One thing you can say for guardian angels:
they guard. They give warning
when danger approaches.
~Emily Hahn

The alarm went off at 2:35 a.m. I could not believe it as I stumbled out of bed to reach the dresser across the room and turn off the loud music. I was exhausted—the mother of an infant, trying to keep a small business going, with a husband who worked nights. Sleep was so precious to me.

I crawled back into bed, thinking evil thoughts about my husband who I assumed had reset the alarm clock. But then I thought there might be another reason. Maybe there had been a power failure. I got up and checked the obvious indicators—the digital clocks on the appliances. No flashing 12:00 anywhere. Everything was fine.

On the way back to bed, I decided to stop and check on our son, asleep in his room. There is nothing more peaceful than watching a baby sleep, all tucked in and wearing cute footie pajamas. As I watched him lie there, something didn't feel right. I leaned in closer to watch him breathe, but he wasn't moving. There was no up and down to his chest.

It had to be there. I put my hand lightly on his chest, hoping to feel the movement. I rubbed him and whispered his name. I didn't want to frighten him, but I was starting to panic. I patted harder. I spoke louder. Still nothing. I grabbed him with both hands and rolled him to his side, and then, finally, he made a little gasping sound and resumed breathing.

He never woke up, and I stood there watching him sleep, astonished by what had transpired. What would have happened if that alarm clock had not gone off at that exact time that night?

They say everyone has a guardian angel, and my son seems to have one who knows how to set off the alarm clock.

— Darci Werner —

What If?

Do you think the universe fights for souls to be together?
Some things are too strange and strong
to be coincidences.
~Emery Allen

I had just put down a grocery bag and was putting the key in the lock when I heard the phone ringing inside. I didn't have an answering machine, so I had to decide whether to miss the call or let my ice cream melt. I dropped the bag, turned the key and ran into my apartment. Rather breathless, I picked up the phone.

It was a woman explaining that a teaching position had opened at a nearby junior high school. She wanted to know if I was interested in interviewing. Since I had thought I would only be substitute teaching that year, I was slightly taken aback. I hadn't thought anything permanent would be available. School started next Tuesday, and it was Friday morning.

The woman on the phone repeated herself. "Are you interested in an interview? If so, you would need to be here in two hours."

I tried to clear my head as I answered, "Yes, I can be there."

After getting the details, I put the ice cream in the freezer and dashed into the shower, hoping my interview suit was pressed and I had a blouse ready to go. I threw myself together and took one last look in the mirror before I left.

As I got out of my car at the school, I noticed a man. He, too, was headed onto the campus of Wilmington Junior High, a sprawling school in the Los Angeles Unified School District. Entering through the iron gates, he made a left turn, so I saw him in profile. He had wavy, chestnut brown hair, a neatly trimmed beard, and was wearing a Harris Tweed jacket. I am a sucker for Harris Tweed.

I followed him into the main office. As he was standing at the front counter, I had to wait my turn three steps behind him. I heard him say to the secretary, "I was called in for an interview." The secretary handed him a clipboard and told him to fill it out. I couldn't help but look over his shoulder as he began writing. From what I could read, his first name was Michael, and he was from Canoga Park. He was applying for the position of English teacher. *Drat,* I thought. *This man is my competition.* I had also been called to interview to teach English, and I wanted this job.

Michael, as I already thought of him, finished filling in the form, handing it back to the secretary. I overheard him saying to the secretary that he had been caught in "miserable" L.A. traffic that caused him to miss an earlier interview at another school. As he turned to sit down, I saw him full-on for the first time. He smiled at me, gave me a quick nod and sat down.

Michael was called in for his interview with the principal. I knew this gorgeous man would get the job, but I sat and waited my turn anyway. Half an hour later, he and the principal reappeared.

"I'll have someone give you a tour of the school. Wait here. When you're through, I'd like you to meet with the assistant principal. It was very nice meeting you." She shook his hand and turned to me. "I guess you're next. Come in." It didn't seem like a very auspicious welcome to me.

The interview was typical in many ways. The principal asked stock questions like "How long have you taught?" and "Why are you interested in teaching at this school?" Then she asked a surprising question, which was completely unexpected for a would-be English teacher. "Can you teach typing?"

Wait, I thought, *typing?* I was an excellent typist, but I had no idea how to teach it. But I wanted a job, and my suspicions were that Michael had already landed the English position.

"You see, we have a position that requires someone to teach four typing classes a day and one class of English. It's a bit unique, but perhaps you would consider it."

It took all my mental strength to not blurt out something stupid. I needed a second to consider, focus, and decide if I could do this. I knew I was a good teacher, but how fast could I learn to teach a skill as specific as typing? Then, unbidden, Michael appeared in my thoughts.

"Is there a full-time English position?" I asked, trying to find out if she was offering the job to Michael.

"When you were called, there was, but I'm sure it is filled," she answered.

What if I took this job? Did it mean that Michael would also be teaching with me? We'd be on the same faculty. We'd get to know each other. Maybe we'd serve on the same committees. I'd get to know this person who in just a few seconds had fascinated me.

I was assuming he was single. At least there had been no ring. Of course I had checked. And he had fabulous eyes. The saying "Nothing ventured, nothing gained" popped into my head.

Putting my hands behind my back, I crossed my fingers. Looking the principal straight in the eye, I boldly answered, "Yes, I can do that."

Many decades have passed since that job interview, and I often wonder what would have happened if I hadn't picked up the phone that day just in time for that interview? What if I hadn't pretended that I could teach typing? What if the gorgeous man hadn't been caught in traffic and had gotten the job at the other school? What if he'd arrived for the interview a few minutes later and our paths hadn't crossed? I wouldn't have taken the typing job if I hadn't seen him.

Michael indeed got the English position, and that year I taught typing and English. Before the school year ended, we were engaged. When we arrived on campus the next year, it was as a married couple. And even though my husband Michael continues to complain about the "miserable" L.A. traffic, next year we celebrate our forty-fifth wedding anniversary.

— Ina Massler Levin —

Step on a Crack

Timing in life is everything.
~Leonard Maltin

I was driving slowly over the border crossing from my mother's place in France, heading back home to Germany, when the border security police stepped into my lane to flag me down. They signaled me to pull over into the parking area. "Your car is leaning a little, and it looks like your tire is fairly low on air," remarked the burly sergeant.

I opened the car door to get out to have a look, immediately stumbling on a big crack in the pavement. *Step on a crack, break your mother's back.* The childhood rhyme flashed through my head. Because I had just seen my mom twenty minutes earlier, I could understand the association. Yet, it still seemed weird to have the thought at that very moment.

I had just been visiting my aging mother, keeping her company for a few days, and stocking her up with groceries and supplies. When my father died, my mother decided she wanted to spend the remaining years of her life with friends and family back in her hometown near Strasbourg, France.

In virtually the same month, as luck would have it, my wife, who is a psychology professor with the American military, was offered a promotion in Germany. The location was just over the border from my mother's hometown, a mere eighty miles away. So, she enthusiastically accepted the position, and we moved to Germany. We were now able to easily visit my mother in France, while supporting her independent lifestyle at the same time.

So, there I was with a leaking tire and no service station in sight, still sixty miles from home. I didn't have a spare tire in my car, which had an air-in-a-can repair kit that I didn't trust. But I was only twenty miles from my mother's place where I was storing a set of winter tires mounted on rims in her garage. I could use one of those tires to safely get home. So, I thanked the officers for the low-tire warning and headed back toward my mother's place. With the help of my repair kit, I hoped I had just enough air in the leaking tire to make it there.

I called my mom to let her know that I was driving back but got no answer, so I assumed that she was watering the plants outside on her terrace. Once there, I rang the doorbell, but there was still no response, so I let myself in with the key she gave me, calling out for her as I went in. I didn't want to creep in and accidentally scare the daylights out of her. I got no response. I checked the terrace and the rest of the place but found no sign of her. She hadn't mentioned anything about leaving home to go visit anybody, so I was completely perplexed.

I opened the door to the basement area and heard a weak moan. Alarmed, I ran down the stairs to find my mother lying face-down in a pool of blood on the cellar floor, her lip badly split and swollen from the impact after falling down the steps. She was fairly coherent but complained of excruciating back pain as I hurriedly called for an ambulance.

I followed the ambulance to the local hospital, and then found myself pacing for hours in the waiting room, hoping for decent test and X-ray results. It turned out that she had fractured her back. Happily, the medical team gave her a good prognosis and had high expectations for a full recovery.

Had it not been for the border police noticing a tire low on air and stopping me, I would never have thought of returning to my mother's place for a spare tire to get me home. She probably would have exacerbated her back injury trying to crawl for help or suffered an even worse fate. Of course, a similar fate could have awaited me. I could have blown out the tire at high speed on the German autobahn, destroying the car with me in it. It was scary to think about all the implications.

As it turned out, my mother's back healed after plenty of bed rest and the use of a back brace and cane. She now keeps a medic-alert necklace around her neck.

The leaking car tire has been repaired, and now I always carry a spare.

It seems even the universe was sending me a message by having the rhyme flash in my head. I put it down to one of life's little unexplained mysteries. In any case, it turned out to be true.

Step on a crack, break your mother's back.

— Sergio Del Bianco —

A Crystal Clear Message

Not everything we experience can be explained
by logic or science.
~Linda Westphal

On a beautiful fall day many years ago, I was holed up in my kitchen baking a bunch of apple pies. My hands were stained brown from peeling, my countertops were sticky, and my sink was full of dirty dishes. The kitchen was a mess, but I didn't mind. The tantalizing aroma of fresh-baked pies made it all worthwhile.

I've always abided by one hard and fast rule when baking: "Clean up before leaving the kitchen!" Only after everything is spotless do I reward myself with a cup of coffee and, finally, the most fun part of all: delivering baked goods to my family and friends.

On this particular day, in the midst of washing dishes, I suddenly heard a clear voice in my head say: "Take Carol a copy of your story." Startled by the unexpected command, I stopped what I was doing and just stood there a moment, listening. *Where did that come from?* I wondered, curious yet wary.

One of my short stories had recently appeared in *Woman's World* magazine, and I had purchased an extra copy to give to my neighbor Carol, who lived next door on the other side of a wooded buffer. There was no urgency to delivering it, though, so I planned to bring Carol the magazine and a hot apple pie after I finished cleaning up.

Shaking off the bizarre interruption, I resumed washing. But, immediately, I heard the voice again, more insistent this time: "Take Carol a copy of your story!"

Totally rattled now, I glanced around the kitchen. The urge to finish cleaning was strong. But the urge to obey that voice was stronger. Despite my annoyance at the untimely directive, my unease was escalating by the second. Commanding voices weren't an everyday occurrence in my life, but similar things had happened to me occasionally before. And, when I'd failed to heed celestial prompts in the past, the consequences had been dire. Like it or not, I'd learned to take heed.

Quickly grabbing a magazine and a pie, I headed out the back door. As I threaded my way through the woods separating our homes, I couldn't help but feel a little foolish for rushing off on a mission because of a disembodied voice. Still, I kept walking.

Reaching Carol's front lawn, I veered away from the house and headed to the nearby business office where she worked weekdays. Shaking off my strange mix of feelings, I slapped on a smile and stepped inside. But my smile quickly morphed to horror when I saw Carol seated at her desk facing me. Through the large picture window behind her I saw orange flames shooting skyward!

"FIRE!" I yelled.

Stunned, Carol whipped around to find a raging inferno not twenty feet from the building. We called 911, and thankfully, the fire was quickly extinguished. No serious damage was incurred. But later, as my still-shaken friend hugged me and called me her guardian angel, I knew I had to set the record straight. Awed and humbled, I explained that I hadn't saved the day — a voice had directed me, and it knew that telling me to take my magazine story to her would make the most sense to me. Somehow that little voice had caused me to stop cleaning the kitchen, saving precious minutes — minutes that made all the difference in spotting that fire on time.

— Wendy Hobday Haugh —

Just Forty-Five More Minutes

If you can heed only one piece of advice from the universe, make it this… Pay attention. Do this and everything else will fall into place.
~Bryan E. Wright

I watched the nurse hang another bag on the IV pole next to me and attach it to the needle in my arm. Then I turned my head and watched the group of medical personnel surrounding a second gurney on which my husband Bracey was lying.

This was not how we had planned our vacation. We were supposed to be on our way to Roan Mountain, Tennessee. My husband had wanted to take me there almost from the moment we'd met eight years earlier, but we hadn't been able to do so until this weekend when we'd decided to go and celebrate Bracey's seventieth birthday,

I hadn't slept well the night before and felt awful when we got up that morning, but I downplayed the severe upper abdominal pain I was experiencing because I didn't want to disappoint my husband. Unfortunately, I continued to feel worse as the day progressed, and eventually I was unable to hide the pain from him.

I was still stubbornly driving, so Bracey texted my sister, who is a nurse. He was relaying her questions to me and then texting my answers back to her. I knew we were getting close to our destination and didn't want to stop, but when I admitted that the pain had moved into my chest, my sister sent Bracey an urgent message: "GET HER TO AN ER NOW."

The very next interstate exit, in Johnson City, Tennessee, displayed a hospital sign, so we followed the signs to the small community hospital on a nearby hill. I was getting checked in at the emergency room, and the triage nurse had just snapped a hospital bracelet onto my wrist, when suddenly Bracey stumbled into me.

"What are you doing?" I asked him in confusion.

"My defibrillator just went off!" he gasped, clutching the counter.

"Oh, Bracey, that's not even funny!" I scolded him. I turned just in time to see his body seize up as his defibrillator fired again and again.

Just then, another nurse came through the emergency room's double doors, pushing a wheelchair meant for me. However, one look at Bracey told him that my husband needed the wheelchair more than I did. He and I shoved Bracey into the wheelchair over his protests, and then the nurse ordered me to follow him back through the double doors. The triage nurse brought up the rear so that she could get Bracey's information logged into the computer.

My initial blood-pressure reading was a scary 200/157, but several hours later all my tests came back clear: no heart attack, no stroke, no plaque, and all major arteries clear. And, thanks to the intravenous medications they had given me, my blood pressure was back down into the normal range, and my pain was gone. I was discharged.

Bracey wasn't nearly as fortunate.

Although his defibrillator had stopped firing, his heart condition was still deemed unstable, so the decision was made to admit him to the intensive care unit. Bracey protested until the staff reassured him that they would bend the rules a little and allow me to stay with him.

Bracey spent two days in the ICU, and the staff was wonderfully sympathetic when they found out that we were supposed to be on vacation. They went out of their way to make sure we were comfortable. Bracey and I were both chagrined, however, when the staff told us that we were only forty-five minutes away from Roan Mountain.

On his birthday, Bracey was moved from the ICU to a regular room. As soon as he was settled in his new surroundings, I went out to our car and retrieved his birthday gifts, which I had brought along on our trip. Bracey was unwrapping his presents when his doctor stopped by to check on him. The three of us were discussing the strange turn of events that had turned our trip into a "non-vacation," and how regrettable it was that we were just forty-five minutes from our destination, when the doctor suddenly turned toward me.

"I advise you to follow up with your regular doctor when you get home, but I wouldn't be surprised if he doesn't find anything wrong with you," he said.

"What makes you say that?" I asked in some confusion.

He hesitated a moment before answering.

"I think you weren't feeling well so that you would be at this hospital when your husband's defibrillator fired. If you had been at Roan Mountain when it happened, we would have still been the nearest hospital. It would have taken you forty-five minutes to get back here, and your husband would not have made it. Instead of celebrating his seventieth birthday, you would've been facing this day as a new widow."

It was a very sobering thought.

When Bracey and I arrived back home, we immediately made follow-up appointments with our doctors — I with my general practitioner, and Bracey with his cardiologist. Bracey had to undergo another cardiac procedure to upgrade his defibrillator to a pacemaker/defibrillator combo.

The doctor in Johnson City was right. My doctor ran a battery of tests on me and could find nothing to account for my abdominal pain or seriously high blood pressure. It was as if someone knew that we needed to be at the hospital in Johnson City… instead of forty-five more minutes down the road.

— Jan Hopkins-Campbell —

An Uplifting Story

Prayer is man's greatest power.
~W. Clement Stone

I was in the kitchen getting dinner ready when my fourteen-year-old daughter, Cassandra, called me from her room. "Mom, can you help me get downstairs?" She had progressive lung disease and was dependent on oxygen twenty-four hours a day. It was impossible for her to ascend and descend the stairs in our home without assistance. I turned down the stove and ran upstairs to her room. Cassandra let out a sigh and closed her eyes. "Mom, I wish it wasn't so hard for me to go up and down the stairs."

"I know, honey. We'll try to work something out."

A month earlier, we had a company give us a quote for an electric stairlift. It sounded wonderful. My daughter would be able to glide up and down the stairs with ease. It would make a huge difference in the quality of her life. Unfortunately, we couldn't afford it along with the medical bills and loss of income associated with my daughter's illness.

Later that day, I called a local organization that lent medical equipment to the community. They had lent us a wheelchair and a shower chair; maybe they could help with a stairlift, too. I held my breath while the phone rang. "Do you have a stair lift I could borrow?"

"We're sorry, but we don't lend or accept donations of stairlifts due to the mechanical nature and storage space they require." Disheartened, I put down the phone and prayed for a solution.

A few weeks later, we purchased a shower chair so we could return the one we had borrowed. Between doctors' appointments and other commitments, a few more weeks passed, and I hadn't found the time to return the borrowed shower chair to the lending agency. It always fell to the bottom of my to-do list.

One day, though, I woke up feeling a pressing need to return the shower chair that day. I lugged the shower chair downstairs, loaded it in my car, and drove to the lending agency. As I approached their building, I saw something metal glistening on the curb. It looked like metal rails, and one of them had a chair attached.

I thought I was seeing things. I parked my car and got out to confirm it was real. I touched the cool metal of the rails and the soft cushion of the attached seat. There was even a remote control taped to a rail. It was a stairlift! I ran in to ask about it. I had to wait a few minutes to speak with the volunteer as she was fitting a gentleman with a cane. "What's the status of the stairlift outside?"

"Someone left it here during the night. We don't deal with stairlifts, so we're hoping the trash collector will take it away tomorrow morning."

"Can I take it away today?"

"That would be great. Go right ahead."

"Thank you so, so much."

I went outside to size it up. There was no way it would fit in my car. I called my husband to advise him of our good fortune and ask him to come with his vehicle, which is much bigger than mine. "John, you have to come right away. I found a stairlift for Cassandra. You need to come help me get it home. It definitely won't fit in my car."

"I'll come, but are you sure it works?"

"I'm sure it will." I knew the stairlift was there for my daughter.

My husband arrived, and we struggled to get the stairlift into his vehicle as it was still fully assembled and we didn't have the tools to take it apart. There was no way I was leaving without it, though. I was worried someone else would take it, perhaps even as scrap metal. We needed a truck fast. The gentleman who was being fitted with the cane was still there and witnessed our dilemma. "I have a truck and would be happy to help you get the lift home, but I can't help load it because of my knee." We gratefully accepted and managed to get the stairlift in his truck. He followed us back to our house.

After we got the stairlift home, we managed to maneuver it into the house and place it on our stairs. It was a perfect fit, as if it had been built for us! My husband is very handy, and before long the stairlift was secured to our staircase and fully installed. He plugged it in, turned it on, and pressed the power button. I heard the purr of the motor. I watched the seat glide up the stairs and back down again. It worked perfectly.

"Cassandra, come try out your stairlift!" She came from her room, sat in the seat with her portable oxygen in her lap, put the safety arm down, and pressed the button. What a glorious sight as she glided down the stairs, and then up again, giggling as she did it over and over.

I am very glad that I followed that urge to return the shower chair that day, after putting it off for weeks. My prayer had been answered through the unexpected provision of a stairlift and a kind stranger to help us get it home.

— Eleanore R. Steinle —

Fleas and Thank You

I think that someone is watching out for me. God, my guardian angel, I'm not sure who that is, but they really work hard.
~Mattie Stepanek

I owe my life to a flea. If I am honest, I'm sure it was more than one flea. I just like how it sounds to say I owe my life to a flea. It makes me stop and think about how you never know what seemingly insignificant detail could end up being extremely consequential. As it turns out, the existence of those nearly imperceptible fleas played a major role in one of the most consequential events of my life.

Cats get fleas. Having owned several cats over the years growing up in small-town Missouri, this was simply an accepted and acknowledged fact of life. Through those years, we had always been relatively lucky. The few times when fleas were apparent, simple flea treatments from the store had been more than adequate to handle the problem. Thankfully, in 2017, that pattern was broken.

My cat, Boomerjax, was scratching at fleas more than he ever had in the two years since I brought him home from the shelter. It had been about the right amount of time since the last treatment, so despite the increased scratching, I didn't assume anything was different. I ran to the store and bought the same flea treatment I had used on him previously.

A few days after applying the treatment, I noticed he had not improved at all. In fact, he seemed to be even more aggravated. A closer look showed his skin was red and irritated. Not wanting to take any chances, I called the vet's office and made an appointment to get Boomerjax some help.

December 6, 2017 felt like any other day. I ran a couple of errands, watched some TV, read for a while, and then started thinking about getting Boomerjax into his carrier to take him to the vet. As with most cats, it usually took a great deal of time and effort to accomplish this task. To my surprise, on that day, Boomerjax did not put up much resistance. At first, I simply attributed the cooperation to the level of misery caused by the fleas. Looking back, I like to believe it all worked together as part of a bigger plan. I had planned for it to take a while, but now we were running early due to the cat's unusual cooperation. I decided to load the carrier in the car and leave for the vet anyway.

The waiting room offered the standard distractions: TV, magazines, and random strangers with their pets. My distraction of choice was playing a mindless game on my cellphone. When Boomerjax was called to the exam room, I quickly grabbed his carrier and exited my game. What I didn't realize was that I had not simply closed the game app; I had silenced the phone entirely. The vet was very kind with Boomerjax and concluded that he was suffering from an allergic reaction to the saliva in the flea bites. I was given some medicine to put in the cat food, and all seemed right with the world.

Before starting the drive home, I pulled out my phone to send a message to my sister about Boomerjax's diagnosis. To my surprise, the display showed I had four missed calls and two voicemail messages. My surprise turned to shock with the first voicemail. It was the first time in my life I had a message begin with the caller identifying himself as a member of the police department. He asked me to call back as soon as possible. With nervous fingers, I managed to push the button to do just that. After confirming my identity, the officer informed me there was a fire at my house.

As I got closer to home, I found the roads blocked in every direction;

I had to be cleared to get through. When I saw my home, I was confused. It looked fine. I was expecting a pile of ashes or at least some visible sign of destruction. One of the firefighters took some information and warned me that the interior did not fare as well as the exterior. When it was finally safe for me to enter, I was walked through the scene. The fire marshal explained exactly what he believed had happened, including the timeline of events.

Due to the materials and design of my century-old house, the fire, which started in old wiring, was contained in the wall until it built up enough pressure to explode through. The full-sized filing cabinet and large freezer that I assumed had been moved by the firemen had, in fact, been blown across the room by the force of the explosion. The fire marshal explained that the build-up of the fire inside the wall would have made enough noise for me to hear from anywhere on the first floor, especially right before exploding through the wall. He felt confident that, had I been home, I would have heard the noise and been investigating—placing me in the immediate path of the explosion. Given the intensity of the force, heat, and flying debris, there would have been little chance of survival.

When the discussion turned to the timing of events, I really understood the important role every small detail can make. The explosion happened shortly after I had left for the vet with Boomerjax. In fact, the first 911 call reporting the fire had come in during the time that I had put aside for wrestling Boomerjax into his carrier. If he hadn't uncharacteristically cooperated, I would have been home and looking for the source of the noise in the wall. And if he hadn't developed an allergy to flea bites for the first time, after our prior successful treatments, we wouldn't have been heading to the vet.

Therefore, I owe my life to a flea, or more accurately to an infestation of fleas.

Amazingly, three years later, Boomerjax has never had fleas again. He's a good boy.

—David L. Bishop—

The West Point Ring

Impossible situations can become possible miracles.
~Robert H. Schuller

As my friend Nancy grew more feeble, I stopped by to check on her whenever I could. Coffee and conversation in her cozy family room were always wonderful. One glorious October afternoon, she asked if I'd help her do something.

"Sure," I said. "If I can."

"I want to stroll through the yard and look at the leaves," she said. "But I can't go outside alone. And I have to take that awful thing." Nancy pointed to the walker that stood in the corner of the room. "I'm just too unsteady without it." I moved the walker and helped her stand and grab hold of it. "Let me empty this out," she said, removing a box of tissues and a folded newspaper from the wire basket that hung from the handlebars. "I want to have plenty of room for leaves."

We made our way haltingly out the door and into the yard. The autumn leaves were breathtaking against the bright blue sky. Red maple. Golden tulip poplar. Best of all were the star-shaped sweetgum leaves, with four different colors — yellow, orange, red and deep purple — all on one tree. I gathered dozens of leaves and handed them to Nancy, who placed them lovingly in the basket. "We'll make leaf bouquets when we get back inside," she told me.

I noticed she was short of breath and asked if she needed to rest.

"Not just yet," she said. "Do you think we could go to the back yard and look for Bill's ring just one more time?"

That's how I learned the story of a class ring that had been missing for more than thirty years. Nancy met Bill in the early 1940s, not long after the United States entered World War II. "Maybe it wasn't love at first sight," Nancy told me, her eyes twinkling, "but it was pretty darn close."

Bill enrolled in the United States Military Academy at West Point. Upon his graduation in 1945, he received a 14-carat gold ring with a garnet stone that became one of his most treasured possessions. His military career with the Army Air Corps, which later became the United States Air Force, spanned more than three decades. It took his family, which eventually grew to include four children, all over the globe.

"We came back home to Tennessee when Bill retired in the late 1970s," Nancy said. "The kids were grown and on their own, and the two of us settled into this lovely home. Bill especially loved our back yard because he was an avid gardener. It was big enough for him to grow anything he wanted, including the little yellow tomatoes that were his favorites."

Sadly, the good times didn't last long. Bill was diagnosed with Parkinson's disease. Though he still enjoyed his garden, he struggled to take care of it. "He grew weak and very thin," Nancy told me. "So thin that his West Point ring was loose on his finger. But he wore it anyway. Then one day it slipped off while he was in the yard. He didn't notice until he came inside and washed his hands. We searched everywhere. For days and weeks, we searched, but the ring was nowhere to be found."

"Bill's health deteriorated so badly that he moved to a long-term care facility, where he died in 1995. We'd been married fifty years," Nancy said. "He was the one and only love of my life." She stayed on at their house, comforted by family and friends as her days filled with new routines. Nancy never stopped missing Bill. And for the next fifteen years, she never stopped looking for his ring.

Not long after Nancy and I took our leaf walk, which failed to turn up the ring, my dear friend passed away.

A decade went by. Bill and Nancy's children decided it was time to empty their parents' beloved home and put it on the market. But they agreed they couldn't let the property go without making one last attempt to find the ring. A friend with a metal detector had tried once with no success. Hoping for a different outcome, the siblings contacted a metal-detecting club in a town more than a hundred miles away to see if they might be interested in searching for it. The men they talked to said they'd like nothing better than to snoop around in someone's yard for a lost treasure. And, no, they wouldn't charge a cent.

In less than two hours, the ring that had been lost for more than forty years was found. It was buried about four inches deep near the spot where Bill had grown raspberries. Nancy's daughter, Travis, was overcome with emotion when she told me the story. "It was a glory moment, for sure," she said. The ring was caked with dirt, of course, but after a couple of minutes under the garden hose, it was good as new, gleaming in the morning light.

"My brothers and I had never stopped talking about Dad's ring," she said. "It just broke our hearts to think it might remain buried forever. It was such a moment of surprise and healing when the men found it. We're so grateful that they volunteered their time to make this miracle happen."

What will happen to the precious family heirloom? Bill's full name was William Robert Jarrell, Jr., named for his father. Bill's oldest son was given that name, too, as was his oldest grandson. Now that grandson has a young son of his own, with—no surprise—the very same name. The ring will be his.

And who knows? William Robert Jarrell V might just be a West Point cadet himself someday.

—Jennie Ivey—

Timing Is Everything

The prayer that begins with trustfulness
and passes on into waiting will always
end in thankfulness, triumph, and praise.
~Alexander Maclaren

Working as a freelancer has its ups and downs. On the one hand, there is a sense of freedom and relaxation when you can work on your own time schedule, taking breaks whenever you desire. But, on the other hand, there is the constant "filling of the pipeline" so that you have a steady workflow producing income.

When you work as a freelance songwriter, there is always that delicate balance between creating art and creating a commodity worthy of pay. I have created songs that are purely for the sake of art, and those tend to enjoy a nice life on my computer. I have also composed songs that produce income because they are created specifically for the purpose of filling a production or publishing need. These songs may not fulfill the "artist cry" within me, but they help pay the bills.

The process of being paid for composing songs varies. In most cases, you earn money by either selling your song outright, or by agreeing to a licensing deal or a royalty deal. When you sell your song outright, you are selling ownership of that song for an agreed fee. This can hurt but sometimes it's the thing to do, especially when income is needed.

A better method is to secure a licensing deal with a publisher or producer. In this scenario, you retain ownership of the song, and the producer or publisher simply pays you a licensing fee to use your song on their project. And, of course, a royalty deal is often the best plan since it can be quite lucrative if the song goes on to enjoy a successful career! In those cases, the songwriter trusts in the honesty of the companies that track sales and compute the royalties.

I have participated in all three of the above scenarios in my journey as a freelance songwriter. The business side of making music is easy to dismiss for those of us who tend to live primarily in the "art" side of that phrase, but you can create wonderful music and still get paid. Most of my songwriting efforts were for children's audio and video projects in the Christian marketplace. God opened some wonderful doors for me to write songs for popular animated videos, audio products, vacation bible school and related children's projects. For a while, there was a steady flow of requests, but demand is uneven, so there can be tough times while waiting for the next opportunity.

Now, here is where the story of God's timing is revealed.

We were living in Aurora, Colorado, where I was serving in a church as a music director. I was still freelancing as a songwriter, but since I had steady work in ministry, the need to secure songwriting jobs was not as urgent. I kept my finger in the pie, so to speak, mainly because of how much I love writing songs.

We were in Aurora for about twelve years, the last few of which were very difficult for our family. It was a season of personal and professional heartache that left us in a terrible financial position. Frankly, it was surprising to me that we were struggling. It was not something I expected.

The last straw was when our minivan fell apart. This was the main transport for our three kids, so we had to get it repaired. I had the van towed to the repair shop and nervously awaited the estimate.

My mouth literally fell open when I heard what it would cost to get our minivan up and running. We did not have the money to pay for the repairs. I gave the shop permission to do the work, and then my wife and I prayed. Unfortunately, when the van was ready, we were not. We still didn't have the almost $1,000 we needed.

I decided to ask if we could pay the repair bill over time. I had no idea if that would work, but it was worth a try.

Before heading to the repair shop, I checked the mail. Honestly, it was just something to do as I procrastinated about the uncomfortable conversation I was about to have.

As I sifted through the mail, one letter caught my eye. It was from a publishing company I had worked with about twelve years earlier. I opened the envelope, and tears filled my eyes as I read the words: "Unpaid royalties." Apparently, this company had never paid me royalties for one of my songs written many years ago. It was a simple oversight on their part, and they apologized profusely for the error.

Then I looked at the check. The amount was almost to the penny what we owed for the repairs on the minivan! I stood in the street with tears in my eyes. Our prayers had worked, and somehow God knew when I wrote that song twelve years earlier, that I would need all the royalties from it on this day.

The name of that song? "Everybody Give Thanks!" And that's exactly what I did.

— Dan McGowan —

Dreams & Premonitions

Lightning Strikes

Out of this nettle, danger, we pluck this flower, safety.
~William Shakespeare

Like his father, my husband wanted to build our home with his own two hands. The shell of our dream sat on a hill with a stunning panoramic view. With the framing completed, it was ready for windows and roofing.

Every day after work, we packed up our two little girls along with our dinner before we headed to the construction site of our new home. Our biggest challenge while we worked on the house was keeping our four- and seven-year-old daughters occupied and out of danger. We set up an area with a little table and lots of toys where we could keep an eye on them. They loved the adventure and were pretty good about staying in their safe spot.

One day, I was loading the cooler with our dinner when I felt a tap on my shoulder. I turned around, but no one was there. I was still trying to figure it out when I heard a voice say, "Don't go to the house tonight." My confusion turned to anxiety.

This particular evening, we were getting a late start and, to add to my trepidation, a storm was predicted. I couldn't shake the foreboding feeling I had. When I felt a tug on my sweatshirt, I looked at two little girls pleading, "Mommy, please, can we stay home?" They had never done that before; they loved playing at the new house. Again, I heard a voice say, "Don't go."

I couldn't ignore the voice or the signs. I turned and pleaded with my husband, "How about taking a break tonight? I feel that something is wrong."

Reluctantly, my husband agreed as we watched the skies darken. However, he insisted that when the storm passed, we needed to check the house. The thunderstorm and high-wind threat never materialized at our townhouse rental, so my unease lifted and we drove to our home under construction.

As we pulled up to our property, we were shocked. The framework for the door into the house from the garage had been ripped from its opening and blown across the driveway. There were char marks along all the nails from the peak of the house to the ground.

"The house was hit by lightning!" my husband cried. "Keep the girls in the car!"

Upon further investigation, we found a zigzag burn pattern across the plywood floor of our daughters' bedroom. Wood had been sheared from the two by fours, and huge jagged pieces turned into projectiles, embedding themselves deeply into the walls of every room.

I shuddered and ran to the safety of my husband's arms. "We could have lost everything to a bolt of lightning. We were lucky the house didn't burn to the gr…" I couldn't finish my sentence because of what I saw next. Our safe play spot for the girls had taken a direct hit from the storm. Studs were ripped from the walls, and the center beam had collapsed onto their table. Lumber with large, protruding nails was strewn around the room, piled on top of the toys. If we had been in our house working like every other evening, our daughters would have been killed.

Later, we learned that a microburst was responsible for this path of destruction on our road. We were more fortunate than others. Neighboring houses had caught fire from the numerous lightning strikes, and there was extensive damage everywhere within a two-mile radius.

Why and how did I hear the voice that warned me away from our construction site that night? And why did our girls uncharacteristically ask to stay home? We'll never know, but it was a miracle that we were spared, and we are so grateful.

— Terry Hans —

A Voice in the Night

Let gratitude be the pillow upon which you kneel to say your nightly prayer. And let faith be the bridge you build to overcome evil and welcome good.
~Maya Angelou

I was living in paradise, and I knew it. My husband, our toddler son, and I lived in a cottage on the Vanderlip estate, Villa Narcissa, the home of the original owner of the Rancho Palos Verdes peninsula south of Los Angeles. The grand, old mansion was built at the beginning of the twentieth century and was surrounded by outbuildings and guest cottages. The cottages were tucked into the hills and strategically placed on curving paths and behind stands of trees to hide them from the main house and offer the highest degree of privacy. Our cottage was the most private, lying at the farthest edge of the property. We often said that it was the "forgotten cottage," just perfect for newlyweds.

From our patio, we could watch cruise ships sail by our cliffs. Past them, we could see Catalina Island in the distance framed by the century-old bougainvillea that crawled over the arches of our gazebo and shaded the terracotta tiles below.

The icons of an era-gone-by with names like Barrymore, Pickford and Gable had played in the pool and wandered the garden. They had spent the night in the same cottages we now occupied after legendary parties and newsworthy antics. European royalty and heads of state still visited on a regular basis and could be seen strolling through the cypress and citrus trees while peacocks roamed the grounds.

Yes, we were lucky to live there.

It had been a perfect summer day. Steven had the summer off, as school was out, and we used the time to just be a family and enjoy our lives. We'd gone for a hike through the estate's grounds that day and had a picnic on the grass before falling into bed and a peaceful sleep.

As the mother of an active young boy, I had no trouble sleeping at night and seldom stirred until my child's voice awakened me in the morning.

So, it was strange that a different voice startled me in the night.

"Get up!" it called to me. "Get up now!"

I was truly tired and wanted to continue sleeping. Eyes still closed, I lay at attention for a moment and then decided the voice was the remnants of some dream and allowed myself to begin drifting back to sleep.

"No!" demanded the voice. "Get up!"

This time, there was no denying it. The voice was real, and the instructions were clear.

I opened my eyes and looked around the room.

The blackout drapes were slightly open, and through the crack a soft orange light flickered through. Silently, I arose from bed and crept to the window.

As I pulled the drape aside and looked out over the hills below, I had to blink to gather my thoughts. Fire had crested the ridge everywhere I looked. Silent orange flames licked the sky and were marching toward us.

I reached down, picked up the phone, and called 911.

"What do you mean you're still there?" asked the dispatcher. "We evacuated everyone off the estate an hour ago! Get out now!"

I threw on clothes with one hand while I stuffed diapers in the diaper bag with the other.

"I bet they didn't even know our cottage was here," said my husband as he gathered up the baby's blanket and slipped into shoes.

In less than five minutes, we'd scooped up our son, tossed a few clothes and diapers in the car, and begun driving down the circuitous road that led off the hill. In a strategic decision, we opted to leave our other car and go down the hill together. Cars could be replaced. Our family could not.

It was other-worldly.

Even though it was 2 a.m., the sky was bright orange. Once outside, the acrid smell of ash and fire stung the eyes and burned into nostrils. To gasp for air meant sucking in searing heat. As we passed the first curve in the road, we were met with fire on both sides of the street. Eucalyptus trees exploded like giant torches. Manzanita burned hot and wild at street level. Amidst the burning trees, neighbors fought frantically to lure terrified horses into the safety of trailers in a life-and-death battle against time. As Steven drove through falling embers and flaming branches, I turned to check on our son in his car seat. The orange reflection lit his face with an eerie yet angelic glow, and his wide eyes held an awe and innocence that will stay with me forever.

Inch by inch, we managed to crawl through the inferno until we could turn off the hill and head to safety

That night, we slept at the Holiday Inn. We each showered and slept in an oversized undershirt we bought at the local convenience store that was open all night. We couldn't sleep in our own clothes, or even bring them into the room, as they reeked of smoke.

Safe and together in our hotel room, I wondered at the voice that had pulled me out of sleep and away from danger. I sent up a silent prayer of thanks before drifting off to sleep, three in a bed, safe with my family.

The next day, they let us go home.

The entire hill still smoldered. The only sound we could hear was the occasional hiss of heat coming off a tree trunk. Debris covered the road, and the slope looked like what I imagine the world would resemble after nuclear war.

Blackness and devastation followed us, curve after curve, as we made our way home. As we entered the estate, signs of the fire were still there. In fact, the fire had been stopped just feet from our door.

It would take time for the land to heal itself, but it would. And so would we. We were safe and whole. We had gotten out in time to save ourselves and give others the space they needed to save our home. The firefighters had clearly worked hard to hold the line just beyond our house. It had been saved — and we had been saved — by that voice in the night.

— Susan Traugh —

Not Yet

Follow your intuition, listening to your dreams,
your inner voice to guide you.
~Katori Hall

Ivory sheets covered a single bed. Soft piano music played in the background as I stood on a fluffy white cloud.

"Where's Mom going to sleep?" I asked my dad. He wore a white gown.

"It's time for me to rest all by myself now," he said.

I reached out to him. "No, Dad, no. You can't! Not now. Not yet!"

I woke up from the dream in a pool of sweat. I'd had the dream that I was dreading. My father, who'd been battling severe heart problems for months, was in heaven. Did this mean he was going to die?

"Are you going to tell him?" my husband asked me later that morning.

"I don't want to scare him," I said, shaking my head after contemplating this concern all morning. "The dream doesn't even make sense. He just had major heart surgery. Everything went well, and he's on the mend. I'm sure the dream was just a consequence of my overactive imagination."

Attempting to forget about the dream, I continued with my day until my mother called.

"We're at the doctor's office. The doctor wants Dad to go to the hospital, but your father is refusing to go."

"Dad has to go," I stated.

"What do you mean?"

I relayed my dream to my mother.

When I got off the phone, I burst into tears. It wasn't my overactive imagination. It was real. Too real. My dream was a warning.

After talking to my mother, my father agreed to go to the hospital.

I saw my dad there when he woke up from the procedure. "Dad, what happened?"

"I don't know. The doctors said everything was fine, and then suddenly my heartrate skyrocketed. They said I had a bad reaction to some medication."

I thought about the dream.

He shook his head. "I thought the docs were nuts until you told us about that dream. And now they're telling me if I hadn't come in, I would've died."

"I'm so glad I told you," I said. "And I'm so glad I listened to my dream."

"Me, too," he said. Still dressed in his hospital gown, my father pulled the ivory sheet up to his chest as he rested on the single hospital bed.

I looked down at my feet just to make sure I wasn't standing on a cloud.

— Keri Kelly —

A Mother's Intuition

The relationship between parents and children,
but especially between mothers and daughters,
is tremendously powerful, scarcely to be
comprehended in any rational way.
~Joyce Carol Oates

I was eating lunch when our second daughter, Melissa, surprised me by stopping by our house. I hadn't seen her in weeks, and her sudden appearance made me wary. She had been an extremely difficult teenager, and she wasn't living with us at that time. She was couch surfing at friends' houses, as best I could tell. It wasn't a lifestyle that suited her very well. She was always thin, but now she looked gaunt.

"Do you want a turkey sandwich?" I asked.

"No, thanks," she said, barely pausing as she walked toward the stairs. "Mom, I'm going to Florida with two boys I met from Arkansas."

When I got to her bedroom, she was stuffing clothing into a backpack. There was nothing I could do to stop her. She was eighteen, so she wasn't asking for my permission. She was telling me her plan. Nothing I said even garnered a response. I followed her out to the car waiting in the driveway.

Two young men immediately jumped out of the car. They came forward to shake my hand. I looked at the young man who seemed to be more approachable. He introduced himself as Doug.

"I'm just not comfortable with any of this," I said.

"I understand, ma'am," he answered. "But I want to assure you that we gave up our serial-killing ways two years ago."

Dumbfounded, I blurted out, "What if you change your mind?"

"No, ma'am, them days are done."

And with that, they were gone.

Eventually, I learned that the two boys were college students on summer break. They were driving cross-country, camping and sightseeing along the way. By September, Melissa and Doug were dating, and they settled back in Arkansas where he was beginning his senior year.

The following spring, Melissa called and asked if she and Doug could stay with us for the summer. We live on Cape Cod, which is a resort area, so they hoped to get high-paying summer jobs in restaurants to save money for Doug to go to graduate school. Even though our relationship with Melissa had greatly improved in our nine months apart, my husband and I hesitated. We didn't really know Doug, and the memories of Melissa's bad behavior in high school — the drinking and drugs especially — were still fresh in our memory.

Every time my husband and I discussed whether to let them stay with us, we came to the same conclusion: It just wasn't worth the risk. We still had two younger children at home, and they didn't deserve a return to the chaos from the past.

When our oldest daughter Jess offered to let Melissa and Doug stay with her, it seemed like the perfect solution. She had an apartment on Main Street, where she lived with her boyfriend and an infant daughter.

Everyone felt pretty good about the decision until one day shortly before Melissa and Doug arrived. Jess called to tell me they had decided to put them in the sunroom on the first floor, instead of the second bedroom upstairs as originally planned. They were afraid Melissa and Doug would wake up the baby if they went out at night or stayed up too late.

As soon as Jess said the word "sunroom," I felt deeply uneasy. I pictured the sunny space with a tile floor and miniature cathedral ceiling. It was a very pleasant room, so I couldn't put my finger on what was making me feel such discomfort. I didn't say anything to Jess, but the feeling didn't leave me after I hung up.

My husband was home at the time, sitting in the living room with me. He overheard my end of the conversation. We were both pretty quiet for a few minutes. After all the hours of discussing the reasons they couldn't stay with us, the decision for them to move in with us took about three seconds.

"Jess and Chris are going to put Melissa and Doug in the sunroom at their apartment," I finally said. "I don't know why, but I just don't feel comfortable about that."

"Do you want them to stay here with us?" he asked.

"Yes."

He said okay, and I felt relief, but it didn't eliminate all my uneasiness.

It turned out to be a strangely idyllic summer. Melissa and Doug were fun to have around. They worked hard at their jobs, but also helped around the house. On their one night off from work every week, they walked our younger children down to the local ice-cream shop for a cone.

That summer ended up being a time for us to repair our relationships and our family. We quickly grew to love Doug as a member of the family. His sense of humor alone won us over.

Then in mid-July, we got a phone call at 2 a.m. from Jess. She was crying so hard that it was hard to understand her. Eventually, I figured out that a drunk driver who was being chased by the police came barreling down the road across from their apartment at a very high speed. Rather than turning left or right onto Main Street, he crashed right into their apartment. They were asleep on the second floor, so they were okay, but the apartment was in shambles.

My husband drove over to pick them all up. We pulled out the sleeper sofa in my office and set up the pack-and-play for our granddaughter, but none of us slept at all that night. The next day, I went with Jess to survey the damage and help her pack some things so they could stay with us while the apartment was repaired.

What I saw made my stomach drop. There was a large, sedan right in the middle of the first-floor sunroom. If Melissa and Doug had stayed in the sunroom for the summer, they would have died.

I don't know if it was mother's intuition or angels who whispered in my ear, but I'm so grateful that I paid attention. Melissa and Doug didn't end up together in the end, but they both moved on to happy relationships with other people. Now I have my daughter, safe and happy, living just one town away where she is raising my two amazing grandchildren.

— Laurie Higgins —

A Rockaway Adventure

It is a good divine that follows his own instructions.
~William Shakespeare

I loved visiting the Rockaways when I was growing up in New York City. You might not think of New York City as a beach community, but there's a long expanse of beaches in Queens and Brooklyn, right on the Atlantic Ocean. The Rockaway peninsula in Queens was a playground for the rich and poor, with trendy restaurants, surfing, boat rides, and a boardwalk along the beach. My friends and I would take the bus there when we were kids. It was an hour from our homes on the other side of Queens, but we loved it.

One hot day in July, my best friend Rosalind and I took the bus there. I was twelve, and she was fourteen. It was perfectly all right with our parents that we went alone. Those were different times, and we were latchkey kids, used to being on our own.

We had saved up our allowance for the fare and snacks, and we were excited about lying on the beach and looking at the other kids. When we got there, we spread our blanket out on the crowded beach and we slid the bathing-suit straps off our skinny shoulders to avoid getting tan lines. All the while, we giggled and chattered like other teenage girls. Then we sat up and opened the brown paper bag we had brought from home, shaking out the sand, and munched on the liverwurst sandwiches my mom had prepared for us. After a while, we flipped over to our stomachs, making sure our backs got enough rays, too. The luckier girls got gorgeous tans—the darker, the better. Some of us got red, burnt and peeled. No sunscreen, no lotion. Even if there had been Coppertone, we couldn't afford it.

When I'd get home from days like this, my mom would yell: "What's the matter with you? You should have covered up!" My brother would snicker and call me "Dummy."

After we'd had enough of the blistering heat, we hid our "valuables" under a corner of the blanket and headed down to the ocean to cool off. The invigorating waves revitalized us.

Then we were ready for the boardwalk. We strolled leisurely, sneaking peeks at the cute guys who never looked back. It didn't matter. We wouldn't have known how to talk to them anyway.

After a long and pleasurable day in the sun, hot and exhausted, we were hungry again. As we prepared to go home, we reviewed our finances and were pleased to see that we had enough for bus fare and a couple of hot dogs. Rosalind went off to get them while I held our place in the line for the bus.

The bus approached just as Rosalind joined me. As she handed me my hot dog, a kid younger than me stepped off the bus and, to my disbelief, swiped the hot dog right out of my hand. As quick as a flash, he ran off, leaving me staring at my empty hand.

As annoyed as I was, I couldn't help but laugh, and so did Rosalind. She took off after the little hot-dog thief.

"No! Forget it!" I called after her. She chased the rascal a few steps, but he was faster, disappearing into the crowd.

Meanwhile, the bus was filling up with passengers. When Rosalind returned, I took a couple of steps up on the bus. One foot was on the first step, the other on the second, and then I stopped.

"Well? Are you going in or what?" Rosalind nudged me, one step behind.

I got a strange feeling. I was being pulled up, and I was being pulled down. I couldn't explain it. It was an instinct or a premonition or something. All the other passengers had either found seats or were standing. I was holding up the bus. The driver was annoyed. He glared at me and barked, "Come on. Come on, kid! In or out!"

My mind was made up. I wasn't sure what I was doing, but I was sure of one thing: We were not getting on that bus.

I returned to the sidewalk, pulling Rosalind with me. The driver took off in a huff.

Rosalind looked at me curiously. "Eva, it's another hour until the next bus!"

I knew that, but it was a feeling I could not ignore. There was something about that bus.

We stood on the sidewalk trying to figure out where the subway station was, hoping we had enough money for the train. A kind passerby gave us directions. We counted our change and discovered we had enough for the fare — but not for a replacement hot dog.

Suddenly, we were startled by loud noises — screeching tires, horns blasting, and the sound of a crash. It was too far down the street to see, but soon we heard sirens coming.

Later, we learned that the bus we were supposed to take had collided with a truck a couple of blocks down the road. The accident was reported on the nightly news. The bus was heavily damaged, and the other vehicle was totaled. Some passengers were injured. Thankfully, there were no fatalities.

It was one of the first times in my life that I had listened to an inner voice warning me of serious consequences.

Although it took us longer to get home on the subway, it didn't matter.

They say everything happens for a reason. I sometimes wonder what would have happened if that spunky kid had not swiped my hot dog. My friend and I might have been seriously injured in that crash.

Saved by a wiener thief!

— Eva Carter —

A Deep Dark Feeling

Learn to trust your inner feeling, and it will become stronger. Avoid going against your better judgment or getting talked into things that just don't feel right.
~Doe Zantamata

His lips were pressed together, and he was staring into the air again. I knew my husband had something on his mind. Although I was tempted to ask him what it was, I decided to wait until he was ready to tell me. I didn't have to wait very long.

A few hours later, after I had given the baby her nighttime bottle, I came into the living room, sank into a chair and sighed. My husband peered over the newspaper he was reading and then folded it and talked nonstop while I listened without interruption.

An opportunity had come up. He had been asked to join the crew of a long-range tuna-fishing boat that would be leaving in two weeks. The payout at the end of the trip would be much more than what he usually made, but he would be gone for a month. He had to give the captain his decision in a few days, but he wanted to make sure I would be okay with him going. He sank against the back of his chair when he finished.

I let the words sink in and considered how to respond. I have always been independent, so I knew I could manage without him for a month. We had relatives nearby and helpful neighbors. It was obvious he wanted to have this experience as well as the benefit of the payout. He had already decided this would be his last year working in commercial fishing, so it would be an upbeat ending before he made a career change. I managed to say, "If you really want to do it, then do it," and watched a smile spread across his face.

Within a few days, a dark feeling started creeping inside me. I convinced myself it was due to exhaustion. The baby hadn't been sleeping through the night, and my husband was gone at night because the commercial fishing boat he worked on fished at night. I promised myself I would catch up on sleep by going to bed earlier and taking an afternoon nap.

The foreboding feeling grew within me. Something wasn't right. I was well past the period of postpartum blues. The upcoming long-range fishing job rolled around in my mind, but I couldn't understand why. My husband was a seasoned commercial fisherman. The boat he was going to work on was only a year old and had the latest in commercial fishing equipment and radio communication. I kept pushing the dark feeling out of my mind whenever it surfaced, but I could no longer deny it.

A week before my husband was scheduled to leave, I knew I had to stop him from going. I could not explain why, but the feeling was all-consuming. I curled up on the sofa and waited for him to come home at dawn.

He was surprised to find me on the sofa and knelt in front of me. When I saw him, tears streamed down my face. It was a sure sign that something was wrong because I am not one to cry easily. I told him what had been happening to me and asked him not to go on the trip. He was reluctant to agree at first but could see that this was an inexplicably strong feeling for me. I wasn't normally like this at all. He called the captain of the long-range fishing boat and withdrew his name from the crew.

The boat left without him but with a few of his friends on the crew. Three days later, the boat and crew were lost in the Pacific Ocean. No bodies were recovered, and only pieces of the boat were found, apparently having been hit by a rogue wave. After that, I knew that I should always pay attention whenever I had a strangely deep, dark feeling about something.

— L.A. Kennedy —

Sight for a Sore Eye

The best thing about having a sister
was that I always had a friend.
~Cali Rae Turner

"I'm sorry," the medical specialist was saying. "There's nothing we can do. These injuries are completely unpredictable. You might regain full sight in that eye, or partial sight, or none at all."

I squinted at him with my left eye because I couldn't open the right one. "There's no surgery to fix it?" I asked, more anxious by the second. My right eye was—or had been—my good eye, my dominant eye. The left one was much weaker.

"I'm afraid not. The problem isn't the eye itself but the nerve connecting it to your brain. And it's too risky to go into the brain to try to correct the problem. But don't worry, lots of people get used to living with only one eye. You'll adapt."

Yeah, I thought, *but I bet most of them aren't editors and proofreaders who rely on sharp eyesight to make a living.* I was single. What would I do if I couldn't support myself anymore?

Six weeks earlier, a serious accident had left me with some broken bones and a brain injury that paralyzed my right eyelid and eyeball. My bones were healing, but the eye remained stubbornly shut and motionless.

My brother-in-law Rick knew I was open to alternative-health practices. He suggested I try cranial-sacral massage, which involves subtle manipulations of the bones in the head, spinal column, and sacrum.

"Sure," I said. "I've got nothing to lose."

"But you have to see my friend Robert for it," Rick added. "He's the best in the city. Your sister knew him and really liked him, too."

My sister Denise, Rick's wife, had died seven years earlier of brain cancer at the age of forty-seven. She left behind a sixteen-year-old daughter from a previous relationship, but Rick had taken her on as his own, and together we'd parented her after Denise's tragic death. The loss had been immeasurable to all of us because Denise was one of the kindest, sweetest, loveliest people you'd ever meet, and the person I was closest to in the world. The year before she died, we'd also lost both our parents. So I had just been emerging from a long, dark tunnel of intense mourning when I had the accident. I didn't know how much more I could take.

I called Robert's clinic and was told there was a one-year waiting list to see him. My heart sank.

"You could see another therapist here," the receptionist said. "Or I could put you on a waiting list for a cancellation for Robert."

I hesitated and then said, "Put me on his waiting list."

"Sure. But note that very few people cancel on him. He really is that good."

Oh, well, I thought. If I didn't get to see Robert within a month or two, I figured I could try another person at the clinic.

Meanwhile, it was fall, and the leaves were turning glorious shades of gold and crimson. I used to love this time of year, but now I hated it because the anniversary of my sister's death was fast approaching. Every October, I felt weighed down with a dense black grief.

Three weeks after she died, I dreamed about Denise. In the dream, she was wearing her dark blue raincoat, which she and I had enjoyed picking out together. She said, "I have to go now. I really have to leave."

"I understand," I replied, knowing, with the weird logic of dreams, that she was dead. I felt a huge pang, but I was also happy to see her again. I watched her walk to the door, where she flashed me her beautiful smile. Then she was gone.

I'd woken up practically sobbing. Since then, I hadn't had a single dream of her that I could remember. I wanted one so badly because being in her presence, if only in a dream, was still better than being in the world without her. Neither she nor I believed in an afterlife, despite our religious upbringing, so I couldn't cling to the notion that we'd ever meet again. Still, I longed for some hint or sign that would make me feel that part of Denise's precious spirit was still alive.

A few days after I'd phoned Robert's clinic, the receptionist called me back. "Robert's had a cancellation this week," she said. "Can you come in?"

Wow, I thought, *that was quick. And how did I make it to the top of the waiting list?* But all I said was, "When's it for?"

"Thursday, one o'clock. October 19th."

My heart stopped for a second. I was speechless.

"Are you still there?" asked the woman.

"Yes, I'm just…" I didn't feel like explaining. "I was… checking my date book. I'll be there."

I hung up the phone and began to cry. My sister had died on a crisp, sunny day early in the afternoon of October 19th.

That Thursday, I went to the clinic, and Robert worked on me. His hands moved almost imperceptibly over my head and down my spine. I felt myself relaxing. As I hovered near sleep, my thoughts strayed to Denise. Was her energy still floating around somewhere? Had she orchestrated all this? And would this treatment actually help, given I could barely feel what Robert was doing?

A day later, my right eye began to open. Four days later, it had opened a quarter of the way and, amazingly, I could see a little with it!

Although I couldn't get another appointment with Robert, who was once again completely booked for a year, I saw another therapist at his clinic for several more treatments. By the end, my eye was almost fully open, and I could move my eyeball. But because it wasn't moving through its full range, I had double vision and had to wear an eye patch. Eventually, enough normal vision returned that I no longer needed it. My left eye grew stronger to compensate for the now-weaker right one, and a year later I was able to drive and even work again.

When I told my doctors and specialists about that first cranial-sacral treatment and its aftermath, they looked skeptical. Two of them told me it was mere coincidence. I simply smiled and silently thanked my sister.

I still have some double vision when I look up and to the right, and that will probably never change. But my optometrist, who saw the MRIs of my brain, thinks I've made a remarkable recovery.

Since that time, I've only dreamed once about Denise — a vague dream in which we were just happily hanging out together. But that's okay, because every time I gaze in the mirror and see my open right eye looking back at me, I think about that particular October 19th. And I smile and thank my sweet sister yet again.

— Marie-Lynn Hammond —

Whisper from Heaven

A dream which is not interpreted is like a letter which is not read.
~The Talmud

A text message came from my college roommate, Erica. "Any chance this looks like the ring in your dream?"

Her mother had died a few months previously in a tragic homicide. At the funeral, I stood with her as she read the eulogy. It was a tribute to a life well-lived, and my friend delivered it with strength and dignity.

In the weeks following the funeral, I thought of Erica and her mom often. I couldn't imagine the pain my friend was experiencing, but I wanted to be strong for her, so I kept my emotions at bay. But bottled emotions will eventually erupt. And one Sunday, while sitting in church, I met them head on. Glancing just a few rows ahead of me, I noticed the back of a woman who resembled Erica's mom. I went from happy to angry to sad in a matter of minutes. My grief had finally surfaced and continued to linger with me throughout the day. That very evening, her mom visited me in a dream.

In the dream, her face was glowing and full of joy. She looked beautiful, just as I remembered, and happy. My attention was drawn to a green-and-gold ring. It looked like a flower, simple and quaint, almost something a child would wear. And then I woke up.

Days later, the images wouldn't leave me, and I knew I was meant to share the dream with my friend. In a leap of faith, I texted the details. She kindly replied, "Thank you for letting me know." And that was that.

We didn't speak of the dream again until a week later when Erica texted me a picture of a ring. The photo took a few minutes to load on my phone, but a smile had already formed on my face. I didn't need to see the ring. I already knew the answer was yes. What I didn't know was the significance of the conversation that would follow.

I learned that my friend had been desperately praying and trying to feel her mom's presence. Because her mother's death was so sudden, Erica needed peace—a whisper from above. She needed to know her mom was okay. As we texted, it became clear that a simple dream about a ring was that assurance.

She told me her mom used to work in a jewelry store. Over the years, she had acquired quite a collection and, as a little girl, Erica loved to peek into her mom's jewelry box. She would look among the pieces, try a few on, and return them carefully. It was one of her favorite memories. Shortly after her mom's death, she found the old jewelry box and began to go through it, examining all the treasures from her youth. The contents were just as she remembered, except for a ring with a green stone that was missing from the collection. The thought of the ring was fleeting, just one ring among many. She simply closed the box and moved on.

And then the following week, I texted her about the dream. My description of the ring wasn't exactly what she remembered, but her mom's green ring still hadn't shown up. Was this a coincidence or something more?

As she continued to search through her mom's belongings, another jewelry box emerged. Erica found the ring with the green stone! Placing it on her hand, it fit perfectly. It was the ring she had remembered from her youth. Thinking of our conversation a week earlier, she took a picture and sent it to me. As I glanced at the photo, I noticed the intricate gold pattern that looped around the green stone, forming the petals of a flower. It was the same ring from my dream!

In our conversations that followed, it was clear that this simple dream gave Erica the assurance she needed. Her mom's spirit lived on, and she was happy. Though no longer here on earth, her mom had found her way home, and was exactly where she was meant to be. While both of us continue to grieve her loss, an unexplained sense of peace and comfort fills our days. Erica and I both know this dream of a childhood ring was more than a coincidence; it was a whisper from heaven.

—Amanda Flinn—

Nurse Buddha

When watching after yourself, you watch after others.
When watching after others, you watch after yourself.
~Buddha

In my dreams, a turquoise Buddha circled my bed, round and round, week after week. It wasn't a particularly pleasant dream nor was it a nightmare. It was more of an informative one, urging me to understand something I knew nothing about.

As the dream continued to appear each night, I felt the need to discern its meaning. I knew nothing about Buddhism, but what I discovered was indeed poignant considering where life had deposited me recently. I learned a turquoise Buddha signifies limitless heights of ascension, embodies the duality of living and dying, and is associated with purity and healing. In other words, this was indeed a message, one that I needed to pay attention to.

I had been diagnosed with stage 2 lobular breast cancer. A double mastectomy was followed by radiation and weeks of chemotherapy. During my second round of chemo, a friend told me I needed to stop thinking about myself and get another pet. I was taken aback by her careless remark. Not only did I have every right to feel sorry for myself, but my beloved cat had passed away just six months earlier. Yet her words kept nagging at me until I sensed she might be right. I did need something to care about, to bring myself back to life, because I had begun to realize that mine wasn't over quite yet.

I spent hours at the local animal shelter one afternoon getting acquainted with each cat. If this was to be my companion, hopefully for a good number of years, I needed to be sure our personalities matched. I found myself standing in front of the last cage and asked the attendant about the cat wedged into the back corner.

"Oh, that's Buddha," she told me. "He's been here a while. He's about three years old, and I gather he had been abused. The lady who brought him in said her boyfriend was going to kill him."

Was this a coincidence, synchronicity, or a miracle? How many cats named Buddha would one find in a shelter on this particular day? He wasn't turquoise; he was a pale orange color with wary, copper-penny eyes. The cat was definitely uncomfortable being held, and the attendant told me if I adopted him, I'd never see him because he would probably hide all the time to protect himself. I could certainly understand that.

From the very first day he came home, Buddha stuck to me like flypaper. He did have issues, and when I removed a clothes hanger from the closet, he would charge at me. But after only a few days, a mutual trust began to surface from deep within us.

Three weeks later, it was time for another round of chemo. Most people don't realize it's not the day after treatment that's hard; it's the next one that does you in. When I awoke that morning, I found all the new toys I had bought for Buddha were surrounding my bed as if a protective castle wall had been erected.

I got through my treatment with the help of Buddha the cat—and perhaps Buddha himself. And even now, if I have just a cold, I wake up to find a delightful assortment of fish, mice, bouncy balls and twirly things arranged around my bed.

I have not had a dream of a turquoise Buddha in more than ten years.

—E.M. Corsa—

Love Shared

The best use of life is love. The best expression of love is time. The best time to love is now.
~Rick Warren

Heading around the interior road of the mall after an early morning fill-up at the gas station, I noticed a woman sitting alone at the bus stop. Her head was resting on her left hand as her elbow secured the large tan purse on her lap. Her bright purple top and backpack straps around her shoulders made her whole presence seem out of place. Was she waiting for the bus? Did mall buses come this early when the stores wouldn't be open for hours? As I drove by, I heard a voice say, "Go give her a bottle of water."

Within seconds, the clear words in my head became a vision as I turned to see an unused bottle of chilled water peeking out from under my purse. And with a glance down the road, my eyes spied a crushed and empty water bottle in the center of the street. That same voice continued, "If not you, then who?"

I wish I could say I immediately pulled the car over and offered the stranger in the purple top a cold drink of water. But rather than act, I rationalized. I muttered out loud, "Okay?" I turned the car around, passed by her again and looked intently at her as I continued driving by. I said to myself, "She looks like she is sleeping. Why would I wake her?" I turned the corner, passing P.F. Chang's, Lazy Dog, the Apple store and a very busy grounds crew with leaf blowers. I made a big circle around the mall, which brought me to a stop sign that positioned me to look at her from afar. She didn't move, and I convinced myself she must be asleep and didn't want to be bothered.

Unable to turn my car toward home, I drove by her again and again as the mind chatter in my head grew relentless. "Why is this such a battle?"

Several hundred feet past her now, I could see a bus pulling up and stopping from my rearview mirror. "I missed my chance!" My first thought was relief. Then came regret with a hefty side of shame. "What is wrong with me? What is so hard about doing the right thing? It's just a bottle of water!" While still arguing with myself, I could see the woman did not move or board the bus. She wasn't going anywhere.

So, around the mall I went… again. Past P.F. Chang's, Lazy Dog, and the Apple store, but this time I waved at the leaf blowers. I knew I couldn't circle again. This was crazy.

Once again, I was stopped at the intersection of decision. I prayed sheepishly, "Lord, if she moves, I will do it."

With a brief look to my left and back, I observed her again and noticed she had lifted her head and adjusted her purse. As she repositioned herself, so did I. I pulled my car into the no-parking bus zone, stepped out with the chilled bottle of water in one hand and a twenty-dollar bill in the other. Each step seemed to fill me with purpose and focus. My eyes were only on the stranger with the purple top. Like an arrow that is released or a wave that reaches its peak, nothing was going to stop me.

"Hi, there!" I blurted out. She looked up as I straddled the bus-stop bench so I could look directly at her. Without hesitation, I told her, "The Lord asked me to stop and give you a bottle of water."

Before I could finish my sentence, she burst into tears and began rocking back and forth. She yelled, "Oh, God loves me! God loves me! Now I know God loves me! Thank you, thank you! It's going to be okay!" As she looked up, big tears came down.

Through her sobs, she admitted how she had just been asking Jesus for help. She began to explain how she came from Florida, spending everything she had to get to Southern California to start a new life with a man she met online. The man never showed up, but God did.

She kept saying over and over, "God loves me! He sent you!"

No words can describe what happened between us in that moment. God used me, a middle-aged, unemployed woman on her way home from the gym, to bring a bottle of hope to a stranger. I thought I was bringing her a cold drink, but instead I was bringing her a miracle — a concrete answer to prayer and the hope she needed.

We sat together for a while as she talked. She had a sad story to tell, but she was no longer sad. She kept saying, "Now I know God loves me." We held hands, bowed our heads and talked to Jesus. I thanked Him and prayed for everything that came to mind. It wasn't eloquent, but it was real.

Before we parted, I grabbed all the cash I had in my purse and found more water in my car along with some snacks I kept in the trunk. We stood at the bus stop hugging and said our goodbyes.

I still have a thousand questions as to why I struggled to act. Why did it take me three circles around the mall and a full-blown argument with myself? Should I have done more? All I know for sure is that while walking toward that woman at the bus stop, a miracle happened. Faith overcame fear, and a heavenly transaction took place between two strangers.

There are opportunities for us to love every day. Maybe our doubts keep us from acting. Maybe we don't want to take the risk or be uncomfortable. Maybe we fear the outcome. That day, I learned how love answers when asked. How love collides in a moment of decision and desperation. How love both gives and receives. I don't ever want to underestimate the miraculous ways that love surprises us. Love can even show up at the mall bus stop as a bottle of water for a lady praying for a drink of hope.

— Constance C. Turner —

Miraculous Connections

The Typo that Changed My Life

You don't find love; it finds you. It's got a little bit to do with destiny, fate and what's written in the stars.
~Anaïs Nin

Coffee dates with my friend Jackie have always been a source of great support and fun for me. As my friend, she is fiercely supportive of me, and is also fiercely honest when it comes to sharing her opinion.

One day, she said, "So what's going on with that guy you've been seeing?"

Shrugging, I said, "I'm not really seeing him anymore. I don't know why, but he stopped calling and e-mailing. I left a voicemail and e-mailed, but he never responded."

Not mincing her words, Jackie set down her latte mid-sip and said, "He's a jerk. Don't call him again. Don't e-mail him again. Do not contact him in any way. He no longer exists in either of our worlds." I agreed, but then I e-mailed him later that night.

The next day, there was no reply. To be honest, I was relieved. I knew sending the e-mail had been a bad idea, and he was obviously not right for me. At that moment, the thought popped into my head that I hadn't used the correct e-mail address. One-hundred-percent certain that I had used the correct address, I ignored the thought, but it refused to go away. So, finally, opening my laptop, I compared the e-mail I'd sent with an archived one. The e-mail I'd sent the night before was addressed to "henrie61"; the archived address was "henre61." One letter difference.

Crossing my fingers, I sent out a quick prayer that the e-mail would go to Henrie61's spam folder. For a week, it seemed that my prayers had been answered. But then one night, I came home from work and found a reply from "henrie61" in my in-box. It read: "Do I know you? Your e-mail sounds as though we have met, but I'm sorry, I can't place who you are. Cheers! Henrie."

I wrote back, explaining that I had typed the address incorrectly and apologized for bothering him. He replied, "No worries. Normally, I wouldn't even have opened your e-mail since I didn't recognize the address. But my old computer quit working, and by the time I got this new one, I had so many e-mails that I just went down the list and opened them all. When I read your e-mail, it sounded like you knew me, so I wrote back. Would you be interested in corresponding? If so, it might be fun to learn about new people and places. If not, no worries. Henrie."

I thought it over and decided that corresponding might be fun. So, I sent a letter back. A month later, Henrie and I discovered that we had even more to learn than we'd thought. He was in Australia, and I was in the U.S. Learning about Henrie as a person and Australia as a country was interesting. Even better was the feeling of being in a friendship with someone who accepted me with no expectations. Someone who would respond and put on his "listening ears" when I talked.

Twelve years after that first e-mail, Henrie moved to the U.S. and we married. I think we were destined to meet. But, obviously, not without a little help.

— Crystal Hodge —

Perfect Match

When positive attitudes meet with faith, courage, consistency and perseverance, miracles tend to happen.
~Edmond Mbiaka

As I step off the hospital elevator, I hear them. Rowdy. The sound of my family burning nervous energy. I peek in the room, trying to pretend I don't know them. My widowed daughter-in-law (the quiet one in the crowd), two of my adult grandchildren, one of my daughters, my younger son and his wife are all crowded into a small room. My son is perched on a hospital bed wearing a barely decent gown. They are all laughing.

"Are you the mom?" a nurse asks as she touches me gently on the shoulder. "They told us you were flying in from California. We've been waiting to meet you." Amusement shows in her smile.

"I don't know whether to admit it or not," I say. "Sorry they're so noisy."

"Don't be," the nurse says, patting me on the back. "They're celebrating, and the other patients enjoy hearing their story. Gives everybody hope."

I greet my family with hugs and avoid telling them to keep the noise down. I'll leave that to the nurses.

My sons, less than two years apart in age, bickered and quarreled when they were small, making us wonder if they would ever get along. Later, despite very different personalities, they became unusually close.

Dave, the older son, was diagnosed with Type-1 diabetes just before he turned eighteen. By the next summer, he had become a counselor and lifeguard at a camp for children with diabetes. His younger brother Doug soon joined him as a counselor. It was there at the camp that the two boys bonded in a new way, each learning to appreciate the strengths of the other. Summer after summer, as Dave attended college and Doug finished high school and joined the workforce, they returned to the camp to work. The friendships they formed there have lasted a lifetime.

To our dismay, Doug was eventually diagnosed with Type-2 diabetes. He faced the challenge much as his brother had, respecting the disease but not letting it control his life. Each helped the other cope, joking and encouraging and always there for one another.

One morning, when they were in their early fifties, Dave was found in a diabetic coma. Just days later, his brother was in kidney failure. Our family reeled with shock.

Painful months passed with one son in a coma and the other one on dialysis. We waited, hoping Dave would regain consciousness, hoping that Doug would be placed on the kidney transplant list, praying for a miracle.

Dave eventually succumbed to medical complications, and his physicians told us he could not have recovered to lead a quality life. Soon after he passed away, his daughter stepped up to offer a kidney to her uncle, who had become increasingly frail.

"Uncle Doug was Dad's best friend. My father would have donated a kidney without hesitating. I'm doing this for them both!" she insisted.

To our amazement, she was an excellent match. There was no talking her out of it. After weeks of tests and counseling, the transplant was finally scheduled. Family members headed to Arizona for the two simultaneous surgeries.

Four years have gone by since that day at the hospital. My granddaughter returned to her active life within weeks of donating her kidney. Doug has been able to return full-time to the job he enjoys and was there to celebrate the birth of his second grandchild.

Do I believe in miracles? Absolutely!

—Judy Opdycke—

A Remarkable Reunion

Important encounters are planned by the souls long before the bodies see each other.
~Paulo Coelho

"The mailman is coming. I need to say something to him in Arabic. Hurry, he's getting close. Please, teach me something. He'll be here in a minute or two."

My future husband, Nabil, squinted to see the mail carrier making his way down the street that I had grown up on. The two of us were in the process of emptying my family home after the death of my father. "Why do you need to speak Arabic to the mailman?" he asked.

"I want to impress him by speaking his native language. My dad once told me that his mailman came from Lebanon and speaks Arabic. He's the son of an Orthodox priest. Hurry, he's getting close."

"Okay, say 'Keefuk inta?' It means 'How are you?'"

"Kee-fuk-in-ta," I imitated, repeating the phrase over and over, trying to make the unfamiliar sounds flow rhythmically, like Nabil did.

I was so excited to greet him that I ran down the steps to the main sidewalk saying, "Keefuk inta, George? Keefuk inta?"

He nodded his head, asking, "Where did you learn Arabic?"

While I was explaining that I had an excellent teacher, his gaze pivoted over my shoulder. He dropped the letters that were in his hand back into the mailbag and stood motionless on the sidewalk, arms, eyes, and mouth open wide. I turned around and saw Nabil running down the steps toward George, a look of astonishment on his face. The two of them hugged.

After a barrage of Arabic, hugs, and even tears, they explained to me that they had grown up together in Lebanon. Their homes in the mountain town of Kab Elias had actually shared a wall. George's father had been the priest at the church located directly in front of Nabil's family home. They used to "hop" over to the church rooftop to hang their laundry.

George and Nabil had played together as children, running through the narrow winding streets of Kab Elias and exploring the mountainside with its many pristine streams. "To hear the water flowing, it's the most beautiful sound," Nabil reminisced. "Really it is. The water swooshing from the mountain and trickling over the rocks. Remember grabbing branches and swinging over the river yelling like Tarzan? And the instant shock when we let go and splashed into the icy water?"

"Drinking that cold water straight from the stream," George added. "So sweet tasting. And don't forget dancing the Dabke on the side of the water. You were the best drummer, Nabil. Dancing 'til we couldn't dance anymore while your fingers set the beat on the derbake drum. I think we all ended up in the water," he laughed.

The two friends continued reliving moments of their childhood. They described to me how, as teenagers, they jumped over the railings of the balconies to sit on the rooftops in the cool mountain evenings. They ate pistachios, baklawa (the Lebanese version of baklava), and fruit. Sometimes, they smoked the narghile, smelling the sweet apple tobacco as they passed the bubbling water pipe around to everyone. They sang, told stories, and shared adventures and dreams into the wee hours of the tranquil, star-filled, pre-war nights in Lebanon.

But the mail must be delivered. George and Nabil exchanged addresses and phone numbers, and George continued down the block.

Throughout the rest of the afternoon and evening, Nabil continued sharing glimpses of his life in Lebanon. He described how the war began to tear apart the country and its people, leaving an emptiness in their lives as friends and family members struggled to survive and fled their homes. They lost track of many dear to them.

George was just one friend whom Nabil had bid farewell to in Lebanon. I could feel the heaviness in his heart as he spoke of the day George left for his new life in America. Nabil had no idea what part of the vast United States his friend would call "home" but wished him well. Over the years, the war intensified. These two young men, now on separate continents, both struggled to survive — Nabil amidst the chaos of keeping his family safe and fighting in the Christian militia and George adjusting to a new life and culture in a foreign land.

After years of fighting, sheltering his family, and living in the bedlam of war, Nabil himself yearned for a more peaceful life. He made the journey to America and began the process of re-establishing himself in the United States. George had no idea Nabil had left Lebanon and moved to the U.S. as well.

But on a gorgeous, sunny spring afternoon in 1992, two childhood friends from a small village on the edge of the Bekaa Valley in Lebanon were reunited on the sidewalk in front of my family home in St. Paul, Minnesota. Some call it coincidence. I call it a miracle.

— Kathleen Ruth —

The Photo in the Paper

When two people are meant to be together,
they will be together. It's fate.
~Sara Gruen

I barely knew the woman. I had only recently fallen in love with her son. I did know, from the few times we had spoken, that she worried about him... a recently divorced, middle-aged man, childless and alone. As she lay dying in her hospital bed, I knew without a shadow of a doubt I could tell her the truth.

"You don't have to worry about him anymore," I said, squeezing her hand. "I'll look after your son."

A few months after her death, we were going through some of her things when we came across an old newspaper. It was nestled amidst a stack of yellowed clippings chronicling weddings, births, deaths and community happenings she had deemed necessary to keep. I had worked at that newspaper one summer while I was a college student.

I eagerly grabbed the newspaper and sat down to have a look. To my surprise, there was my twenty-year-old self staring at me from a front-page picture. "*Chronicle* hires summer student," the cutline proclaimed.

Scrawled in some white space at the top of the page was "Grandma's obituary, page 7" in my mother-in-law's handwriting.

I know the two articles being in the same issue—the issue she had saved for twenty years — is nothing more than a coincidence. To this day, though, I don't know why she didn't cut out the obituary, add it to the stack of clippings, and discard the rest of the newspaper as she had done dozens of times before.

The logical answer is that she simply couldn't find the scissors that day, so she put the whole issue away for safekeeping, intending to clip out the obituary later. I don't expect the obituary being in the same issue has any meaning whatsoever. It's almost a given that she didn't save the paper because my picture was on the front.

But still, what an amazing coincidence. I like to think that she somehow sensed the girl on the front page would fall in love with her son one day. I like to think she hoped for it.

That old newspaper is fodder for a romance novel, a tale of happily ever after, the plot twist of a mother blessing the relationship she foresaw long before anyone else and from beyond the grave. After spending a long career telling other people's stories, filling newspapers with stories about their lives, maybe it's time to tell my story as I now approach my twenty-fifth anniversary with that lovely woman's son.

— Lynne Turner —

As Good as Gold

Life is a series of thousands of tiny miracles.
~Mike Greenberg

My mother didn't have a lot of nice jewelry when we were growing up, but for her fortieth birthday she bought herself a very expensive, one-of-a-kind, heavily braided gold bracelet with a lovely circular charm attached. My sister's and my name were engraved on it.

When my mother died at the age of seventy in June 2000, I inherited the bracelet. I also inherited a few other small gold bracelets and rings that I gave to my best friend Deb and her daughters. The braided bracelet, however, was another story. It was quite unusual and beautiful, and even though I found myself looking at it more than wearing it, I would never part with it no matter what.

In June 2010, out of curiosity, I brought it to a gold dealer. Even with its clasp broken off and the charm missing from its loop, I was told it was worth enough to pay for a two-week trip to Hawaii, airfare and hotels included. Sold! They told me it would be melted down, so I took a picture of the bracelet and walked out the door.

We had a wonderful time in Kona.

Over the years at family events — weddings, funerals, and celebrations — I would curse myself for selling the bracelet. It was an extraordinary connection to my mother, whom I missed dearly.

In June 2014, four years after my trip to Kona, my best friend

Deb and I went to a local club to hear some music. She said, "I have a great story to tell you."

Her daughter, Michelle, had bought a purse from a thrift store. As she was switching things over from her old purse to the new one, she discovered a Ziploc bag filled with jewelry in the side pocket. She contacted the store and told them she had found something valuable inside the purse. Three months later, when no one claimed the jewelry, it was hers to keep. Before making a beeline to the pawnshop, she showed the jewelry to her mother. Although Deb could never see herself wearing it, she bought one of the bracelets from her, knowing Michelle could use the cash.

As Deb finished her story, she reached under our table and pulled a little bag out of her purse. She opened it and laid a bracelet on my cocktail napkin. "What do you think? Isn't it gorgeous?" she asked. Tingles raced up my arms, and tears blurred my vision. I knew immediately that it was my mother's bracelet. The unique braided design. The small loop, which had previously held a charm, was still attached. The once-broken clasp had been replaced with fourteen- not twenty-two-karat gold; the difference in color was obvious.

When Deb didn't understand my reaction, I told her the story about selling my mother's bracelet to pay for my trip to Kona. This was that bracelet, and it hadn't been melted down! I wrapped it around my wrist and felt the extraordinary connection once again. Deb insisted I keep it, but I had already taken a vacation to Kona on that bracelet. It was hers to keep. My mother had been very fond of Deb, so I could hear my mother saying, "Why did you give Deb and her kids all my cheaper jewelry when I died? This is what you should have given her if you didn't want it!" Well, my mother found a way to do it herself.

What stars must have aligned for this to happen? The gold dealer must have decided not to melt down the bracelet. It was bought by a customer who, four years later, left it by mistake in a purse donated to a thrift store (in another county, by the way), which was bought by my best friend's daughter who decided, before pawning it, to show it to her mother. My best friend bought the bracelet from her daughter.

When I have a family event to attend, Deb appears at my door with the bracelet. I gratefully accept, wear it, and return it to her. It's a gift from my mother.

— Shelley Friedman —

Knock, Knock

Don't believe in miracles — depend on them.
~Laurence J. Peter

I tried not to worry, but I was scared. The job I had lost was a good job, and I was good at it. It wasn't my fault that I lost it; it was just what happens when a government contract isn't renewed. I accepted my lot and filed for unemployment benefits.

My full-time job now was finding a full-time job. I searched diligently and tried everything I knew to find work, but without success. Weeks went by. If I didn't find a job soon, I wouldn't be able to pay the rent on my apartment — a modest two-bedroom in a four-story walkup. And then what?

It was the early 1970s, and job hunting was done the 1970s way. Print copies of your résumé. Peruse the Help Wanted ads in the local newspaper. Mark the jobs you think you might qualify for, even if you think they're long shots. Write a hello-I'm-wonderful cover letter, put it in an envelope with your résumé, and mail it to the employer. Tell everybody you know that you're available for work and ask them to help get the word out. Make phone calls and knock on every door.

One Saturday morning, the knock came on *my* door.

Silently grumbling, I arose and walked down the hall, temporarily abandoning my collection of Help Wanted ads and stack of résumés on the kitchen table. Why was it that every time I got my toddler settled down with her toys and started my job search, someone interrupted me?

"Hi," said a smiling woman in jeans when I opened the door. "I'm

Melba. I just moved in upstairs. Can I borrow your phone for a minute? I'd like to call the phone company and ask them to turn mine on."

A neighbor in need — of course, I would help. "Hi, Melba. Sure, come on in. I'm Carole," I said, leading the attractive woman who looked about my age — early thirties — to the phone anchored on my kitchen wall. "Help yourself while I run into the other room and check on my little one."

Returning a few minutes later, I found Melba holding the phone to her ear and looking down at my résumé on the table. Apparently, the phone-company rep had placed her on hold for a moment. "Coffee?" I asked, holding up my glass coffeepot for her to see.

Putting her hand over the mouthpiece of the phone, she responded, "Yes, thank you." Barely glancing at me, she continued to look down at my résumé on the table.

Soon, her conversation was finished, and I invited her to sit down. She did and picked up one of my résumés. "May I look at this more closely?" she asked. "I gather you're looking for a job."

"Yes," I said, "and spending all my scarce money on paper, envelopes, and postage stamps."

"Well, your search is over. You're exactly the person I'm looking for."

I was puzzled. "What? What do you mean?"

A cup of coffee later, she had told me exactly what she meant. She was special assistant to the CEO at her company, and they had been searching for someone to fill a staff vacancy for which I was uniquely qualified.

Our conversation continued for several minutes as I elaborated on my experience. I answered her questions, and she answered mine. It was the most informal job interview I'd ever had, I would reflect later. I was happy that the company she represented provided a very needed service that I would be proud to support.

"Can you come in on Monday? I'll introduce you to my boss, but that's just so you and he can get to know one another. He has delegated hiring authority to me," she said, telling me the salary. "I haven't found anybody who is even halfway as qualified as you are for the job. How soon can you start?"

I was incredulous. "You mean, just like that?"

"Well, you'll have to fill out all the forms and pass the reference checks. But, yeah, just like that. I mean, if you like us."

"Like you? No, I don't like you," I replied. "I love you."

She laughed. "I'll slip one of my cards underneath your door as soon as I find one in the boxes I'm unpacking," she said, with one of my résumés in her hand as she walked to the door.

I let her out and leaned back against the closed door. What had just happened? Was she for real? Was this divine intervention? Perfect timing? Had I found a job without even leaving my apartment, making a phone call, or knocking on a door?

Yes, as it would turn out on Monday morning when I signed the official offer of a job that seemed tailormade for me. It would support my daughter and me for a couple of years until both Melba and I moved on to even better opportunities in our careers — but not until after we had built a friendship that endures to this day.

It was a fateful day. No, not the day I found a job. The day the job found me.

— Carole Harris Barton —

Patty's Sign

The bond between friends cannot be broken by chance;
no interval of time or space can destroy it.
Not even death itself can part true friends.
~Saint John Cassian

My friend Patty and I were enjoying a burger and a beer on a winter's evening after playing some indoor tennis. We were sharing small talk when she said, "I've gotta make a doctor's appointment. I've got this swelling." She pulled the neckline of her pink moisture-wicking sports shirt aside, and I saw that there was, indeed, a swollen place on her collarbone.

"Huh," I said. "Does it hurt?"

"No," she replied. "I'm not too worried about it."

Patty and I had met at work, realized we shared a love of music, sports, and good conversation, and had become fast friends. She encouraged me to join a tennis league, and I encouraged her to join the church choir, resulting in our lives intersecting in ways that were both personal and professional.

When, after several rounds of tests, Patty was diagnosed with lymphoma, I was shocked. She would beat it, though, I told myself. She ate well, had never smoked or used drugs, drank rarely and in moderation, exercised regularly, managed her stress, and took good care of herself. There was no way that someone like that would become sick and die. That just didn't happen.

She started chemo and lost her hair but didn't let anything stop her from working, continuing to participate in church choir, and indulging in her beloved sports. She and I had lunches, went to ballgames, and stayed in close touch. So, I knew when the first round of chemo didn't work and, also, when the second didn't. When the third course of treatment didn't appear to be changing her condition, she told me that the more things she tried that didn't work, the lower her chance of survival.

I was stunned. How could nothing be working? And yet, that seemed to be the case. Months went by, and it became clear that Patty wasn't getting better. Finally, she told me there was just one thing left to try. It was a longshot, but she was going to give it a go for her husband. He wanted to make sure no stone was left unturned. She wanted to make sure nobody had any regrets in the end.

Days and then weeks went by. Patty didn't even bother to tell me that this last-ditch attempt to save her didn't work. I knew. I could see it, and I could sense it in her change of attitude. Patty started preparing herself for her death.

One day, when I had brought one of our favorite lunches of soup and a sandwich by her home, where she was continuing to attempt to work remotely, she asked, out of the blue, if I would consider singing for the memorial service of "a friend." A lump caught in my throat. She was starting to think about her own funeral, and now that she had said the words out loud, everything became very real. As I looked at her, the expression on her face was so earnest that I burst into tears. And they were ugly tears. I sobbed so hard that I could not catch my breath. Through my waterworks, I could see that she was crying too, which made me feel worse.

Finally, I managed to croak out, "I can't sing. Nobody wants to hear sloppy blubbering in the key of D."

She stopped crying, and so did I. We looked at each other. "Maybe you could try it in the key of C then?" she asked. And then we were laughing. Tears ran down our faces as we sobbed and laughed at the same time. And after we'd calmed down, I told her that in all seriousness, I didn't think I could sing at her funeral because I would cry, and it would be awful. But, I said, I would be glad to try to speak.

"Yeah?" she said.

"Yeah," I replied. "And I'll say nice things about you."

We started talking about death. About how we all will face it and how weird it is that we all go through it, but nobody knows what it's like. How we had faith that what comes after life is good. And that we will still be connected with our loved ones who are living.

"I want to be able to give people signs," Patty said. "I want them to know I'm there."

"Okay," I said with enthusiasm. "Let's agree on a sign that you can give me."

"Well," Patty said, "I've heard of people leaving pennies as a sign after they have passed."

"Don't be cheap," I said. "Couldn't you at least make it quarters?"

"Greedy," she replied.

We both laughed and never spoke of it again.

Patty died in July that year. I saw her a couple of days before she slipped away in her husband's arms. She had grown so frail and quiet. That last time I was with her, she had withdrawn and wasn't saying much. She'd reached that point in her journey when she was no longer entirely in this world but hadn't completely left, either. She was lying in her recliner, her eyes large in her thin face. I leaned over her and touched her shoulder. "I love you," I said. "I will remember you always."

"Me, too," she said faintly. That was the last time I heard her voice.

I did speak at Patty's funeral. I wrote what I wanted to say and rehearsed it until I knew I could get through it without crying. I hoped that it expressed what I thought of my friend, how much I admired and enjoyed her, how much fun she was, and how much she meant to me.

A couple of weeks after her funeral, another friend visited me at my home. We had a glass of wine and talked about Patty, death, and whether we believed in the afterlife. Then I recalled the conversation I'd had with Patty when she'd said she wanted to leave signs for her loved ones. I shared our discussion and my smart-alecky comment about her thinking enough of me to leave quarters instead of cheaping out with pennies. My guest asked if either type of coin had shown up. "No," I replied. And I was a little sad. I'd hoped for a sign from Patty.

I wanted evidence that she still existed and was still with me.

That night, after my guest had gone, I went to my room, hung up my robe, and threw back the bedcovers. I heard a loud chinking noise at the foot of the bed. There, on the floor, tossed from the bedspread, were seven shiny quarters. I stared, open-mouthed. Where had those come from? They hadn't been there when I'd made the bed that morning. I never brought loose change into my bedroom; it went into a jar downstairs.

A warmth lit me up from inside, and I smiled, then giggled. There was only one explanation: Patty had given me her sign.

— Melissa McCoy —

A Tale of Two Mollys

Often a healing takes place in ourselves
as we pray for the healing of others.
~Michael E. DeBakey, MD

Our poor dog had already vomited twice that day, so I thought I would call the vet in the morning. But that night, she woke me with her barking, and as I cleaned up yet another mess in the wee hours of the morning I saw that there was blood in her vomit.

I jammed on flip-flops over my socks and started the hour-long drive to the emergency vet. Molly was elated, sticking her head out the window and wagging her tail as she hemorrhaged internally. My mood was less jovial.

The vet wanted to do some testing, so I settled down to wait in the front room. I had already received a scolding from my husband, who was unhappy about being awakened to news that his wife was off spending hundreds of dollars at the emergency vet instead of waiting till daytime to go to the regular vet. The seats were hard, the room was cold, and my phone had six percent left on the battery.

"Why me?" I whined.

In response, an elderly man walked in the door. The waiting room was partitioned with four-foot, cubicle-type walls to give people privacy, but sound can't be compartmentalized. A technician brought him a dog, telling him she still hadn't eaten. His wail overwhelmed me, although in reality it was probably no louder than the sniffling coming from the other areas of the room. "Please eat, Molly. I can't lose you," he moaned.

I felt so much compassion for this man and his dog. "Please, Father, please help that dog eat, and also please comfort that man," I prayed.

Then I heard a voice. "That's good. Now go pray with him."

There are so many men and women in the Bible whom I admire for their faith, courageousness, and obedience to God's instructions. I have not stood before any cruel kings or stormed a battlefield, but I'd like to think I am the same kind of servant who is always willing to move when my name is called.

"No!" I told God. "No, I do *not* want to do that! Everyone is going to look at me, and he'll probably get mad!"

But the thought returned. "Go pray with that man, quickly." I got up and feigned interest in a rack of old magazines so that I could look over the partition.

He was trying to get his dog's attention with a bowl of mush he had brought from home. The dog was trembling and tense, and she looked like she had given up on herself.

Quickly scanning the rest of the room, I saw lots of people. There were technicians up front, office staff behind the desk, and people hiding behind the partitions, not to mention the people walking in and out the door. I took a deep breath, turned, and went back to my seat. I would be too embarrassed to approach the man.

But the urge returned. "Okay, Father," I prayed. "I will do this, but please give me the words because I don't know what to say. Please, calm me!"

I whirled out of my seat and sat down with the man and his dog.

"My dog's name is Molly, too." It just came out.

He looked at me, broken and weary. "It's been four days, and she hasn't eaten anything. They said if she doesn't eat today, she won't live. My wife of fifty years left me. I just moved here a few months ago. All I have is Molly."

I grabbed his hand, put my other hand on the dog, and began

praying the worst prayer ever to have been prayed. It hit all the points.

"Please help the dog eat and give this man comfort and peace."

It was genuinely heartfelt, but it was clumsy, awkward, and spoken through gulping sobs. When I finished and looked up, we were surrounded by people. A technician was standing there, people who were previously concealed behind partitions had emerged, and new people were at the front desk.

The man squeezed my hand, interrupting my embarrassment. "You can probably tell I don't go to church but thank you." Then a technician took them to an exam room.

I went back to my seat, satisfied that my job was done, although perhaps not done well. I checked my phone, now down to five percent. There was a text from my husband: "Couldn't this have waited a few hours for the regular vet?"

The man and his dog returned. He looked destroyed. "Please eat, Molly," he begged. Suddenly, he cried again, but it sounded different. "She ate! She ate the whole bowl!"

I charged out of my seat, draped myself over the partition, and pointed. "That is an answered prayer!" This time, I knew everyone had heard me, and it wasn't embarrassing.

Molly was gently snoring and lying on her side with one little leg bent into the air, the empty bowl beside her. The old man looked at me in amazement.

"You're an angel!" he said.

"What? Oh, no! I am no angel. Ask my mother-in-law!"

"Come here, angel," he beckoned me.

There was a lot of hugging, and unfortunately some pictures taken of his dog and me in my pajamas.

Finally, the staff brought out my own Molly. Turns out she had a mild ulcer, probably due to something she ate. We don't call her the Hoover for nothing.

As I was checking out, the man came up for one last hug. "I wish there was something I could do to repay you."

"I am not the one who did something for you," I said. "But if you insist, do this: read the Gospel. Read it with your heart, remembering what happened to you today."

I took out my phone. It had just enough battery left to send one text.

"No," I wrote my husband. "It couldn't wait."

— Michelle Civalier —

The Wrong Number

I believe that tomorrow is another day,
and I believe in miracles.
~Audrey Hepburn

A gruff voice on the phone warns there is a problem with your tax return or your Social Security account that you need to fix immediately. Or a bright, excited voice announces that you have been selected to win a cruise to the Bahamas; all you have to do is send a small processing fee.

When do they call? Just as your fork is about to enter your mouth, or just as you've taken off your last piece of clothing for a shower, or just as you've dropped into the sweetest afternoon nap. And it's usually a recording, because they don't want to waste their time on hang-ups, even though they're happy to waste your time on answering the phone.

After a couple of these bogus calls one day while trapped in the house during the COVID-19 lockdown, I said to my wife, "Just once—just once—I'd like to get a call from a stranger that is worth getting! A call from a real person!"

My wife said, "Don't get upset. Just hang up." But I stalked around the house planning what I'd tell the next spam caller. Once a human being took over from the recorded message, I would say, "Gee, I'm busy now. Give me your home number, and I'll call you back tonight." Or to amuse myself during the lockdown, I'd keep the caller on the line for an hour with pointless questions. Why, I'd…

Then, in one of those coincidences you beg for and never expect to happen, the phone rang. Aha! I was ready. "I'll get it!" I shouted, but Carol stepped in front of me and picked it up.

"Hello," she said sweetly. Since we're older and a little hard of hearing, we keep the phone on speaker. So, I stood beside her to see what gimmick the robo-voice would spring on us. Instead, a woman said, "Oh, thank goodness, you're home."

"All day," my wife said. "Shelter in place, right?" She threw me a questioning glance, but I didn't recognize the voice either.

"I'm going crazy here," the woman said. "It's really getting to me. I'm so glad I can talk to you. How are you?"

"Oh, okay," Carol said. "Spending time online today." She mouthed to me, "I have no idea." Since this was obviously a wrong number, I expected her to cut the call short. Not Carol. We joke that her Chinese fortune cookies always exhort her to show patience even though she already has enough for both of us and all our children. She let the stranger go on about how tense she felt at grocery stores and the bank these days. Carol's demeanor changed. She's a retired therapist, and the woman's tone alarmed her. She said, "Are you all right?"

"Not really. I'm scared, honey, and upset."

"What's the problem?" Carol asked.

"I'm so down. It's this disease all around us. Cooped up here, no one to talk to, and alone. I really am scared to go out or see anyone. I want to crawl into bed with the covers over my head."

"Oh, no."

"Actually, honey, I'm depressed. I don't know what I'm going to do. All these people sick and dying. All this turmoil. It feels like the whole world is falling apart. You're so far away. There's nobody here for me."

"Yes, there is," Carol said. She took a breath. "Now, please tell me who you are."

The woman stopped sharply. "Who are you?"

"I'm Carol."

"Oh, no! I thought you were my daughter. I'm so sorry! I should go."

"No, wait," Carol said. "Don't hang up. I'm concerned that you're so down." At this point, I was concerned too, hanging beside my wife, hoping this suffering, anxious woman would stay on the line. Later, Carol told me she was worried about possible suicide. The pandemic was causing such stress that therapists manned hot lines in some cities to help people through the crisis.

The woman said nothing but didn't hang up. Carol agreed it was awful to be afraid of every person outside your home, and then suggested that it might help to focus on nature. Maybe she should take a walk with the sun on her face and hear the birds sing. They would reassure her that life would return to normal. The woman only sighed. Carol asked, "Have you ever been depressed before this?"

A muted voice replied, "Yes."

"When?"

"About ten years ago."

"Did you take medication?"

"Yes."

"Are you still on it?"

"No, I stopped."

"Well, maybe you should look into starting it again. Your brain needs it. It's nothing to be ashamed of, a chemical imbalance. A horrible event like this COVID-19 can trigger depression again. Many people feel like you do. You probably just need a little help to get through this."

Another long pause. "How do you know so much about how I feel?"

"I've worked with people who were depressed. And I'm locked down, too."

"You are calming me down."

"That's good. Please call your doctor—and your daughter. I'm sure she'd love to hear from you. She's probably just as lonely as you are."

"Oh, not so much. She has children. My grandchildren."

"You can talk to them, too. It's especially difficult for active children these days. I'm sure they'd love to talk to Grandma. It'll be good for them—and you. Skype or use Zoom so you can all see each other. But I won't get off the phone until you promise me you'll call your doctor."

"I will," the woman said. "I will! Right away. Oh, thank you for talking to me, Carol. I feel so much better knowing somebody is out there. Thank you so much!" She hesitated. "Sometime, maybe, I could call you again?"

"Sure. It's the best wrong number I've ever had."

They said goodbye with promises to keep in touch. Carol and I looked at each other. "Well," she said, "you wanted a call from a real person."

— Garrett Bauman —

Answered Prayers

The love between a mother and daughter
knows no distance.
~Author Unknown

A murky shadow marred my mammogram and sonogram. It was suspicious enough for my doctor to order an immediate excisional biopsy. I knew breast cancer in younger women could be particularly aggressive and deadly. I was fifty-four. That was strike one.

And if there is a family history of the disease, double the odds. My grandmother had died of breast cancer, so strike two.

I read the directions concerning the upcoming biopsy. But lurking in the back of my mind was another fear: claustrophobia. What would happen if my dread of closed spaces reared its ugly head?

The night before surgery, I stepped out on the back deck and looked at the stars. "Our Father, who art in heaven, hallowed be thy name… Protect me tomorrow from both cancer and anxiety."

As my husband steered us into the hospital parking lot the next morning, my breath quickened, although I tried to slow it down. From years of practice, I drew one deep breath in, exhaled one slow breath out, and tried to keep my apprehension at bay.

I checked in at the outpatient counter surrounded by the stark odors of antiseptic cleansing and other people's fears. Then a technician called my name, and my husband gave me the thumbs-up sign.

But I wasn't reassured. Not one bit. What if I sensed the walls closing in? What if I suddenly couldn't breathe? What would happen if my heart beat so fast that I went into cardiac arrest?

I knew that cancer was a far worse diagnosis than claustrophobia, but I remembered how, in the middle of a panic attack, immediate survival is the only frantic thought.

Alone in the small, curtained-off changing area, I fought to remain calm. The same technician wheeled me through a hallway, while I kept my hospital gown closed with a clenched fist. All around us, the constant whir of machines and medical chitchat buzzed in my ears.

Then I met my surgeon—a pleasant man with a professional manner. I forced myself to concentrate as he repeated the instructions. In this room, two technicians would mark the incision site. Next, I would go to the O.R. for sedation and the biopsy.

Then he left. *Wait!* I wanted to shout. *Don't leave me. I want the sedation now.* Then my eyes shifted to a mammogram-like machine.

I heard one technician say, "We'll strap you in and then map the site. A radiologist will insert a thin fiber-optic needle into the incision spot. You'll only need to be completely immobile for ten minutes."

Ten minutes strapped and immobile? I could feel the imminent panic attack clawing its fingers into my chest.

I mumbled, "I'm claustrophobic."

"We'll work fast." The technicians seated me on a padded chair next to the machine and buckled me in. A few minutes after they marked the spot, the radiologist appeared and inserted the needle. Then he left, and the technicians told me they would step outside for a few moments.

By now, my goal was to stave off hyperventilation.

Alone in the room, I lowered my eyes to peer at the skinny needle protruding from my chest, and I gulped air. Then I repeated the only part of Psalm 23 that I could remember, "Yea, though I walk through the valley of the shadow of death..."

Then I frantically began to babble, "Hail Mary, full of grace..." while my heart thumped wildly in my chest, and my lips cracked with dryness—two classic signs of impending panic. An eerie silence pervaded the room, broken only by the tick-tock of the clock on the wall.

And then a voice sounded from behind me. "You're okay."

What? I was sure I was alone. I couldn't turn to see, but the intonation was resonant and clear.

"I'm right here with you."

The voice belonged to a woman.

For a brief moment, I had a wild thought. *Was the Virgin Mary in this room?*

But the voice carried a familiar cadence.

And then the realization hit—it was my mother's voice. Even though she had died almost thirty years ago, I could recognize her speaking anywhere.

I couldn't move. I couldn't talk. I wanted to tell her everything, but no words came.

A few seconds later, a total calmness washed over me. My mother, who had bandaged my scraped knees as a child, stood with me in that room.

The air stilled, and my breathing relaxed. The ragged edge of the panic attack subsided, and the drumming of my heart returned to normal.

The door opened, and the radiologist walked in with the two technicians. Was I ready to be wheeled into the surgery?

I didn't ask them if they had seen anyone else in the room when they entered. I knew what the answer would be. But I also knew that my mother, or at least her spirit, had been there long enough to soothe a frightened child.

How could this even be possible? I don't know. But I do know she was there.

And my biopsy result? Cancer-free. So far, I had beaten the odds.

—Linda Harris Sittig—

Love That Doesn't Die

A Gift Rediscovered

I cannot forget my mother. She is my bridge.
~Renita J. Weems

I rummaged through a forgotten box left behind a year ago when I relocated my office to the bedroom vacated by my newly married daughter. I doubted the box contained any useful items until I saw a birthday gift my mom had given me years ago. It was a thoughtful gift, meant to encourage me to chase a dream that seemed impossible at the time. But now, it was perfect.

As I held the gift, my grief rose to the surface again. It was only a year ago that I had given Mom a copy of my first novel, just in time, as she was in hospice. That novel was the impossible dream that had prompted Mom to give me the birthday gift long ago.

Mom had interrupted the hospice nurse as she was adjusting Mom's pain medication. "My daughter wrote that book." She beamed with pride as she pointed to the pristine cover and undisturbed pages. "That's her name on the front."

Every nurse who visited heard about my book. I felt like a little girl, delighted I'd made my mom happy. But my heart also ached. My novel hit bookstores weeks before Mom started fading fast from stage 4 metastatic breast cancer. She struggled to read it, but after a page or two, she'd close the book, too fatigued to concentrate, and say, "I promise I'll read your book when I feel better." I assured her I knew she would, but the truth was Mom would never feel better.

I spent months taking care of Mom, ensuring she would spend

her final days in her home as she wished. Making her my priority was a privilege I cherished, but it required me to neglect other important things in my life — my family, my classroom, and especially my writing, which felt less and less important. The physical and emotional toll of losing more of my mom each day made me wonder if I'd write again. Maybe one book was enough, I told myself, even though the characters inside my imagination stirred on occasion to remind me they were still there.

After Mom passed, her unread copy of my book found a new home in my office, although I didn't spend much time there myself. My daughter's November wedding was approaching, and after that, our home would be filled with family for Thanksgiving and Christmas. My desire to write dwindled even more.

But the holidays passed, and a new year promised new beginnings. One snowy day, I opened my laptop and started my next story, unaware that life was about to start an unexpected chapter of its own.

Within a few weeks, my husband was diagnosed with leukemia. He was admitted to a hospital two hours away where he spent a total of ninety-two days over a ten-month period. When he was finally discharged for what we hoped was the last time, I couldn't imagine writing again. It had been more than a year since I last hugged my mom, and even longer since my first book had been released. It would be my only book, I decided. Too much life had happened — real life with real people, not make-believe with made-up characters.

But then I rummaged through that box in the basement and discovered the long-forgotten birthday present from Mom.

It was a book, well-worn, with a tattered cover that read, *Chicken Soup for the Writer's Soul: Stories to Open the Heart and Rekindle the Spirit of Writers*. Coincidence? I opened it for the first time in years. Inside was Mom's handwriting. Waves of grief, longing and comfort swirled inside me. Inside she wrote:

Karen, maybe this book will give you a little inspiration.
Happy Birthday
Love, Mom

I brushed my fingers over her words. It was almost enough to make me think about writing again. I turned a few pages. I scanned the table of contents. Then I opened it to the middle where a bookmark had been placed. It was facedown, revealing the back where Mom had written my birthdate along with: "Love, Mom."

I turned the bookmark over. My heart pulsed. On the front was a poem titled, "Don't Quit." How could she have known then how much I would need those words now?

Today, the book rests on my desk beside my laptop where I can see it every time I sit down to write. It's the "little inspiration" Mom hoped it would be, a daily reminder not to quit, a gift rediscovered.

— Karen Sargent —

Heavenly Comfort

Love is something eternal; the aspect may change,
but not the essence.
~Vincent van Gogh

It was a particularly gloomy day, and I was sitting on the couch in the upper part of our split-level home, staring out the window, deep in thought and consumed with sadness. We had buried my ex-husband two weeks earlier. He was a recovered alcoholic, thirty-six years old, and had committed suicide due to depression.

At that moment, a semi-deflated Mylar balloon from his funeral came floating up the stairs from the basement. It worked its way around the bannister at the top of the stairs and traveled across the living room, stopping squarely in front of me. Written on the balloon were the words "Thinking of You," and it had pansies on it. His family used to raise pansies. I was so stunned that I reached out instinctively to touch it. It then moved in a triangular path and stopped at the framed Serenity Prayer that hung on our wall. It bounced up and down three times and then moved on to a large potted plant that was nearby. The plant was from his funeral. The balloon then came back to me and stopped.

At this point, I sensed he was reaching out to me. The balloon left me and drifted over the railing and positioned itself at the front door. My ten-year-old son was just getting home from school and opened the door. I quickly explained to him what was happening. We watched it float back up the stairs and down the hallway. That evening, as I made my way to the bedroom, I noticed the balloon had positioned itself directly behind my queen-sized headboard, precisely in the middle. I drifted off to sleep and woke in the middle of the night to find its string wrapped around my hand that was now under the pillow on what had been my ex-husband's side of the bed. The following morning, the balloon was on the floor, on his side again — deflated.

I can't explain any of this. However, I do know it brought us much comfort, knowing he was nearby and thinking of us. His spirit was alive and well.

— S. Jacobs —

Let Me Know When You Get There

Death ends a life, not a relationship.
~Jack Lemmon

Mom wanted to stay at home until the end, but I was no longer able to manage her care without help. As a former nurse I felt that I should be able to do that for my mom. So, it was with a heavy heart that I realized it wasn't possible. My brother and I talked with her about the move to the hospice facility. I promised her I would not leave her side until her time was over, so I packed a suitcase and climbed in the ambulance with her.

My brother and his wife followed in their car and went in with me while the staff at the hospice got her settled and comfortable. The next day my sisters and brother-in-law came, and because of the weather forecast, which included many feet of snow and record cold, everyone that lived any distance away brought a bag. We all wanted to be there for the last moments of her life, just as she had been there from the beginning of ours.

When she passed, we each gave her a final kiss goodbye and packed up to go to our respective homes. Although I lived two hours away, I had been staying with Mom for the past five months since we began the journey of letting go. I went back to her log cabin where we used to sit on her porch swing and watch the world go by. Memories of my mom came flooding back. She was always waiting for me on the porch when I arrived. Now I would never smell her baking my favorite oatmeal cookies or making a pot of vegetable soup again. I was already missing her presence, which had been such a reassuring force in my life. I had been lucky to have her first as my mother, and then as my friend.

I had said my goodbyes, but in my heart I was waiting for her to let me know she was okay. I had spoken with her about that very thing when we started her hospice care. She had promised she would somehow communicate to me that she was okay and had arrived at her final destination.

I started talking to myself. No one was there to listen, so I poured my heart out to the pine walls and the sunny yellow kitchen in her home. I said many things out loud. I told her I loved her and would miss her. I did laundry, mine and my mom's. I folded mine and hers. And when the last nightgown that was Mom's was ready to be put away, I dropped it on the floor. I did not have the energy to pick it up.

I sat down and cried at the foot of her bed. It was the bed where we were all created and where we were all held as infants. It would no longer be where my mom slept. I crawled into the empty bed in the empty house and reminded my mom that she had promised to let me know she was okay after she was gone. I fell into a restless sleep.

I awoke to the warmth of someone beside me. I felt calm and peaceful. I drew the covers up higher and went back to sleep. In the early morning, I woke with a start. I remember thinking that my husband must have arrived and crawled in next to me, but there was no one there. I shook it off as a dream until I saw the body print on the covers next to me. And the nightgown that was my mom's was folded neatly at the end of the bed.

I called my brother and sisters because I thought one of them must have come over while I was sleeping. My brother drove over to see if I was experiencing some sort of hallucination from the stress of our loss or the lack of sleep. He looked at the bed where the imprint was. The only person we both knew who could make that kind of short-stature imprint was Mom. At 4'8", she was small but mighty. I told my brother about feeling someone lie down beside me. I should have panicked because I was alone in the house, but I felt only a calm stillness and warmth. I knew it was my mother.

The second time I felt the warmth of someone lying down beside me was a few months later. I was sleeping on the couch in my brother's upstairs loft. I was alone up there, too. I was back in town to help sort through Mom's belongings. It was time to finish settling the estate. It had been a difficult time, and I was ready to go back to my own home. My car was loaded with some of the keepsakes I wanted to take with me to remind me of my mom and her home. I slept fitfully that night, and once again, the couch and the covers I used showed the same evidence of a short person lying down next to me. I felt only warmth and calm. No panic, no disturbance, just peaceful. My brother also witnessed the imprint in the couch.

It has been several years since my mom left us. She always said, "Let me know when you get there" every time I drove the two hours to my own home. And she also said it to each of her kids and grandkids as they left to go to their own homes. We teased her about it mercilessly. But we all knew it was because she loved us and wanted to make sure we were home safely. So, as we said our final goodbyes to her, I told her she had to let me know when she got there. I fully expected that, somehow, she would do just that if it was in her power to do so.

I had another dream recently where my mom spoke to me. It was a wonderful dream. She was showing me her new residence, which was filled with bright light and sunshine. It was everything she had always wanted in a home. It was on the water, with birds, butterflies, and beautiful scenery in vibrant colors all around. I remember asking her how she could afford such a beautiful place. She reassured me that she could stay there forever.

I can't come up with a rational explanation for the folded nightgown or the sense of peace, calm and warmth I felt when someone lay down next to me. I have been told that I must have been dreaming or hallucinating. I only know that Mom was letting me know that she is in heaven, at peace in her forever home and fulfilling the promise she made to "Let me know when you get there."

In my brother's home, the spirit of my mom remains. He still has my mom's bed and dresser. And whenever I stay with him and sleep in Mom's bed in the guest bedroom, a sense of peace fills me. It is as if her presence is still there, comforting me and letting me again feel the love she always gave me. It is like no other feeling I have ever felt, and it is a precious reminder of the unending love she gave us throughout her life. Everyone who has ever stayed in that guest room comments on the sense of peace and the restful sleep they have in that bed that once belonged to my mom.

— Kathleen E. Jones —

Little Gifts of Comfort

Those we love don't go away; they walk beside us every day.
Unseen, unheard, but always near; still loved,
still missed and very dear.
~Author Unknown

On November 22, 2005, my life was turned completely upside down when my fifty-six-year-old husband, Sid, died suddenly from a massive heart attack. The shock and grief that followed were almost unbearable. It became a struggle just to drag myself out of bed each morning after another sleepless night.

As the months dragged on, I found solace in small things. I pored over photo albums, trying to relive the good times rather than sink completely into the mire of an unhappy present. It was almost impossible to face an uncertain future, but I tried. Sid would want me to go on and find the "new normal," despite his loss.

Strange coincidences began to occur that seemed to slightly ease my pain. I was driving to work one day, crying my eyes out again. Through my tears, I caught the license plate on the car in front of me.

The letters on the plate read "SJB." I lost my breath. Those were my husband's initials. A warmth enveloped me, and I stopped sobbing. It had to be my beloved Sid reaching out to me.

I hesitated to tell anyone about the incident. Yes, it was a coincidence, but to me it was more than that. It was a sign, and I didn't want anyone to tell me otherwise. For the first time, I felt a tiny bit of comfort.

I finally opened up to members of my grief group and found that others had similar experiences. One widow confessed that she sometimes smelled her husband's cigarette smoke in their home even though he had been gone for months.

Another said that several times when she couldn't see any light at the end of the dark tunnel of grief, a special song would suddenly float from her radio speaker. It was weird that an old tune she and her husband had dubbed "their song" would miraculously play when she was completely drowning in sorrow.

We believed these occurrences were our lost loved ones giving us the comfort we needed to get through a terrible ordeal. Maybe someone else wouldn't understand, but the men and women in my grief group did.

A few months after Sid's death, a couple we had known for forty years came to visit. We wept and laughed as we reminisced about our times together.

Jim and Loretta wanted to get married when we were all freshmen in college but didn't even have the money for a license. Jim sold his shotgun to Sid so he and Loretta could wed.

The first morning of their visit, Jim came out of the guest room. His face was pale, and he whispered, "That gun I sold to Sid years ago is in our closet. Did you know it was there?"

I honestly did not realize that Sid still owned it, and I certainly had not stored the gun there. In fact, I had just cleaned out that area and never saw the gun leaning up against the wall.

How did it get there? Maybe I had overlooked it, but we all agreed it didn't matter how it ended up in a rarely used guest-room closet. We were convinced the shotgun appeared out of nowhere to help us deal with our sadness. We held each other and cried bittersweet tears.

Finding one of Sid's cigarette butts was even more bizarre. He smoked a certain brand and I complained if he threw them anywhere but the trash. He would crush his cigarettes out, dip the butts in water and place them in a small can we kept in the garage for yard trash.

No one had smoked anywhere near our home in the months after Sid died, but I continued to use the bin for clippings. One morning after dumping the contents into the curbside container for our weekly pick-up, I was shocked to see a distinctive butt in the bottom of the small can. How did that happen? Could I have missed one of Sid's cigarette butts for weeks on end? I didn't think so.

Another amazing experience involved a woman I met right after my husband died. Sandy was my age, and we began going out to eat together. It was nice to have a new single friend as I tried to adjust to life alone.

One day, she happened to mention that her son was an emergency-room doctor. We both sat stunned as we suddenly realized he was the physician who had frantically tried to save my husband that awful November morning.

He had been very kind to me that day. I don't remember much, but I do recall how he put his arms around me and whispered the words that would change my life forever. "We did everything we could. I'm so sorry."

Despite the cold surroundings and devastating news, I felt Sandy's son truly cared as he patiently answered my tearful questions about what happened to my beloved husband.

Out of the almost 100,000 residents in my hometown, how did I end up becoming friends with the mother of the doctor who was on duty the day my husband died? We both agreed that it was a strange coincidence. That bond reassured me that Sid was reaching out to me again.

I decided then that it didn't matter what people outside my grief group thought. If I was comforted by the sometimes almost eerie happenings, then so be it.

I began openly sharing my experiences and even looked forward to events that I considered signs from heaven. It was incredible how many people confessed that they, too, had similar miraculous happenings that gave them hope after a loss.

There is life after death, although it is forever altered. I have learned to cope with grief and take consolation in my memories and comforting coincidences. It has made moving forward easier.

After all these years, I still occasionally experience things that are totally unexplainable. I no longer try to analyze the events. I accept them as gifts that make the long journey through grief a bit more tolerable.

I consider the episodes divine intervention. Each and every time, I smile through my tears, close my eyes and feel Sid's loving presence surround me.

I whisper, "Thank you for communicating with me again. When your spirit embraces me, I know you are okay. You are still very missed and always will be, but I'm okay, too."

— Melinda Richarz Lyons —

Words of Love

Those we love never truly leave us.
There are things that death cannot touch.
~Jack Thorne

My mother-in-law, Christine, developed crippling arthritis, heart disease, and shoulder problems. She had difficulty walking and often fell. It was clear she could no longer live on her own.

"Your mother can live with us," I said to my husband George, her only child.

Our college-aged children had vacated their rooms. After twenty-five years of marriage, I'd mellowed enough to welcome her into my home and possibly remove some of the distance between us.

When she ate the food I cooked, I was happy. Her appetite was my only compliment.

There were challenges. Soon after she settled in, she slipped in the bathroom. We remodeled it and installed a shower with safety rails and a bench.

"No more baths for me," she lamented, but then I overheard her tell a friend her new bathroom was beautiful. Secondhand praise would have to do.

"It's better at Judy's house than I thought it would be," she told my mother.

"Christine likes you," my mother told me. "Some people have trouble putting their feelings into words. It's not the way she was raised."

I knew Christine hadn't learned to express her feelings, but a part of me longed for affirmation.

"When you have time, could you bring me a cup of tea? Now," she said.

I smiled at what once would have been an irritation, brought two cups of tea, and joined her in what would become an after-dinner ritual. She shared glimpses of her past as my reward.

I learned Christine was just sixteen and living in Poland when German soldiers invaded and took her away from her family. She spent most of World War II in indentured servitude on a German farm.

"I missed my parents but always had food, and the farmer was kind. He saved paper for me to put in my wooden shoes when they gave me bloody blisters."

Understanding softened the bite of her words. Would I have been strong like her? How could I mind when she examined clothes I sewed and pointed tiny flaws or insisted that I stood on the wrong side of the ironing board even after I explained I was left-handed? I relaxed and learned that smiles, even fake ones, made me feel better and brought us closer. She shared more of her life.

She met Edward in a resettlement camp after the war. They had no money so he had a jeweler fashion a ring from a German silver dollar. They married, had a baby while in the camp, and came to America when George was two. She never saw her parents again. I wasn't sure what I would have done.

I admired Christine's strength. She was brave to start a life far away from all she knew. She found a job in a Polish store and learned the language of her new country. Edward, who had been a university professor with a degree in engineering, found work building gas stations. They paid their bills the day they received them and never bought anything with credit. They were generous with everything except compliments.

My admiration grew. I wanted Christine to be happy with us. I enrolled her in our town's senior center. She resisted but found friends and joined in activities she enjoyed.

"Your daughter-in-law must love you," I heard one say when I dropped off a cake on Christine's birthday. She didn't reply, but her eyes glistened.

Over the next eight years, her shoulder problems escalated. I held her hand as her doctor extracted seven vials of liquid from her shoulder.

"This will ease the pain, but it's only a temporary fix," he said. "You're going to need surgery."

She was afraid and frustrated. She lost her mobility and spent most of her time in her room. Shoulder pain rendered her cane useless. She missed the senior center. We hired an aide to stay with her while we worked. I spent more time with her and encouraged visitors.

"Should I get the operation?" she asked.

"I can't decide that for you," I said.

She chose the operation. The surgery went well until she developed an infection in the hospital and spent a week in intensive care before she went to a rehabilitation facility.

"Take me home. I'll die if I stay here," she said.

"Mom," said George. "Do your exercises, get strong, and then we'll bring you home."

She pulled her hand away.

"I love you," he said.

"We both love you," I added.

She turned her back to us and closed her eyes.

She died in her sleep a week later. I wished we'd brought her home when she asked, but the doctor had said she wasn't ready.

She'd been afraid. I asked the choir to sing "Be Not Afraid" at her funeral mass. They chose "On Eagles' Wings" instead. I cried at the omission.

"Don't be afraid," I whispered.

I prayed she found peace. I missed her.

It was part of my job to accompany high-school student volunteers on service projects. They were excited about the new site, the center where Christine had died. I hesitated as we approached the facility, took a deep breath, and caught up with my students.

The activity director gave us a list of residents requesting visits. I stayed in the background as my students walked from room to room.

We approached the room that had been Christine's. My chest tightened, I took a deep breath, followed them in, and stood near the door.

The students read poetry to the woman in Bed 36B. The woman in 36A called to me.

I approached the bed where Christine had died, bit my lip, and leaned toward a tiny lady with a gummy smile. She sandwiched my hand between hers. Her skin felt like dried leaves.

"Would you sing something for me?" she whispered.

I sang "Take Me Out to the Ball Game." When I finished, she squeezed my hand and looked into my eyes. Her forceful, familiar voice made me shudder.

"I love you," she said, "and I wasn't afraid."

— Judy Salcewicz —

The Garden Visitor

Mothers hold their children's hands for a short while,
but their hearts forever.
~Author Unknown

It was a new year, 1981, and spring was finally here! We had moved into our beautiful new home and acreage a few months earlier. We were looking forward to better days ahead since the previous two years had been full of challenges and sadness.

In 1979, soon after construction began on our house, loan rates soared to 16 percent when the oil industry collapsed, and work slowed to a snail's pace at the concrete plant where my husband Don worked, causing paychecks to be cut nearly in half. Those days were rough, but they couldn't compare to the sadness of losing Don's mom, Nita, to congestive heart failure in May of that year.

Don and Nita had been as close as any mother and son could be. She was his confidante — his "rock" — and her sudden loss was terribly difficult for him. He missed the daily visits with her for coffee, swapping stories about family and friends, and sharing their differing views on politics. There was never a day that went by without him thinking of her and wishing he could talk to her just one more time.

Although Don never shared his thoughts and feelings of depression and grief with me, I could sense his pain. But as the months passed, I could see his sadness slowly lift as he watched our house being completed.

By the time spring was approaching, Don's eyes began to sparkle whenever the subject of planting a garden came up — our very first garden, a symbol of hope and new growth. He had purchased all the necessary tools, including a rototiller, and enough onion sets and seeds for nearly ten acres!

Finally, the day came to put Don's garden ideas into motion. He had just started the tiller as the sun was appearing on the horizon. I could hear the tiller running and decided to look out the window to watch the progress.

As I lifted the blinds, while squinting through the sun's glare, I didn't see the tiller, but I saw Don standing at the edge of the garden. A woman was standing beside him, dressed in a black coat and wearing a head scarf.

That's odd, I thought. *Why would someone be wearing a coat on a warm morning like this? And the head scarf — that's strange, too. Perhaps she's a neighbor who is just curious about the garden. Oh, well, I'll wait for Don to come in and ask him who she is.*

A few minutes later, Don came in through the garage to the kitchen. I noticed that he had a strange look on his face.

"Who was that woman you were talking to?" I asked.

"What woman?" he asked.

"The woman who was beside you at the edge of the garden," I replied.

"I don't know what you are talking about," he answered.

"Look, I saw her! Now, who was she?" I said, my curiosity now turning to frustration.

I couldn't understand why he denied seeing the person whom I had seen. His denial was hurtful to me.

Suddenly, I felt tears welling in my eyes. I looked at Don's eyes, and they began to fill with tears, too.

"Sheryl, it was Mom! I saw Mom," Don revealed. "One minute I was tilling, and then all of a sudden, Mom was standing beside me. It seemed like time was standing still.

"She asked me, 'Donnie, what are you going to plant?'

"'Mom, I'm going to plant green beans, okra, tomatoes, squash and peppers,' I answered. "'That's nice,' she said. "And then, Sheryl, she disappeared, and I shut the tiller off," he said. "It was so strange. One minute, she was there, dressed in dark clothes, and the next minute, she was gone. I walked away thinking maybe I had dreamed it. But then, when I walked into the house, and you started asking me about her, I was shocked that you seemed to know about her visit. I didn't know how to react or what to say to you, other than to deny it. Then when you kept pressing me about her, I realized it wasn't a dream after all because you saw her, too. We both saw her!"

At that moment, we realized we had experienced the same vision at the exact moment in time! We held each other and cried.

We shared details of that special event with only a few family members and friends. We could tell that some of them doubted our story, but we didn't care. We knew it was true, and that's all that mattered.

Don believes his mom may have appeared for a reason — to let him know she was okay and to help mend his broken heart. As to why she appeared to me, I can only guess that it was simply for confirmation to Don that her visit was real.

From that day forward, Don became a happier person. He seemed to enjoy life and his family more and was hopeful for the future.

Now, many years have passed since that special spring day, but each time garden season rolls around, Don remembers that day with fondness and can't wait to plant those vegetables. Each seed he plants reminds him of the day his mom came to see his garden.

— Sheryl K. James —

With This Ring

The love game is never called off
on account of darkness.
~Tom Masson

It was a sunny afternoon in October, and we were sitting in our living room, chatting and sharing the newspaper. Gary glanced down at his hand and said, "I'm missing my wedding ring."

"It's got to be here somewhere. I'll help you look," I said.

We searched every inch of the house. We searched his truck and my car. We searched the garage, the workshop he had been building in our back yard, the front and back lawns, the flower beds, and the driveway.

No ring.

"When do you last remember seeing it?"

"I'm not sure. I'm worried it flew off my finger when I tossed an apple core out the truck window the other day."

My husband of almost thirty-seven years looked close to tears.

In May of that year, Gary had been diagnosed with diabetes, and one of his symptoms that our doctor chalked up to the diabetes was weight loss.

"That's normal," he said. "It's nothing to worry about."

Then one day in September, Gary choked on his supper.

The next day, he was fine. But it happened again. And again.

Our doctor arranged for a surgeon to perform an endoscopy in a nearby hospital, and after the procedure we went home to await results.

Neither of us mentioned the word "cancer," but it was definitely on my mind.

The follow-up appointment with the surgeon was good.

"Your esophagus was constricted, so I stretched it," he said. "It also has a lot of ulcers, so you need to take this prescription and eat only soft foods for a couple of weeks to let everything heal."

The "C" word was not uttered.

By mid-October, Gary was no better. Swallowing remained a struggle, and he lost more weight.

We went back to the surgeon, who said to give the diet and medication more time and let him know if things didn't improve.

After another week, Gary was unable to swallow any soft foods at all, and his daily weight loss continued.

He switched to soups, milkshakes and protein drinks, and took a short-term leave of absence from work.

And to top everything else off, he lost his wedding ring.

Gary and I had been childhood sweethearts and soulmates, and we married at the age of nineteen. Our simple white-gold wedding bands, engraved with our names and our wedding date, had been on our fingers since 1972, and now his was gone.

I made a mental note that if we didn't find his ring before Christmas, I would buy him a new one and have it engraved with the same words as the original one.

But that wasn't in our future.

Gary died on December 13, 2009, exactly one month after finally being diagnosed with stage IV esophageal cancer that metastasized into his chest cavity, liver, adrenal glands and lungs.

I thought I would never stop crying.

How could the man I had loved since childhood be dead at the age of fifty-six? How would I find the strength to continue living without him?

I had no answers.

Days and weeks drifted past. I arranged for someone to plow my driveway and mow my lawn. I learned how to do simple maintenance projects around the house and to call someone when I needed additional help.

I learned to navigate life as a woman alone, missing her soulmate, and to dance the dance of the "new normal" into which I had been unwillingly thrust.

But it was tough.

When Gary was in the hospital, I took him a spare laptop to use for e-mails. The morning he died, I brought it back home and tucked it away in a drawer.

A few months later, my son turned it on again. While browsing, he found a note that Gary had written to me shortly before his death.

"Honey, remember, I have just moved on ahead to get the water hooked up and your lawn swing set up, and I will be waiting for you. Just make sure you don't come too soon. I'll wait for as long as necessary until we are together again."

His note almost broke me.

The fall after Gary died, I flew to Alberta to spend a few weeks with my brother and sister-in-law. I arrived back home shortly after my thirty-eighth wedding anniversary.

My son met me at the airport and drove me home. After he carried my bags in from the car, we sat in the family room to catch up.

"Mom," he said, "I have something to show you. I know that it's going to make you sad, but I think it's going to make you happy, too."

I had no idea what to expect.

"Okay, show me," I said, and he pulled Gary's wedding ring from his shirt pocket and handed it to me.

Of course, I cried.

"That's impossible. Where did you find it?"

"It's really weird, Mom," he said. "I was in the garage a few nights ago and saw something shiny on the floor, right in front of the overhead door. I figured it was a bottle cap or a quarter, so I went over to pick it up. When I did, I realized it was Dad's wedding band."

I shook my head.

"That doesn't make any sense," I said. "We've been in and out of that garage a million times this past year, and your dad and I searched it thoroughly last year when his ring first disappeared. How could it just show up now?"

"Mom," my son said, "it really was just sitting there, in the open, as if someone had carefully laid it on the floor for me to find."

That night, sleep eluded me.

Where had Gary's ring been for the last thirteen months? Why did it show up now?

I tried and tried to come up with a logical explanation for its reappearance, but I couldn't. After a few days, I decided to simply be thankful that it had been returned.

I took the ring to a jeweler and had it resized to fit me. Now I wear it to honor Gary's memory and the love we shared.

But I still don't know where it had been or how it found its way back to me.

Could it have been an anniversary present from Gary, a sign from him that love really is eternal? I am a skeptical person by nature, but I have no better explanation than that.

I recently wrote the following note to Gary: "Thanks for turning the water on, dear, and for setting up my swing. I'll be along to join you when it's time. And, oh yes, I'll be wearing your ring."

— Sylvia Morice —

Sewing a Legacy

You may be gone from my sight,
but you will never be gone from my heart.
~Henry van Dyke, Jr.

When I was twenty-four years old and pregnant with my first child, Grandma G. suddenly left this earth. Just days after her passing, our family cleaned out her apartment. This being the first death of a loved one in my adult years, I was devastated by the process of sorting through her belongings. I felt like an intruder in her home and sick at the sight of family members rummaging through her possessions, picking things to keep for themselves.

Grandma's jewelry box had been emptied onto her bedspread, and people were sifting through it like they were at a garage sale. "I love this necklace," my cousin said. "I'm keeping it." I didn't want any of it. These were Grandma's treasured items, not a giveaway.

"Stacy, you should take the sewing machine. You learned to sew in 4H, right?" I don't remember who said it first, but everyone agreed that I should take it. I was the only one who'd learned to sew and didn't have a machine. I shook my head. "No, I can't. It's Grandma's."

I remembered visiting my grandparents' farmhouse as a young girl. The area where Grandma sewed doubled as the play area. My sisters, cousin, and I knew that the sewing machine was not to be touched, nor was the sewing stool, which was so tempting. The seat of the stool opened to a secret compartment that held threads, buttons, and lots of mysterious gadgets. It was off-limits to children (although I may have peeked once or twice).

My cousin paused from sifting through jewelry and said to me, "Would you rather we donate her sewing machine and a stranger takes it?"

I hadn't thought of that. The suggestion made me sick to my stomach.

My cousin was helping me to grasp the reality that Grandma wouldn't use the machine again. It was no longer hers. But I could make it mine and remember her and all the projects she'd sewed with love. My discomfort over ransacking Grandma's place was replaced with humility that I could be the keeper of Grandma's meaningful possession.

The sewing machine sat in a corner of my living room for months — not out of sight, nor out of mind. It felt too sacred to touch. Possessing the sewing skills of a nine-year-old, I was unworthy of messing with Grandma's machine. Then it dawned on me that perhaps I could learn the craft and continue her legacy. A year later, I decided it was time. I bought pretty fabric and a pattern to make my daughter a dress. I removed the machine from the corner and set it on my dining room table. Lifting off the lid, I saw the spool she'd placed, the needle threaded by her arthritic fingers. I had second thoughts, wanting to leave everything just as she had left it. I liked thinking she was in the middle of a project that she would be returning to.

But I wanted to continue her legacy. How special would it be for me, her granddaughter, to place my fingers where she'd placed hers? To learn to use those mysterious gadgets in the stool? To sew clothes for my baby girl as Grandma had done for me? I could do this.

I took a deep breath and lifted the machine out of the bottom part of the case… when a pink scrap of paper caught my eye. I picked it up and read my own address on the paper. I gasped, and my heart swelled with joy and wonder. Grandma had ripped the return address label off an envelope I'd mailed to her and must've placed it in her sewing-machine case.

The label was confirmation that Grandma wanted me to have the sewing machine. I didn't know how God had orchestrated the events, but I knew that my address label was proof that I was the rightful new owner of Grandma's sewing machine. I cried happy tears. This precious treasure was residing at its new address.

In addition to my daughter's dress, I've sewn curtains for our home, Halloween costumes, a wax-museum costume for my children, and masks for family and friends during the COVID-19 pandemic.

I'm so grateful for the divine intervention that helped me to heal and experience joy despite my grandmother no longer being physically present with me. I keep the return address label in the stool and find myself in awe every time I see it. What a precious gift.

— Stacy Boatman —

A Miraculous Message of Love from Beyond

Love recognizes no barriers. It jumps hurdles,
leaps fences, penetrates walls to arrive
at its destination full of hope.
~Maya Angelou

One Saturday evening in early October, a Facebook notification popped up on my phone. I was surprised to see it was a message from Sandy, my mom's best friend from high school. Mom and Sandy grew up together and had been in daily e-mail communication for years. I can't imagine how many messages they sent to one another over the decades.

I didn't know Sandy well as she had lived out of state most of her life, but I wondered if Sandy knew that the day was difficult for me. It was the third anniversary of Mom's terminal cancer diagnosis. I had been with Mom when she got the awful news, and I'll never forget how she handled it with such grace.

Mom passed away four months after her diagnosis. The last time Mom used her computer, she sent a message to Sandy telling her that she was leaving her home and was headed to her next adventure.

A few months earlier, a story I had written about selling Mom's car had been published in *Chicken Soup for the Soul: Angels All Around*.

It was the fourth time my work had appeared in the *Chicken Soup for the Soul* series, and I was honored. I knew Mom would have been proud of me.

I opened the Facebook message. Sandy had written to say that she ordered the book on Amazon but couldn't find my story.

"Is there a second edition?" she asked.

"There's only one edition. It's on page 274," I responded.

After a few messages and pictures back and forth, I realized she had purchased the wrong book by mistake.

Then she said something that shocked me.

"I saw the wonderful story you wrote about your great-grandma! You won't believe it. It was in the Dollar Tree store!" she said.

I had no idea what she was talking about. I had written a story called "A Great Grandma Forever" that was published in *Chicken Soup for the Soul: Miraculous Messages from Heaven*, but that was six years earlier.

"In Dollar Tree?" I asked.

Sandy explained that she had been shopping in a Dollar Tree store in North Carolina when out of the blue she picked up a book called *Miraculous Messages of Love from Beyond*. She said it was a small book, only seventy-five pages. She picked it up, looked at the contents, and immediately saw my name.

"There were a few books there, but I went right to the one with your name," Sandy said. "I was so surprised and happy to see it."

I was completely shocked and amazed when Sandy sent me a picture of the little book. I was thrilled my story had been reprinted in this tiny *Chicken Soup for the Soul* book at Dollar Tree.

I got goosebumps and a few tears just thinking about it.

"I usually don't look at books in that store," Sandy said.

"Maybe Mom tapped you on the shoulder and directed you to the book," I suggested. I couldn't imagine another explanation for it. Nobody else had mentioned the book to me.

"Your mother wanted me to see it," Sandy said.

"I think so, too," I said.

I couldn't stop smiling.

It was too late on Saturday night to go to Dollar Tree, so I waited until the next day to drive to our local store. I was giddy with excitement Sunday afternoon when I pulled into the parking lot.

I walked to the book section and was overwhelmed with all the books piled on the shelves. If I spotted it, it would be like finding a needle in a haystack.

After a few minutes, I sat down on the floor in the aisle of Dollar Tree. I didn't care what the employees thought—I was on a mission! From that viewpoint down low, I saw several *Chicken Soup for the Soul* titles, including the one Sandy mentioned. The books were so small. The width of the book spine was about 1/4 inch. I'm not sure how anyone could have found them down there.

I pulled out my phone and messaged Sandy. "I found the books! Thank you so much for letting me know."

I wanted to jump in the air and shout from the rafters that my story was published in this tiny book, but instead I grabbed four copies and headed toward the checkout.

As I was standing in line, I had a strong feeling that Mom was right beside me, beaming with pride. I could almost feel her energy, as if she were hugging me. As the cashier rang up my order, I tried not to cry. I thought about the likelihood of Sandy ordering the wrong book, randomly finding this little book at Dollar Tree, and then contacting me and telling me about it. Sandy and I rarely communicated. It seemed more than a coincidence.

I walked out to my van and sobbed.

I'll never forget that Sunday in early October when I found that book because it was my forty-ninth birthday. I couldn't imagine a better birthday gift from Mom.

Since that day, I have visited a handful of Dollar Tree stores and have never found that book again. I like to think Mom knew about the publication and sent a message to her best friend Sandy, just like she always used to do.

Mom really did send a miraculous message of love from beyond.

—Tyann Sheldon Rouw—

Dimes from Heaven

Forgiveness does not change the past,
but it does enlarge the future.
~Paul Boese

My mother and I had a challenging relationship from the moment I was born. I remember as a young child thinking my mother was always angry or sad. She was always yelling or crying. I didn't understand. I suppose on some level I blamed myself. I tried to be a good little girl, but I was never good enough for my mother to be happy. I didn't understand. Whatever mood my mother was in, she took it out on me.

If my mother was angry, she would yell at me and spank me with her hand, a paddle, a belt, a wooden spoon — whatever was handy. If my mother was sad, she would hug me, rock back and forth, and cry. I could never figure out what I did or didn't do to trigger my mother's anger or sadness.

When I was eleven years old, I had a health class and learned about alcoholism. I finally understood. I knew my mother drank beer every night, but I did not know what beer did to a person. Intoxicated. I was intrigued and learned people's moods could fluctuate when intoxicated. I no longer had to blame myself, but it didn't help my relationship with my mother. It only made it worse.

I stopped blaming myself and started blaming my mother. I would plead with her to stop. My pleas angered her and only caused the chasm between us to widen. By the time I was in my teens, our relationship was too fractured to repair.

I felt guilty about my relationship with my mother. I would try different things to try and get closer to her. Nothing seemed to work. I struggled buying Mother's Day cards; they seemed insincere. I'd get a blank card and just write "Happy Mother's Day" because anything else seemed shallow. The mother/daughter bond seemed forever lost.

In my late teens, my mother started collecting dimes. She would save them all year and cash them in for vacation or Christmas. I remember her saying, "Nobody collects just dimes. I want to be different." I also started collecting dimes, and I would give her a bucket of dimes a couple of times a year. It seems trivial, but to my mother and me, it was a connection.

The exchange of dimes went on for a few years. My mother was so excited to receive the dimes. It wasn't for the money. It was because we were both trying. She continued to drink alcohol, which kept anyone from getting close to her. It was like she had erected an emotional wall around herself. She had her wall and her dimes. There was nothing in between. The dimes I gave her were a tiny window in that wall.

My mother eventually had a debilitating stroke. She was a chain smoker and chain drinker. The two vices did her in. My mother could no longer talk. In the home, she had to use a cane to walk. Outside the home, my mother was in a wheelchair. She had to have her food cut up for her and have help eating. She could no longer care for herself.

My mother forgot she drank and smoked after the stroke. She never did either again. She was a shell of herself after the stroke. It was like she was there, but she wasn't. I watched the toll it was taking on my father to care for her. I bought their house from them and moved back in to help Dad care for my mother.

My father and I took care of my mother for thirteen years after her stroke. My father had to take early retirement to care for my mother, and I helped as much as I could while continuing to work and go to graduate school. I had tried to get past my mother's wall produced by alcohol and cigarettes. Now her new wall was the stroke. I'd look in her eyes, and they were vacant.

In graduate school, I took a class on death and dying where I had to write a paper on death for an assignment. I chose my mother. I wrote that by the time my mother died, she would have died three times during my life: once by alcohol and cigarettes, once by the stroke, and finally when the day came that she would leave this earthly plane. My professor thought it was interesting. I thought it was tragic.

Over the course of the thirteen years that my father and I took care of her, we made many trips to the emergency room. She had chronic bladder and kidney infections. The last one did her in. I think she finally gave up. The next step was hospice.

The doctor said she would probably not live until the weekend. It was Wednesday, but she lived two more weeks. It is sheer torture watching someone die. No food. No water. Just moistening the lips. My mother never regained consciousness. I put pictures of the family around her hospital bed in case she woke up and nobody was there.

I got the call a little after midnight. The nurse said my mother had passed, and she had been with her when it happened. My father, younger brother and I went to the hospital. She looked peaceful, like her soul was finally at rest.

A few days after her funeral, it started. The dimes. I started finding dimes every single day. Randomly. Everywhere. Anywhere. At first, I thought it was a fluke. It kept happening. I found at least one dime every day for eight years. Not quarters or pennies, just dimes. I know it was my mother. I know in her spiritual state she could finally tell me she loved me. Her wall finally came down.

One day while we were having lunch, I told my niece about finding dimes. She thought it was fascinating. As we left the cafe and walked around the corner, there on the sidewalk were three dimes! This happens quite frequently. I will share the dime story with someone, and they will either find a dime that day or we find one together. The dimes are a bridge, a connection between worlds.

It has been sixteen years since my mother passed away. I don't find dimes every day anymore. I do find dimes if I am trying to make a decision about something and need reassurance I am on the right track. I find dimes when I'm working too long or under stress. I know it's my mother. I realize now that my mother was depressed and self-medicating. The dimes are her way of saying she's sorry.

I know my mother loved me the best she could. I wish it had been different, but I am not angry with her. My mother did not love herself. The dimes are a sign from the other side that tells me she gets it now. That she loves herself. That she loves me. It is a thin veil between the worlds. When we keep our mind and heart open, love enters through the cracks. In the end, it is all love.

— Darlene Parnell —

Holiday Miracles

The Christmas Diamond

Miracles come in moments. Be ready and willing.
~Wayne Dyer

I remember holding my mother's hand when I was a little girl and being mesmerized by the bands she wore on her right ring finger. The rings had belonged to my mother's mother, and her mother before that, and had been handed down through the generations. They were the only things remotely of value that any of the women had ever owned.

The engagement ring consisted of a small center stone surrounded by even smaller diamonds. I remember using one finger to gently trace the outline of that delicate gold band, so thin and frail from years of wear. None of the women ever had the means to have it repaired.

As a teenager, I used to beg my mother every single day to let me wear those rings, and she never would. Then, one sunny Saturday when I was seventeen years old, she gave in and let me borrow them to wear on a date. That very morning, my mother had announced that—after twenty-three years—she was finally filing for divorce from my abusive father. As she slipped the rings onto my finger, she made me promise that I wouldn't let anything happen to them, and that I'd return them to her the second I came home. Eager to finally have a chance to wear them, I gave her my word, childishly crossing my heart as I did so.

I never had a chance to keep that promise.

That night, while I was away, my father came back to the rundown rental house we had all shared, armed with a revolver. Without saying a word, he shot everyone in the house, killing my mother and brother and badly injuring my sister before taking his own life.

I wore those rings every single day for seventeen years.

Then, a few years ago while decorating the Christmas tree at work, I looked down to find that the center stone was missing from my mother's ring. For three days straight, I searched everywhere for the diamond. I swept the entire room where I had been decorating, pulling everything apart and retracing every step. I methodically sifted through every speck of dirt and debris, and checked every sequin, bead, and piece of glitter three or four times. The stone never did turn up, and finally I had to accept that it was just gone forever.

Thinking about the situation in the days that followed, I realized something. Although I had really hoped to find the diamond, I never felt desperate about the situation. The minute that I noticed it was gone, my very first thought was, *If you don't find it, you'll just have it replaced. No big deal.*

Had the same thing happened to my mother, I know exactly how she would have felt — we would never have had the money to fix that ring, and it would have been lost to her forever. These were her mom's rings, the only thing handed down to her, and they were probably the nicest things that my mom had ever owned. She meticulously cared for them and wore them with great pride. Knowing how much they meant to her, it would have been a huge blow, and she would have been frantic over the whole ordeal. I could picture the desperation in her eyes as she looked for that tiny stone, and I knew she would have been crushed when she didn't find it.

All that my mom ever wished for us was that we would have it better than she did. She wanted more for us. She wanted us to leave behind that poverty and desperation she so often felt. In many ways, that wish has come true, and I know she'd be proud that I didn't have to worry over that little diamond or anything else. So, even though I really hoped that I would find the stone that had been hers, I decided that I would have the rings repaired, and she would understand.

That Christmas, when it was time for the decorations at work to come down, I was in a terrible mood. It had been a chaotic several weeks, and I was busy and tired. I took the decorations from the tree and wrapped the ornaments for storage. But when it was time to put away the tree, I couldn't find the box anywhere. Agitated, I grabbed the tree by the base and dragged the entire thing across the property, outside and to the storage building fifty or so yards away from my office area. There, I threw it into the corner and slammed the door, leaving it forgotten for an entire year.

When the following Christmas season rolled around and it was time to pull out the tree and put it up, I found it exactly where I had left it. By then, it had been covered up with other discarded junk — empty bags, a broken weed eater, and a piece of water hose that had been chewed up by a lawn mower. I kicked all these items out of my way and dragged the pathetic artificial tree out of its corner and into my office. There, I began the painstaking process of shaping this battered and abused piece of junk into something that slightly resembled a pine tree.

While doing so, I thought about my mom — about those rings and the day that she gave them to me — and breathed a silent apology to her that I had lost her diamond. Suddenly, just as I had that thought, I got so cold that I physically shivered, and the skin on my arms broke out in goosebumps. All at once, as I pulled up one of the little branches of the tree, a sparkle caught my eye. It was a tiny diamond, just lying there, as if someone had put it on the branch of the tree, stood back and waited for me to find it.

Scarcely daring to breathe, I reached out with a shaking hand to pick up the stone. Gently, I laid the diamond in the palm of my left hand, convinced that I was imagining the entire thing, that I would blink and nothing would be there after all. But it was there.

Somehow, after having been up for the entire season the year before, after all the abuse that I had bestowed upon that tree, after having been pulled across a parking lot and abandoned in a pile of garbage for an entire year, the diamond was there. It just didn't make sense. How could that tiny speck of stone still be on the tree, perched on a branch without having fallen out anywhere? It was a miracle, plain and simple.

That day, I got the best Christmas present I ever received. It was not the diamond, although I am thrilled to have the same stone that my mother cherished back in my possession. No, the best present was the confirmation that my dear mom, whom I miss so much that it hurts, never left me at all. She is here, every second, watching over me still. I know it, as sure as I know that diamond was never in that tree until the second that I felt a chill come over me, and my mother laid it there for me to find.

— Candy Allen Bauer —

The Night Santa Claus Cried

Every day holds the possibility of a miracle.
~Author Unknown

Four-year-old David was giddy with excitement as we drew near to the front of the line to see Santa Claus. He stood on his toes to see over the shoulder of the taller boy in front of him. "We're next, Mama," he said, grabbing my hand and pulling me forward.

Santa gently patted the back of the little boy who scrambled off his lap and turned to us. He held his hand out to David, barely giving me a glance. "Come, sonny. Tell Santa what you want for Christmas." He smiled indulgently as David rattled off an impossibly long list of toys he'd seen advertised on TV. "You know, son, I have many boys and girls to bring gifts to. I may not be able to bring you everything you want, but I think I can bring the things you'd like most."

David looked puzzled. "How will you know which things I want most?"

Santa gave a low chuckle. "Santa knows." For the first time, he really looked at me. The twinkle left his green eyes, and he swallowed. He turned to Mrs. Claus, who was passing out candy canes to the kids as they left. "I think I need a quick break."

Something in his face made her react quickly. "Boys and girls, Santa will be back in a few minutes. He just needs a little break."

Santa gently slid David off his lap and stood to follow Mrs. Claus. Although he tried to turn his head away from the kids, I was standing right in front of him, and I saw the tears in his eyes as he hurried away. I saw him grab Mrs. Claus by the arm and say something to her just as I was turning to leave. She looked back at me and motioned me to come forward. For a moment, I was too stunned to move, wondering what was happening and how it could involve me. She gestured again, this time almost frantically.

I grabbed David's hand and followed them into a small storage area in the rear of the store. Without saying a word, Mrs. Claus abruptly left the room. Santa stood staring at me, his green eyes glistening with tears that he somehow managed to keep from falling. I knew that if David had not been there, this man would have been sobbing. But why? And what did he want from me?

"Beth?" he whispered hoarsely. "You are Beth. I know you are." He swallowed. "I've looked for you for years, honey." He saw the confusion on my face, and he took the cap off his head and tore the fake glasses from his nose. "My hair and beard used to be red, but they turned snow-white quite some time ago. I'm your daddy, honey."

I reeled back on my heels. Daddy was an alcoholic, and Mama left him when I was seven years old. I saw him once in a while for the next few years, whenever he managed to stay sober long enough to come for a visit. Then Mama was transferred to another state with her job, and I never saw him again. He was always good to me, even when he was drinking, so I missed him terribly. But Mama was bitter toward him, and she never let him know that we were moving.

As I stared at the man in front of me, I began to see remnants of the father I once knew and loved. I especially remembered his green eyes that always seemed to shine when he looked at me. My own eyes were filling with tears, but I couldn't speak past the huge lump in my throat. I had resigned myself to the fact that David would never know his grandfather, yet here he was standing in front of us in a Santa Claus suit, of all things. But I had some of my mother in me, too, because I instantly doubted if I wanted my son to grow close to an alcoholic grandfather or not.

As if he could read my thoughts, he said in a rush of words, "I've been sober for ten years, honey. I started playing Santa Claus when I worked for the mall during the Christmas season one year to make extra money. The man who usually had the role got sick, and they couldn't find a replacement. My manager looked over at me and said, 'Joe, you'd make a good Santa with all that white hair and beard. How well can you do a ho, ho, ho?' I found that I actually liked it, and I've been doing it ever since."

He swiped at his eyes to knock back a stray tear. "Honey, I've searched for you everywhere. But I never dreamed I'd look up and see you in one of my lines." He looked down at David, who was utterly perplexed and not understanding anything that was being said. A huge smile spread across his face, and dimples that looked exactly like David's creased his cheeks. "I'm a grandfather," he whispered, reaching out for me.

I stepped into his arms, and as we embraced, I could smell the familiar scents that I had forgotten until that moment. The clean, familiar smell of his soap and after shave filled my senses as I clung to him.

David, eyes big with surprise as Mama and Santa embraced, stepped forward and put one arm around Santa's waist and one arm around my waist. Santa and I both laughed. David didn't yet know it, but he was meeting his grandfather. Ten minutes ago, I thought that my son would never know this man. But as I watched him place a big hand lovingly on David's head, his eyes sweeping over the boy as if he couldn't get enough of him, I instinctively knew that this man was in our life to stay.

I invited Dad over for dinner. David was overjoyed that Santa would be having dinner with us. I had a lot of explaining to do, but as I watched the small boy and the man in the Santa suit grin at one another, I knew that everything was going to be just fine. I could already see the beginning of a bond between them. Dad's green eyes shone when he looked at David, just as they always did when he looked at me when I was a girl.

When we got home, my husband, Glen, was making spaghetti for dinner. "Did you two have a good time?" he asked.

David ran to him and jumped into his arms. “Daddy, guess what! Santa Claus is coming for dinner tomorrow.”

Glen looked at me over the top of David’s head, his eyes full of questions.

I laughed. “I’ll explain later,” I said.

— Elizabeth Atwater —

Gramma's Gift

A grandmother is like an angel, who takes you under her wing. She prays and watches over you, and she'll gift you anything.
~Author Unknown

The Christmas season could only really begin once my grandparents arrived for their annual December visit. The moment they pulled into our driveway, our home would light up with their love and delight in spending time with their family.

Gramma, in particular, relished the joy of the season. She'd hum Christmas carols as she wrapped gifts and addressed her hand-painted cards. We would bake chocolate kringle cookies and read stories in front of the tree. On Christmas Eve, we'd sing "Silent Night" on the ride home from church, while I snuggled against her in the back seat and looked for Rudolph's red nose in the dark sky.

Years passed, and Gramma shared our traditions with my three children, her great-grandchildren. They learned how to melt chocolate for the kringles and roll out the pie dough without handling it too much. They read the same Christmas stories, curled up on Gramma's lap.

We always said Gramma was the closest person to a real angel on earth. She was serene, patient and always positive. She never, ever spoke a bad word about anyone. She was devoted to her family, and Christmas was the time of year when her beautiful spirit really shined.

When Gramma had a stroke at age ninety-seven in February 2019, we knew it was time to say goodbye. She'd lived a full and happy life.

I drove to Pennsylvania with my fourteen-year-old daughter Lucie to see her in hospice care. During the two-hour drive, I tried to prepare Lucie for what was happening. We talked about life, death, and the afterlife. I told her how some people believe that our spirits carry on and are still present after death. I shared with her some of the stories I'd read in my job as a Chicken Soup for the Soul editor, putting together our latest book of stories about angels and miracles, *Chicken Soup for the Soul: Angels All Around*.

We said our goodbyes. Gramma wasn't able to speak or respond, but we could tell she was listening. Lucie handled it with composure beyond her years, and in our final parting, she said, "Send us a sign when you're gone, Gramma, a sign that you're with us."

Months went by, and one day Lucie asked me if I'd seen any signs from Gramma. No, I hadn't seen any signs. I wondered if I should have told her those angel stories and created those expectations. Now she was waiting for a sign, in the literal way that a teenager would. What if there was no sign? I worried that she'd be disappointed and think Gramma was just gone forever.

The Christmas season arrived, and it seemed that Lucie had forgotten about watching for Gramma's sign. But we all felt an emptiness in the season without her. We tried baking chocolate kringle cookies, but they turned out flat and didn't quite taste as good. We sang "Away in a Manger," but it sounded off-key.

December festivities kicked into full swing, and I became too busy to dwell on missing Gramma. In fact, I was too busy even to enjoy the spirit of the season. It flew by without a moment of appreciation for my bright-eyed children and their excitement for our family holiday traditions.

On Christmas Eve day, I saw our mail carrier deliver a stack of cards to our mailbox, but I was frantically doing all the things a mom does the day before Christmas — wrapping, cleaning, baking, cooking, and preparing. *I'll collect the mail tomorrow,* I thought.

After hosting dinner for thirty people, I collapsed into bed. But instead of falling into a dreamy Christmas Eve slumber, I tossed and turned in my regret that I had been too busy to even pause and enjoy my family during this special time of year.

Christmas morning, I was exhausted. I had a cup of coffee and smiled through the flurry of unwrapping. Once it was over, my husband took the kids to his parents nearby to see their cousins and open more gifts. At last, I had some time to myself. I went for a quiet walk and reflected on all the wonderful Christmases I've had. I thought about Gramma and promised myself to be more positive like her, to take more time to enjoy the small moments in life.

Back home, I went by the mailbox and grabbed the mail before jumping in the shower. I stopped short when I saw the card at the top of the pile, addressed in Gramma's distinctive cursive handwriting. And then my eye went to the return address: Thelma A. Church, with her home address. I ripped open the card. It was Gramma's hand-painted Christmas card, a lovely watercolor she did every year:

Dearest Jamie, Tom, Lucie, Emmett and Clara,

To all 5 of you —

What a precious family! It will be so nice to see you on Christmas.

Save a few hugs for me.

Love you,
Gramma

It was last year's Christmas card that hadn't been delivered. It had a December 2018 postmark, and there was a slight error in our address, so it hadn't made it to our house last year. Somehow, it had ended up in our mailbox on our first Christmas without Gramma.

There was no logical explanation. I quizzed family members and even asked our mail carrier what happens to undelivered mail. Was there a chance it was in a box of lost Christmas cards that were redelivered the following year? She shook her head. "No way," she said. "That's just a Christmas miracle."

Gramma gave me the gift of knowing she was with me on Christmas Day and every day. I slept like a baby that night for the first time in weeks, with Gramma's card propped next to my bed.

— Jamie Cahill —

Daddy's Last Christmas

He was a father. That's what a father does.
Eases the burdens of those he loves.
Saves the ones he loves from painful last images
that might endure for a lifetime.
~George Saunders

My daddy had been sick for several years with Alzheimer's and Parkinson's disease. Before the diseases robbed him of his mind, he had earned a bachelor's, master's, and doctorate degree in theology, and had been a pastor since he was sixteen.

During the previous forty years, all at the same time, he worked as an editor, a chaplain for the local fire and police departments as well as the state highway patrol, and hosted a weekly radio show. Not only did he pastor a local church, he was considered the town chaplain and wrote for two local papers.

Last year, the months leading up to Christmas were extremely hard because we knew it would be Daddy's last. Our family loved the season, but what we usually celebrated as a joyous and eventful time had a dark cloud hanging over it.

Daddy could still walk a little but had hardly spoken since late October, and anything he did say made absolutely no sense. He didn't recognize any of us, not even my mom, his wife of sixty-plus years. His children and grandchildren were all strangers, except for me. I look so much like a younger version of my mother that he often called me my mom's nickname: "Barbs."

In early November, I sat with him listening to music while my mom took a much-deserved nap. Suddenly, he looked me straight in the eye and said with complete clarity, "I know Christmas is coming, and I want you to do me a favor. Your mom loves bracelets. I want you to find her a silver bracelet with two charms on it: a double heart and a pair of boots. (My daddy was from west Texas and constantly wore boots, even to the beach.) I also want to get the three of you kids a sterling boot charm."

I thought it might be nice to have a note from Daddy to go along with the gifts, so I asked if he thought he could write his name. But this great wordsmith had been robbed of even being able to scrawl his own name. I wrote out both words, and after many tries, he managed to scribble out "George" and "Dad." He told me what he wanted on the two notes. I would type them out and place his name on each one. One note for Mom: "For the love of my life." And for us kids: "Always remember the way I was." Then he turned on a dime and became the man we didn't know again.

Those were his last thirty minutes of lucidity. He didn't speak another word to anyone. Christmas was emotional for all of us except for Daddy. He didn't know any of us and spent the day unpacking and packing his Christmas stocking. No one knew about his gifts but me. My brother opened his first, and the tears began to flow. My sister wouldn't open hers.

A few weeks later, he was gone. But that last Christmas, we received gifts even more precious than silver or gold. We got one more look into the mind of the man who loved us so much that his last thoughts were of making us happy. While it was a bittersweet Christmas, it was one our whole family would cherish for the rest of our lives.

—Jennifer Clark Davidson—

Love Finds a Way

Anyone can be an angel.
~Author Unknown

I was no Scrooge. But, to be clear, I was no Tiny Tim either. My usual response to a holiday greeting was muted at best, usually a generic "You, too" or "Same to you." I was a typical cynic, burdened with the doubts and misgivings of my generation. Preoccupied with surviving, I did not have time to ponder the meaning of life or the answers to its many questions. Christmas was just another tradition demanding my time and effort for the sake of my family.

And so it happened that I was running errands a few weeks before the holidays one year. Work was busy, the family was making plans, and my to-do list kept growing. My mom had undergone very successful treatment for cancer, and there were many people to thank for their help and support. She had added quite a few names to her Christmas card list and sent me to the card store and post office almost daily.

It was on one such trek that the box appeared.

I have to admit that it was odd. Traffic getting off the interstate was slow and, as luck would have it, I got caught at the longest stoplight ever. Glancing out my window at the wintery scene, I noticed a small box on the side of the road. It was covered in an inch or two of snow and wrapped in Christmas paper. It did not seem like trash. The paper was intact, and the box lay flat on the ground as though carefully placed there. I tried to ignore it, but curiosity won. I shifted into park and jumped out to retrieve the small gift. The light changed, and a honking horn delayed any further investigation. I tossed the package on the back seat and resumed my chores, my newly acquired treasure forgotten.

A few hectic days passed, and once again the package caught my eye as I drove home from work. I took it inside and carefully opened it. I don't know what I had expected, but I was shocked to find a beautiful gold bracelet, adorned with precious stones and sparkling charms. The stones were onyx, ruby and emeralds. The charms were inscribed with words like patience, perseverance, courage, and hope. On the reverse side were inscribed the words: "Love finds a way." It took my breath away. How could anyone have lost such a wondrous gift? For whatever reason, I made it my mission to find the owner. I could only imagine someone frantically searching for what must have been a heartfelt and expensive gift.

Ads on the Internet and in the newspaper did not yield any results, save a few crank calls trying to guess — and steal — the Christmas gift. Disappointed, I looked at the bracelet, still imagining the sense of loss and frustration someone felt. Then I realized that the box had the name of the jeweler emblazoned on the top. Perhaps he would remember the owner, or the owner might return to order a replacement. There might be a happy ending to the story after all.

The next day, I took the piece back to the jewelry store, explained what happened, and asked the jeweler to return the bracelet to me should he not be able to identify the proper owner. I told the jeweler I would call in a few weeks to see what happened, but I really had no intention of doing so. I put the matter in his hands and left the store to go about my business, satisfied I had done my part.

Two weeks later, the package was long forgotten when we were invited to a Christmas party, attended by patients, their families, and the staffs from the doctor's office and the hospital. Chatting with such warm and wonderful people was as therapeutic for me as it was for my mom. Her hospital roommate was doing well, her favorite nurse was as funny as ever, and one of my mom's favorite aides, Angelica, told us of her recent marriage. Her face beamed with excitement and pride as she told Mom all the details of the wedding and the future plans she and her husband had made. She was very excited, and her energy and joy were contagious.

A short time later, Angelica's sister arrived. Her name was Mariam. She was as beautiful as her sister but spoke with a slight impediment. I had assumed she worked as an aide at the hospital, but she was working in the gift shop as a clerk. She told us how much she loved her job. She was grateful for it since she had her own medical challenges, having been recently diagnosed with an inoperable brain tumor that might eventually take her life. But no matter. She was determined to live a full and happy life, and Mariam knew she could count on her sister for love and support. In fact, Angelica had introduced her sister to my mother, and the two were a great support for each other. No wonder Angelica was so good at caring for others. She knew firsthand how difficult it was to see loved ones suffer from their illnesses.

The group was hushed into silence, and one of the doctors proposed a toast to all the patients, living and deceased. He talked about fighting the good fight against disease, and the courage, patience, perseverance, and hope it took to face the enemy. The doctor thanked everyone who was there to show their support and love for all the patients. He then ended his speech with the phrase, "We never give up because..." And all the patients and staff responded with "Love finds a way!"

I was stunned. The meaning of the phrase slowly sunk in, and I realized that the forgotten bracelet was meant for someone in that room. I looked around at all the smiling faces and the joy that filled the room. I felt ashamed of myself and my failure to follow up with the jeweler and work harder to find the bracelet's rightful owner.

I was lost in my thoughts when Mariam asked me to come with her to be with my parents. She sat down next to my mother and began to tell her a story. When Mariam was in the hospital, her roommate's family had gotten their daughter a gift. But before they could give it to her, she died. Her family held onto it for almost a year. Her father, so devastated by her death and bitter about life, did not want the gift in his home any longer and wanted to prove that love was a lie. So, he took the gift, and after driving around the city, he tossed it out the window, thinking that someone else would find it and put it to good use.

A couple of weeks ago, his brother the jeweler called to tell him that a man had come into the shop to return a bracelet he had found along the road. He did not leave a name or number. He left the store, and when the jeweler opened the box, he recognized the bracelet right away. He raced outside, but the man had already gone. The jeweler told his brother that he was convinced it had been an angel, sent by God to return the bracelet and prove the power of love. The grieving father was overcome with emotion and realized that he was wrong about love. He knew where the bracelet belonged and wanted someone brave and kind to have it. He called Mariam and asked her to give it to someone who fought the good fight. Mariam chose my mom.

Mom still wears the bracelet, and every time she does, I greet her with, "We never give up because…" I never did tell her of my small part in this Christmas story. Better to think of the "stranger" as an angel because, in that moment, I was not my usual self. I believe I was led by angels to be part of the bracelet's journey—not that I am worthy or better than anyone else, but because love finds a way.

—James Gaffney—

A Saturday Night in Central City

Wherever there is a human being,
there is an opportunity for a kindness.
~Lucius Annaeus Seneca

In search of a night's entertainment during a snowy Christmas vacation, we stumbled upon an intimately small casino in Central City, Colorado. The town had once thrived during the Gold Rush, and had been revived as a gambling town in the 1990s.

After a short time in the casino, I began to feel uneasy in this room of "one-armed bandits." Most of my quarters were already lost, and I was bothered by the noise of all the machines and the sounds of other patrons hitting jackpots. Suddenly, I heard a voice calling out in my direction.

"Howdy!" rasped a tall stranger, extending a thin, muscular arm for a hearty handshake.

"Hello," I offered back, catching my breath.

He smelled of alcohol, and though his eyes were a soft pale blue, I first noticed his thin, leathery skin and worn gray jacket. I felt my guard go up and my body stiffen.

"I'm Jeff," he rasped. He must have noticed my son and daughter because he followed with, "Are you folks having fun tonight?" As I looked up into his blue eyes again, I wondered why he had singled us out.

But an answer was expected, and I blurted that we weren't doing too well on the machines.

"Where are you folks from?" he asked cordially. This made me even more wary as I wondered why a stranger in a casino would care to know.

"New York," I clipped, almost curtly. "And we'll probably be leaving soon."

Seeing his hand reach into his pocket, I tensed, sure now that something was about to happen. "Here," he said, smiling and holding out a stack of quarters in my direction. I smelled his alcohol again, backed up a couple of steps and firmly shook my head.

"Oh, no! I can't take these," I said with determination.

"Trust me. I'm a Texan who's made sacks of money in black gold! Go ahead. I want you to use the coins," he replied.

I was now becoming sure that I had seen him watching us from the casino staircase.

"They are your quarters. I don't want them," I said, doing my best to appear polite and not cause any ruckus.

"I insist you use them," he said, placing about twelve quarters in my hand.

I took the quarters from his rough hand as I heard the man say, "I'm from Houston." I could not believe that a stranger would be so friendly.

"Use that machine!" he said as he pointed to the one that had taken my quarters.

"Oh, no!" I argued with the new acquaintance, now known to me as "Jeff." "That's where I lost my money!"

"Go ahead... play on that machine," he urged as if he knew something I didn't.

As I played and quickly lost six quarters, he coaxed me to keep on feeding his coins into the same machine.

"Three at a time," he called out. "Put in three coins at a time."

The second time that I followed his advice, and put in the last three of his quarters, I heard what seemed like the loudest ring I had heard that night. *Does this man have some control or power over what is happening?* I wondered as the coins showered from the one-armed bandit.

"Won't you take some?" I turned to him and questioned. Now it was his turn to back away, refusing even the few quarters from my jackpot that he had given me. Excitedly, I filled my plastic container with the winnings as my son looked on in disbelief. Jeff had gone over to the side of the room where I could feel his blue eyes still observing me.

Unable to stay away from him now, I needed to learn more about this person who was responsible for my change of fate. I prodded him into conversation, and he told me that he had most recently lived in Kansas and had a six-year-old daughter named Jessica. He also confided that he had won $600 the day before and lost $1,200 that morning.

I am still not sure what prompted Jeff to give me the lucky quarters. Was he lonely, or did he just enjoy watching people have fun? It felt good knowing that my trust in human nature had been restored, as I found out that it is possible to meet a nice stranger in a gambling town.

We said our goodbyes and shook hands. I remember thinking it was the most unforgettable experience that I would have that evening. I bounded up the steps, feeling light-footed on my way to the cashier's cage. I walked past a blur of blackjack, roulette and poker tables. Standing before the cashier, I exchanged my coins for $500 in $20 denominations.

Quickly stuffing the crisp bills into my wallet, we rushed down the steps as I pictured the lobster dinner and champagne that I would choose for dinner. I was planning a quick exit to my car, which was parked down the road. With our first steps outside, I felt the crunch of new snow under my boot. Looking around brought a picturesque view of the old mining town, now with a new, pristine quality.

The wind blew gustily as we pulled tightly on our coats to wrap the collars around our necks. The cold felt raw and piercing as a shiver went through my body.

As we crossed the snow-covered road at an angle, we saw a figure huddled against the side of the casino. He was under a blanket with his knees up, leaning against the building and facing away from the street. Curiosity led me to examine further.

We walked to his side, looked down and saw an old man with snow on his scalp and long whiskers. He was under a worn Army blanket.

I reached over and touched his arm. "Come with me," I heard myself say to him in disbelief. He looked up at me, his dulled blue eyes taking on a momentary look of wonder. He hesitated but then slowly got up. Together, we crossed the street to a motel just as small as the casino we had come from.

A petite lady with spectacles stood behind the desk, seemingly not sure of what to make of the three figures who had entered her motel. Unable to stop myself, I readied for what I was about to do.

"The gentleman needs a room for tonight," I announced, "...and a hot meal."

Reaching into my wallet, I grabbed a wad of twenties from my winnings and moved them toward the motel clerk. She looked surprised and started to say something about it being more than was needed, but I would have nothing of the money as long as this man was left out in the snow.

"Can you get him some warm food?" I asked. A smile appeared on her face, and I heard her say, "Sure" and "Thank you."

As we turned to leave, the old man turned to me and murmured, "I served in World War II" and "Bless you."

Looking back now, I know that this was the most unforgettable moment of this very special evening. I was the one who found "black gold" that night, as I had been presented with the best Christmas present ever. This homeless person had transformed me into a better person and given me a feeling that my family and I would take back home and keep with us forever.

— Shelly Sitzer —

A Matter of Hours

Believe in miracles. I have seen so many of them come when every other indication would say that hope was lost. Hope is never lost.
~Jeffrey R. Holland

It was nothing more than a plaster five-and-dime-store nativity, but to me it was as perfect as fine china. During the Christmas season, I loved nothing more than rearranging it over and over, moving animals closer to Baby Jesus or positioning the angels to keep a careful watch over the tiny figurine in swaddling clothes. I remember the glow on my mother's face as she'd turn from the kitchen sink to see me at the piano, strategically placing the sheep in a circle around the shepherd or arranging the three wisemen in a triangle as they carried their precious gifts to the manger.

The small figurines had belonged to my dad's grandparents, and I was touched when the nativity was given to me the January I moved into my first apartment. My mother was boxing up the Christmas decorations when I stopped for a visit. She placed the aged pink shoebox in my hands and told me she wanted me to have the family heirloom I loved so much as a child. I was getting married that September and moving to Massachusetts, and she wanted to ensure I would have the set to display the following Christmas. I lived in the upstairs apartment of a home owned by two very kind senior citizens who lived downstairs, and they generously allowed me space in the attic to store items. That is where the pink shoebox containing my childhood treasure was safely tucked away.

Our first Christmas as husband and wife came, and I couldn't wait to decorate our tiny apartment. We purchased a table-top tree and a few decorations to brighten our home. I began searching the closet where items I'd brought from home were stored, but I couldn't find the pink shoebox that held my treasured nativity. A great sadness poured over me as I realized I must have left it in the attic of my apartment in Pennsylvania. I called my landlord and she agreed to look for the missing box. Only a few minutes passed before she returned to the phone to report she couldn't find it. I felt confident it was there, but pleading my case got me nowhere. I was devastated.

A few years later, we moved back to my hometown in Pennsylvania. As Christmases came and went, I reflected on the memory of my simple nativity. I wondered if my daughters would have loved it as much as I did, and I visualized them arranging and rearranging it as I had.

Thirty-four years had gone by since I left my apartment when I picked up the morning newspaper one day and saw my landlord's husband's name in the obituaries. His wife had passed away long before him, and now they were both gone. Immediately, panic set in. What if my nativity was still tucked away in the corner of the attic? What if the house was put up for sale, and all the contents were cleared out? I would never see my beloved family heirloom again.

My head was spinning when a name popped into my mind. Of course! The name was that of my landlord's grandson's wife. She was close to my age, and I vaguely knew her in high school. Maybe she could tell me what was to become of the house. Perhaps she could solve the mystery of the missing pink shoebox.

I quickly found her on social media and sent a message spilling out the whole story of the lost nativity. In no time at all, I got a response stating her son was moving into the house, and he was in the process of cleaning out the contents. She was more than happy to have him look through the items he had ready to donate to a charitable organization.

The next day, I received another message from her. She believed her son had located the missing box. The anticipation I felt as I drove to the house was almost overwhelming, and my hand was shaking as I reached for the doorbell. A young man came to the door, and I identified myself. He politely asked me to wait while he went to another room to retrieve what he suspected belonged to me. As he returned, he was clutching a familiar pink shoebox. I nearly gasped at the sight of it, and I profusely thanked him. He told me it was a good thing I hadn't waited any longer; the box was just hours away from becoming a charitable donation.

I loaded my precious pink package into the car and joyfully transported it home where I sat down on my living-room floor and gently opened the lid. There it was, each piece wrapped in tissues just the way my mother had given it to me that January day so long ago. Tears streamed down my face as I unwrapped the delicate figurines, smiling at each one the way one would smile when reunited with an old friend. After the tearful reunion, I mindfully placed my precious nativity in a safe place in my own home, never to be abandoned again.

Every Christmas since that day, my beautiful treasure has been placed in a spot that can easily be reached by my young granddaughter. I derive such joy from watching sheep being herded, angels watching over the Baby Jesus, and the wisemen bearing gifts — from whatever position she chooses.

— Tamara Bell —

The Magic Red Sweater

Christmas is the day that holds all time together.
~Alexander Smith

When I slipped the new crimson-red sweater over Mom's head and gently pulled it down for her, she magically came to life just like Frosty the Snowman. "It's Christmas Eve, Mom," I whispered joyfully.

She slid her frail fingers over the silky-smooth wool and smiled up at me to show her approval. This was the first time I'd seen her genuinely happy in months. My heart melted!

I'd moved in to become Mom's full-time caregiver ten years earlier after a stroke robbed her of the ability to speak or adequately communicate by other means. It also left her with diminished use of her right side.

Although the journey hadn't always been easy, it had most certainly been a wonderful opportunity to give back to a special loved one. Mom was a trooper and tried to make the most of every day. Her never-give-up attitude made my job far less strenuous over the years.

Sadly, symptoms of dementia began to present themselves two years earlier, when she was ninety-five. In addition to her poor communication skills, Mom was nearly deaf, which made it difficult to determine the severity of the dementia in the beginning—or perhaps I just didn't want to see it. Now, unfortunately, it was crystal clear to me, evidenced by her lack of interest in her surroundings, her withdrawal from family and friends, and her bouts of frustration and paranoia.

Because we were never sure how Mom would be feeling from one day to the next, we hadn't hosted our family's traditional Christmas get-together at her house since I moved in. Instead, the kids had been taking over the hosting festivities at their homes.

But this year was different. With the realization that Mom was experiencing fewer and fewer moments of clarity, along with the possibility that she might not be with us for another year, I decided that she deserved the best Christmas possible — one celebrated in her own home surrounded by her loved ones.

When I mentioned this idea to the kids, everyone loved it. We decided to gather on Christmas Eve since it had always been Mom's favorite time of the season.

My son found us a beautiful ten-foot fir at the neighbor's tree farm and helped me string lots of brightly colored lights. I dug out all the ornaments Mom and I had used on our trees throughout the years and hung them one by one until the entire tree was adorned with beautiful, precious keepsakes.

We even moved the living-room furniture around and faced Mom's recliner toward the tree so she could enjoy the warm, festive atmosphere from the best vantage point. This also gave her an unobstructed view of the front door, which would allow her to see each of our guests as they arrived for the big night. Things were looking good!

To my disappointment, however, Mom was not in her best form for the entire week prior to Christmas Eve. Her yelling was nearly constant, and I worried that she wouldn't be able to experience all the joy and love I so wished for her. I also worried that others wouldn't have a good time if they saw Mom either extremely agitated or completely withdrawn.

But, to my overwhelming delight, things changed miraculously just hours before our family began to arrive. I'll never know for certain if it was the magic in the red sweater or some other remarkable intervention, but Mom was instantly transformed into her formerly vivacious self. She truly sparkled with the spirit of the season!

Mom's complexion glowed, as did her bright eyes and rosy cheeks. Even without make-up (which she gave up wearing years ago), she was absolutely beautiful.

After brushing out her thick, wavy white hair into soft curls, I fastened her favorite diamond necklace around her long, slender neck and handed her a mirror. Her smile reflected it all.

"Wow, Granny looks amazing!" "You look so bright and festive, Granny!" "She looks happy, Mom!" "Your smile is so beautiful, Granny!" "She is so alert!" "Granny looks younger than the rest of us!" Sincere, astonished compliments flowed freely as each of our guests walked through the door and headed straight for Mom to give her a warm hug. Each was in turn rewarded with a huge, radiant smile as Mom's frail, soft hands clasped lovingly around theirs.

She not only recognized everyone but was delighted to see them, contrary to the past year when she hadn't acknowledged those around her. All five of my children and their families were able to come, which thrilled me beyond measure. It was a priceless night to say the least. We took lots of photos, including several of our five generations, and Mom's smile was (for the first time in years) genuine and from the heart, rather than forced. She loved every moment, including our visit from Santa, who hadn't made an appearance at our home in years.

After the last of the kids trickled out the door shortly before midnight, Mom and I sat together looking at the tree lights and soaked up the beauty of the silence. I reflected on Christmases past when my father, brother and husband were still with us. It saddened me, but at the same time, I was so thankful that we still had Mom.

Deciding it was time to call it a night, I made my way over to get Mom up from her chair and ready for bed, and noticed unexpected tears trickling down her rosy cheeks. My heart melted as I guided her walker to the bathroom. It had been a big night with lots to take in.

As I tucked her into bed and whispered, "Good night, Mom. Merry Christmas," she was still crying but unable to tell me why. I wondered if she somehow sensed that this beautiful evening of clarity would end soon, and she'd once again slip back into the clutches of the devastating dementia.

But that would be okay. We were blessed with the best Christmas gift ever—having Mom back for the most magical night of the year.

—Connie Kaseweter Pullen—

Room at the Inn

The gift which I am sending you is called a dog,
and is in fact the most precious and
valuable possession of mankind.
~Theodorus Gaza

"A puppy, Mamma. That's all I really want for Christmas."

"Troy, you know Christmas is for toys or things we really need," said Mom. "If you had a puppy, I'm afraid you would treat it like one of your old stuffed animals and get tired of it. A pet is a big responsibility."

My shoulders sagged. I'd been asking for a puppy for more than a year and, even though I was only seven, I knew I would never treat it as a toy.

Christmas Eve arrived. My parents were of modest means, but always managed to make the holidays happy. I knew they wouldn't get me a puppy, but I would act thankful for whatever gift I did receive this year. And I had faith that some day, somehow, I would get that puppy.

The family was finishing dinner when I heard something. Sometimes, raccoons rustled around our porch, especially on a cold night. I excused myself from the table and opened the front door. I was shocked by what I saw—a small, very round, fluffy dog. It looked up at me and whined.

My mother soon stood next to me. We both looked at the little dog, then at each other. Mother opened the storm door and the dog waddled in without hesitation.

“Okay,” Mom said. “It’s too nasty for an animal to be out in this weather. We’ll give it a place to sleep until your father can find out who it belongs to… before we open our presents tomorrow.”

“Mom, he has no tags. Maybe someone just left him ’cause they couldn’t feed him. Maybe he has no home.”

My mother sighed. “He is a she, Troy, and she looks well fed, as stuffed as your teddy bear, I’d say. She’s certainly no puppy.”

“Can I play— ”

“She could be sick or have something wrong with her. You need to get to bed, young man. Tomorrow is a big day, you know.”

My father agreed we could put our guest up for the night. I asked to stay up long enough to help Mom find a wicker basket in the basement and a woolen blanket to place inside it.

Mom lifted the pooch into the makeshift bed and set a pan of water nearby. She also put newspaper on the kitchen’s linoleum floor in hopes the animal would understand its purpose. I peeked at the visitor one last time as Mom closed the kitchen door.

“She’ll be fine. Just remember that we must find out who she belongs to. Now get up to bed and dream of sugarplums.”

Mother kissed my cheek as did my father as I trundled up the stairs. “But she has no tags,” I murmured as my parents remained downstairs as always on Christmas Eve. I had difficulty getting to sleep. If the excitement of Christmas Day wasn’t enough, I kept thinking of the round fluffy dog shut in our kitchen. She hadn’t barked or whined once since she came inside, and she seemed happy to be given a warm bed. Maybe no one wanted her anymore. Maybe…

Finally, I was asleep, dreaming of the lost dog in its basket rather than sugarplums or presents under the tree.

***

“Troy, wake up. It’s Christmas.” My mother gave me a little shake. “Get dressed and come down.”

It took me a moment to remember our overnight guest. Fear struck me. What if my parents had taken the dog away before waking me? I pulled a robe over my pajamas, stepped into my slippers (a gift from the previous Christmas), and padded down the stairs.

My parents were not next to the Christmas tree in the living room as I would have expected, but rather by the kitchen door. They waved me toward them.

"What's wrong?" I asked, concern in my young voice.

My father led me into the room. I cautiously looked at the basket. My eyes grew large as I tried to comprehend what I was seeing. Next to the little dog were two squirming smaller creatures no bigger than my hand.

Newborn puppies, their eyes tightly shut, nestled against their mother's tummy.

"It seems a miracle of sorts happened overnight," said my mom. "Maybe this little mother-to-be was sent to us for safety."

Like Baby Jesus, I thought.

The subject of what to do with the little mother and her babies did not come up during the day. Presents under the tree were opened later, almost as an afterthought.

No one ever claimed her, so she and her pups became part of our family. The mother would be named Love for bringing more of it into the Seate household. I named the pups — Faith for the female and Hope for the male because I'd had faith that my wish would somehow come true.

And so it came to pass that on this night of miracles, a miracle occurred. Not only did my dream come true, but a new family of three had found a home full of warmth and love.

— Troy Seate —

Unexpected Christmas Gift

Butterflies are nature's angels.
They remind us what a gift it is to be alive.
~Robyn Nola

It was a few days past Christmas, and I was taking advantage of the after-Christmas sales. My basket was full of wrapping paper and boxes for the next year as I made my way up and down the aisles. I was searching not just for wrapping paper but also for items for our new tree. It wasn't a replacement tree but an additional one that let us make the most of the high ceilings in our new home.

At more than nine feet tall, the new tree reached higher than any we'd ever had. It soared nearly to the top of the ceiling. The thousands of lights twinkled and danced, delighting Grace, our eleven-year-old daughter. Even though we had plenty of ornaments we'd collected over the years, we still had room to add a few more on the new tree. The new tree didn't even have a tree topper yet. As I rounded the corner of the next aisle, I saw a few shelves of toppers that would be perfect.

Amid the stars and Santas, my eye was drawn to an angel. She was lying on her side and turned away from me, but I could see the wings made of feathers on her back and a flowing white dress. At eighteen inches tall, I knew she would be perfect for the new tree. I checked her delicate face for breaks and her dress for tears, and placed her in my shopping cart.

This Christmas had been unusual, and I was still struggling with a bad mood as I shopped. Traveling over Christmas to visit our oldest son was exciting but tiring, and took us out of our routine. As a military family, we were used to adapting as our Christmases changed from year to year. What made this one significant, however, was that our oldest was beginning his life away from us. Gone were days of a little boy in snowman pajamas. Now a young man was making his own way and establishing his own traditions.

Regardless of where we lived or where we were visiting, Christmas was our favorite time of year, and my husband and I went all out on decorating the house. We loved a kitchen full of cookies, a room full of family, and a tree full of lights. I had come by it naturally since my dad loved Christmas more than any holiday. One of his favorite things to do was play jokes on us by wrapping up rocks or things he found around the house, keeping us from correctly guessing what was under the tree. His eyes would shine as we'd realize the box we were certain held something fun held an old flashlight wrapped in a pair of socks.

Even as he aged, Daddy still loved Christmas. As his health started to decline, each Christmas had been tinged with the thought that it might be the last we shared with him. Eventually, we did celebrate our last Christmas with him, though none of us knew it at the time.

The day after he died was a beautiful, sunny day in May. We sat on our back porch with our closest friends, watching six-year-old Grace play in the yard. Although it was officially spring, the trees and flowers were just starting to bloom in Alabama that year. The nights were still cool, and the color wasn't quite full yet. Despite that, as Grace stood in the yard, she became surrounded by butterflies. She stood still, arms extended, as dozens of butterflies circled her, landing on her arms, nose, and hair. On her face was a sweet look, not quite a smile but clearly content.

"Grace," I said with what was probably my first smile in days. "Where did all those butterflies come from?"

In her six-year-old, matter-of-fact way, she immediately replied, "They're from Grandpa because he loves me."

It was her absolute certainty that struck me. This sweet, little girl was able to experience love in a time of loss that I hadn't been able to grasp yet. I knew, right then, that the God who created the universe was the same God who gave a beautiful gift to Grace. He let a little girl know her Grandpa loved her when he couldn't tell her himself.

A friend cried when I told her this story. She recounted how, to Native Americans, butterflies represented messages from loved ones who had passed away. Some people scoffed at the idea that God would send butterflies as a message from heaven. I knew, however, that a God who loved us enough to send His son to the world at Christmas loved us enough to cheer a little girl's heart. It hadn't been just Grace who was comforted by this unexpected expression; it was all of us.

In the years since Daddy died, butterflies became symbolic. When I saw a butterfly in a garden or flying nearby, I felt a wave of thankfulness. It was a reminder that God and Daddy loved us. As the years slipped by, the loss hurt less, and I grew to appreciate those reminders more.

By this Christmas, he had been gone five years. I wished he had been there to see my children grow up. He had been absent for a high-school and college graduation, swim teams, triathlons, marching bands and a host of other rites of passage. He was never far from my mind. I missed unimportant conversations as much as seeking his company at times when I needed to be reminded how much I was loved.

Since we traveled for Christmas, I felt off-kilter. Our suitcases were still not upacked, I hadn't prepared a big Christmas meal, and I needed to wrap the rest of our gifts. We had to celebrate before our youngest son headed to Florida with his university's marching band. I wasn't feeling any Christmas spirit. We hadn't done our usual traditions. Coupled with the exhaustion from traveling across the country, I was emotional and tired.

I unpacked my shopping bags and called to my husband as I reached for the angel tree topper. I grasped her from the bottom, bringing her up out of the bag.

"She's beautiful," he said.

I turned her toward me to make sure she had made the trip unharmed and fluff up her dress before we put her atop the new tree. No one, including me, expected the tears that sprang to my eyes. I took a long look at her and wondered how I could have missed it, especially since it wasn't something we usually associate with Christmas.

The angel in my hand held something in her hand, too.

It was a tiny, delicate butterfly. The tiredness and crankiness left me, and a sense of peace washed over me. My gift that Christmas was knowing God loved me enough to provide a special way to tell me my daddy loved me, too.

— Susan Poole —

Weird and a Little Bit Eerie

The most beautiful thing we can experience
is the mysterious.
~Albert Einstein

"Looks like Mary and Joseph left town..." I said to my friend as we stared at the partially empty manger stable in front of our house. Sometime during the night, our Mary and Joseph figures had disappeared—except the thieves forgot to take Jesus.

At Christmastime, we didn't like to go overboard on decorating. But one thing we always did was to have a place for our holy family in the front yard. We really liked our manger set. Our Mary, Joseph, and Jesus figures were rendered in childlike forms, like something one would see in a children's Christmas pageant.

The following year, with no sign of Mary and Joseph returning, we began our search for a new Holy Family the week before Thanksgiving. We went to all the local stores and malls but couldn't find those childlike figures. Our last chance was a one-hour drive to a Christmas shop, which promised they had everything Christmas. They did, except not our figures.

On the way home that night, we passed a local hardware store and saw a Holy Family in their window. I turned the car around, and as we pulled up to the front of the store, we saw our Mary, Joseph and Jesus displayed big and bright.

Inside, the salesclerk told us they had a couple of the manger sets in the back, but the price was a little more than we wanted to spend.

"If you can wait two days, the set will go on sale for Black Friday," the salesclerk told us.

"That will work," we said, and headed home.

With the next day being Thanksgiving, we decided to bring some of our Christmas decorations down from the attic. Then we could start to decorate on Friday after we brought our new family home.

I climbed the ladder to the attic. All our Christmas decorations were packed in boxes set together on a wood sheet covering the open rafters.

As I started to go through the boxes to hand down to my friend, I spotted a large box in the opposite corner of the attic.

When we had first moved into our home, the only thing left in the attic was a roll of insulation.

After crawling over the rafter boards to the box, I pulled it up on its side. The box looked like it had never been opened. It was secured with the original tape.

I cut open the box with a utility knife and pulled back the lid to reveal a ball of plastic.

When I pulled out the ball of plastic, I couldn't believe what I saw.

Shocked and somewhat stunned, I yelled down to my friend, "You're not going to believe this!"

Under the ball of plastic were three brand-new Mary, Joseph and Jesus figures — the very ones we had been searching for all week, still factory-wrapped.

It was weird and a little bit eerie.

We kept asking ourselves how a brand-new box of the very Holy Family figures we were looking for could appear in our attic. There was no logical reason... and we never found one.

Even though it's been several years since the night we discovered our new Holy Family, our excitement has never faded.

Every Christmas, when we set our manger set out in the front yard, we remember how they came to be "our" Holy Family.

It was the night we received our Christmas miracle.

— Kam Giegel —

Meet Our Contributors

Monica Agnew-Kinnaman is 102 years old and served in an anti-aircraft artillery regiment in the British Army during WWII. She holds a doctorate in psychology and is the author of a nonfiction book about dog rescues, three children's books and numerous short stories. Dr. Kinnaman has lived in Colorado for more than sixty years.

Becky Alexander teaches at the International Guide Academy and leads tours to Washington, D.C., New York, Toronto, and other destinations. When not on the road, she writes magazine articles, curriculum, and inspirational stories. Born with one arm, Becky speaks at schools to encourage kids and teach them about prosthetics.

Mary M. Alward lives in Southern Ontario. She has one grown daughter and two grown grandsons. When Mary isn't writing, she loves spending time with her family, reading, crocheting and spending time with friends.

Michelle Armbrust is a wife, homeschooling mom, and writer. She is mom to a tween daughter and tween son. Passionate about helping women learn to study and love the Bible, Michelle is currently working on her Master's in Theological Studies and developing a line of Bible study journals.

Elizabeth Atwater lives in a small Southern town with her husband Joe. She discovered the joy of reading in first grade and that naturally seemed to evolve into a joy of writing. Writing brings Elizabeth so much pleasure that she cannot imagine ever stopping. She sold her first story to a romance magazine when she was seventeen years old.

Carole Harris Barton, author of *Rainbows in Coal Country*, and *When God Gets Physical*, is retired after a career in government service. Her stories have appeared in *Chicken Soup for the Soul: Dreams and Premonitions* and

Mysterious Ways magazine. A wife and mother, she lives with her husband Paul in Dunedin, FL.

Candy Allen Bauer has written dozens of short stories and has been featured in *Working Mother* magazine and on MSN Family. She is currently working on a compilation of short stories about growing up poor in Southern West Virginia. Candy lives on the Eastern Shore of Maryland with her husband Andrew and their five children.

Garrett Bauman and his wife Carol have weathered the COVID-19 isolation by exploring new creative ventures like stained glass and wall hangings. They have learned to Zoom with their children and grandchildren who are spread across the eastern United States. Garrett has had sixteen stories published in the *Chicken Soup for the Soul* series.

Linda Monaco Behrens completed her first novel, *Sarah's Gone Away*, on her seventieth birthday. She has two children and two granddaughters and has lived in upstate New York for more than half her life. Retired, Linda likes spending time with her family and friends, traveling, gardening, and, of course, writing.

Tamara Bell left her career as a real estate agent in 2018 and is currently living her life-long dream of writing and working at an antique shop. She and her husband Paul have resided in Cooperstown, PA for thirty-eight years where they raised two daughters. Tamara is an avid supporter of animal rescue and historic preservation.

David L. Bishop and Boomerjax relocated to Montana following the fire. David continues to write amid the beauty of the mountains. He maintains his passions for reading, sports, and politics, while never missing a chance for good conversation with friends. Boomerjax has adjusted nicely, no longer suffering from fleas.

Stacy Boatman enjoys running, kayaking with her friends and high school sweetheart-turned-husband, and reading on her front porch — a retreat from the beautiful noise of her daughter, three sons, and Labradoodle. Stacy is a pediatric nurse and author. Her debut novel, *Bittersweet Goodbye*, was published in 2018.

Jamie Cahill is a freelance writer and a reader for Chicken Soup for the Soul. In her freelance career, she's written about everything from oil markets to French pastries to blockchain technology. She lives in Greenwich, CT. When she's not busy with her three children, husband and dog, she loves to travel and read.

Eva Carter is a freelance writer and photographer who has worked as a financial analyst in the telecommunications industry. She is from Czechoslovakia, raised in New York and resides with her Canadian husband in Dallas, TX.

Michelle Civalier had a run-in with Jesus in 2016 and hasn't been the same since. Hallelujah! This is her fourth story published in the *Chicken Soup for the Soul* series. She has authored several other short works. Maybe someday she'll find time to write something longer than 1,200 words. E-mail her at michelle_civalier@cox.net.

Kelly Cochran writes humorous mystery novels. In her free time, she enjoys genealogy research, exercising on her Wii Fit, and watching competitive reality television. Kelly lives outside Austin, TX with her husband and three dogs. E-mail her at Kelly@KellyCochran.com.

Steve Coe was told by his English teacher that he would never make it as a writer and hasn't stopped writing professionally since. He has four children, all boys. As a consequence he is prematurely bald and likes to distract himself with board games, sports and attempting to make something approaching music.

Gwen Cooper received her B.A. in English and Secondary Education in 2007 and completed the University of Denver Publishing Institute in 2009. In her free time, she enjoys Krav Maga, traveling, and backpacking with her husband and Bloodhounds in the beautiful Rocky Mountains. Follow her on Twitter @Gwen_Cooper10.

Beverly Kievman Copen is an entrepreneur, author and award-winning professional photographer. She has more than forty-five years' experience in marketing and communications in business, developing programs and presenting them throughout North America and abroad. She has authored five published books, numerous articles and stories. Learn more at www.beverlycopen.com.

E.M. Corsa is an artist and writer with a deep respect for nature. Her sketchbooks are her love letters from nature, filled with drawings and notes used as reference material for her work. E-mail her at ofcorsa3@gmail.com.

Barbara Davey received bachelor's and master's degrees in English and journalism from Seton Hill University. She is an adjunct professor at Caldwell University where she teaches writing to undergraduates. She and her husband live in Verona, NJ, where she does her best to avoid the kitchen.

Jennifer Clark Davidson grew up as the middle child in her family, with an older sister and a younger brother. She and her husband have been married for thirty-six years, and have two married children, two in-laws (considered their third and fourth kids), two beautiful granddaughters, and two grand-dogs. She is currently setting up a podcast.

Sergio Del Bianco has a background in fine arts and psychology. He is an artist and writer interested in the intersection of art, psychology, and the humanities. He resides in Europe with his spouse and a growing family of rescue animals. Contact him at sergiodelbianco@yahoo.com or through Twitter @DelBianco97.

Holly DiBella-McCarthy, a retired public-school teacher and special education administrator, has published several journal articles and two books. She spends her time creating folded book art, traveling and writing. Holly adores family time with her husband and three adult children. E-mail Holly at mychicforhome@gmail.com.

When **Rosanne Ehrlich** escaped from the entertainment industry, she started teaching English as a Second Language at Bergen Community College. Currently she is at work on a collection of short stories and, as a grandmother, trying to get the names of the Disney princesses straight.

Tammie Rue Elliott began observing and capturing her world in words and stories as soon as she learned to read and write. Today, she is a professional author. Her first novel, a mystery, was set in Virginia Beach. Her current novel will be completed in early 2021.

Sheila Petnuch Fields holds a bachelor's degree, cum laude, in journalism. She has been published in newspapers and magazines. During the pandemic, she crafted *Awakened Heart: Meditations to Empower the Feminine Soul*. She is the creator of AwakenedWoman.me, Mom to three men, and Gramma to one precious boy.

Amanda Flinn is an award-winning author, blogger and book nerd from Southeast Missouri. She absolutely loves living the small-town life with her husband, three boys and two rowdy rescue pups. While being a wife and a mom is her main gig, she's passionate about using her words to positively impact others.

Jean Flood has been writing poetry since childhood and prose for quite some time. She lives in the beautiful Hudson Valley with her three rescue cats and the occasional raccoon that visits for snacks. As a mom of one, Jean enjoys hiking, wandering beaches for shells, photography and off-beat road trips.

Shelley Friedman received her B.A. in English Lit/Creative Writing from San Francisco State University in 1980. As with many of her fellow English majors she went on to work for the airlines, followed by a ten-year stint as a courtroom clerk. She plays tennis, hikes, meditates, hangs out with friends and travels.

Lorraine Furtner has had inky fingers since her childhood and is a published journalist, poet, playwright and fiction writer. This is her fourth contribution to the *Chicken Soup for the Soul* series and she's a frequent contributor to Foundlinghouse.com. Follow her on Instagram @write_as_raine and lorrainefurtner.com.

James Gaffney is a writer and entrepreneur from Pennsylvania. His first book, *How Shall We Pray?: 30 Steps to Prayer*, was published by Catholic Book Publishing. After teaching college writing and communication courses, he wrote and published an app for study skills. His company can be found at Inspirational-Publishing.com.

When **Kam Giegel** was little, she would sit on a large rock by her backyard creek with pencil and paper, dreaming of being a writer. Today she is living that dream, loving the adventure of writing e-books, articles, newsletters and copy. Visit her two sites at LittleStepsCount.com and KamGiegel.com.

TG Gilliam started writing at the insistence of family members. She has a blog detailing visits to old Texas dance halls and has written short stories for family. This is her first published story.

Carol Graham received the Woman of Impact Award and Author of the Year for her memoir, *Battered Hope*, and the global award for One Woman Fearless given to women who have faced their fears and made the world a better place for women to thrive. She hosts a talk show, *Never Ever Give Up Hope*, and has rescued more than thirty dogs.

Lacy Gray is the pen name for writer Cynthia Brown of Clarksville, IN. Having previously been published in the *Chicken Soup for the Soul* series, she looks forward to retirement and plans to spend her "golden years" continuing to touch readers with her stories and poetry at lacygray.com.

Wendy Hairfield has a B.A. in Journalism from Temple University. After a rewarding career in public relations promoting environmental programs, she is now a freelance writer who enjoys photography, biking, and gardening. She has a daughter and stepson and lives in the Seattle area with her husband and two tortoises.

Marie-Lynn Hammond is a writer, editor, and singer-songwriter who lives in Southern Ontario. Half French, half English, and an Air Force "brat," she's known for her songs and stories about her fascinating family. A passionate animal advocate, she spends a lot of time with cats and horses. Learn more at marielynnhammond.com.

Terry Hans is a three-time contributor to the *Chicken Soup for the Soul* series. She is compiling a collection of humorous stories drawing on a forty-five-year career as a dental hygienist. Terry has two accomplished daughters and four athletic grandsons. Terry and her husband are happiest when cheering at one of the grandsons' games.

Wendy Hobday Haugh recently relocated with her husband Chuck to the Adirondack Mountains of upstate New York. A freelance writer and naturalist, she looks forward to writing and observing wildlife during the long winter months ahead. This marks Wendy's seventeenth story to appear in the *Chicken Soup for the Soul* series.

Kat Heckenbach graduated with honors from The University of Tampa with a B.S. in Biology and now homeschools her daughter while writing and making sci-fi/fantasy art. She is the author of the YA fantasy series *Toch Island Chronicles* and urban fantasy *Relent*, as well as dozens of speculative fiction short stories.

Bill Hess is a former United States Marine and has been a firefighter and a nationally registered paramedic for over thirty-six years. He is a father and grandfather and enjoys spending time with family, building hot rods and riding side by side with family and friends. Bill plans to write more true-life stories of inspiration and real-life miracles.

Laurie Higgins is an award-winning journalist who writes about health, food, gardening and family. She is a regular contributor to *The Cape Codder* newspaper and *Cape Cod Health News*. She and her chef husband live in Brewster, MA. Laurie enjoys hiking, photography, camping, cooking and spending time with her grandchildren.

Crystal Hodge is a previous contributor to the *Chicken Soup for the Soul* series and is delighted to share the story of how she met her husband in this edition. To read more of Crystal's work visit medium.com/

@crystalhodge1202. E-mail her at crystal@crystalhodgewriter.com.

Jan Hopkins-Campbell is a professional watercolor artist, author, mom of two adult children, and grandmother to one amazing grandson. When not at the department store where she works full-time, she enjoys painting, drawing, photography, antiquing, and reading. This is her third story published in the *Chicken Soup for the Soul* series.

Laurelyn E. Irving recently retired after a career in higher education and conflict resolution. She is travelling around the United States in an RV with her husband, Larry, and two spoiled black cats, Samantha and Sabrina.

Jennie Ivey lives and writes in Tennessee. She is the author of numerous works of fiction and nonfiction, including many stories in the *Chicken Soup for the Soul* series. E-mail her at jennieivey@gmail.com.

S. Jacobs, retired and young at heart, resides in Northwest Pennsylvania. She enjoys playing competitive games and staying active. Retirement is spent learning new skills, reading, and traveling. She is blessed with a loving husband who cooks, caring children, and four lively grandchildren. Her passion is helping the homeless.

Sheryl K. James retired after a thirty-five-year career in the federal government. She and her husband of fifty-five years have one daughter and two granddaughters. Sheryl enjoys playing her electric piano, writing music, and painting with acrylics. Throughout her life, she has written poems for family and friends.

Latonya Johnson ghostwrites everything from children's books to Christian romance. She frequents her family-owned recording studio in the Virginia Beach area where she composes chart-topping songs with the love of her life. LaTonya is in the throes of building a global healing ministry, one local brick at a time.

Kathleen E. Jones, a former nurse, is now a freelance writer. She has been published in *Chicken Soup for Soul: Inspiration for Nurses*, *Chicken Soup for the Soul: New Moms* and *Woman's World*. She writes for kids and edits for writers, in addition to leading a writing group locally.

January Joyce, a retired civil servant with twenty-eight-plus years in state and federal systems, spends her rocking chair years with a wine glass in her hand, crafting stories.

Keri Kelly is an award-winning author and comedy writer. She earned an MFA in fiction and studied comedy at Second City. She's written comedy for Erma Bombeck Writers' Workshop, Little Old Lady Comedy, and Capstone. Keri lives and surfs at the Jersey Shore with her family.

L.A. Kennedy writes short stories and creates works in polymer and papier-mâché clay in her studio while supervised by three family cats: Tortie, Marble, and Willy. Her ongoing project is refurbishing the inside and outside of the fixer-upper bought after losing the family home to a wildfire in 2018. E-mail her at elkatnca@aol.com.

Wendy Keppley counseled troubled teens and taught college courses for high-school honor students. She enjoys family, especially her grandsons, and writing life stories. Wendy also loves yoga, kayaking and reading. Motivated by the pandemic, she and her husband look forward to many new endeavors. E-mail her at wendykep@gmail.com.

Ina Massler Levin was a middle-school teacher and later, the editor-in-chief at an educational publishing house. In retirement, she has been indulging in her love of travel and ballroom dancing with her husband Michael. Ina also loves time with her family, especially her granddaughter Elianna Mae.

Melinda Richarz Lyons received her Bachelor of Arts in Journalism from the University of North Texas. Her articles have appeared in many publications. She has also authored four books and lives in Tyler, TX.

Nicole S. Mason is an attorney, mentor, author, speaker and coach. She is the recipient of the 2018 50 Great Writers You Should Be Reading award. Nicole is married to her college sweetheart, and they have three sons. She enjoys reading and encouraging others. E-mail her at contact@nicolesmason.com.

Monica McClure received her Bachelor of Science, with honors, from the University of Wisconsin-Green Bay. She resides in Green Bay, WI where she works at a liberal arts college. She is married to her best friend, has two German Shepherds, and enjoys biking, running, and devouring novels.

Melissa McCoy works as an administrator for the UNL College of Law. She holds a Ph.D. in English literature and enjoys reading, writing, and playing tennis. She is previously published in *Chicken Soup for the Soul: Miracles and More* as a co-writer with her husband Paul Muff. The two are currently finalizing their first novel, a western.

Dan McGowan is a songwriter, actor and television producer. He has a passion for creativity, joy and laughter. Dan lives in Camarillo, CA with his wife and their dog, Tess.

Jennifer McMurrain has won numerous awards for her short stories and novels, including hitting #1 on the Amazon Best Seller list with *Quail Crossings*. She has eighteen novels and collaborations published. She lives in Bartlesville, OK with her family. Learn more at www.jennifermcmurrain.com.

Lynn Maddalena Menna, a retired educator, is a Young Adult author. She lives in Hawthorne, NJ, with her husband, Prospero, and cat, Tiger Lily. E-mail her at prolynn@aol.com.

Christina Metcalf believes in the law of twos/second chances. She has twin boys, two bonus kids, and two dogs. She and her husband, Bart, finally got married a year ago after a broken engagement when they were twenty-two, making this not only the second marriage for both of them but also the second time around with one another.

Robyn Milliken has her Master of Arts in Sociology. She lives in sunny Florida with her family. Robyn enjoys the beach, reading, spending time with family, daydreaming and writing.

Sylvia Morice writes fiction, creative nonfiction, essays and poetry. Her work has been published in Canadian literary journals and magazines and she has self-published several eBooks. Sylvia is retired and lives in Atlantic Canada.

Loretta Morris is a retired special education teacher and is currently a part-time youth services assistant at her local library. She has been a member of the Naperville Writers Group since 2013 and has been published several times in their yearly anthology, *Rivulets*. She enjoys writing both fiction and nonfiction.

Rachel Dunstan Muller is a children's author and a professional storyteller to audiences of all ages. She lives on Vancouver Island, off the west coast of Canada, with her husband and their two youngest children. Learn more at www.racheldunstanmuller.com or www.indigoforest.ca.

Nell Musolf lives with her husband, three dogs, two cats and variety of adult children in Minnesota.

Anne Oliver, a native of West Virginia, holds bachelor's and master's degrees from the University of Georgia. She and her husband, George, reared three Army brats during his thirty-one years with the Army. (HOOAH!) She enjoys reading, writing, and looking forward to further adventures.

Judy Opdycke received her B.A., with honors, and her M.Ed. from

University of San Diego. She is the mother of six, grandmother of eight, and great-grandmother of two. Judy enjoys creative writing, meetings with her writing group, and time with her family.

Darlene Parnell has a master's degree in Social Work from Indiana University. She has a private practice in counseling and life coaching in Fishers, IN. She plans to continue writing inspirational books, stories and poetry. E-mail her at darleneparnell@att.net.

Susan Poole received graduate degrees from The University of Alabama and the University of Maryland and has worked in the marketing and communications field for more than twenty years. A native of Vernon, AL, she traveled the world during her husband's career as a U.S. Marine. They have three children and now reside in Alabama.

Connie Kaseweter Pullen lives in rural Sandy, OR, near her five children and several grandchildren. She earned a B.A. degree, with honors, at the University of Portland in 2006, with a double major in Psychology and Sociology. Connie enjoys writing, photography and exploring nature. E-mail her at MyGrandmaPullen@aol.com.

Author of the romantic location mystery novel, *NOLA*, **Molly Jo Realy** is an award-winning writer and author coach. Known as the Bohemian Hurricane, she encourages people to embrace their unique talents to come alive and stay wild every day. She is addicted to cats, coffee, and pens, in no particular order. Learn more at mollyjorealy.com.

Mark Rickerby is an author and screenwriter. His stories have appeared in more than twenty-five *Chicken Soup for the Soul* books. His other works are listed at www.markrickerby.com. Look for *Harmony*, a western TV series he co-created/co-wrote, coming soon! His greatest sources of joy and inspiration are his wife and his daughters Marli and Emma.

Tyann Sheldon Rouw received her B.A. from the University of Northern Iowa and her MSE from Drake University. She lives in Iowa with her husband Chris and their three teenage sons. You can find her blog at tyannsheldonrouw.weebly.com where she writes about her family's adventures. Follow her on Twitter @TyannRouw.

Manoshi Roy has a Master of Science degree. She has two girls and is a textbook content writer. Manoshi is an accomplished short film director and a children's book author. She enjoys travelling, sketching and doing numerology readings for her friends.

Kathleen Ruth earned her B.A. from St. Catherine University in St. Paul, MN and her M.A. in TESOL from the University of Central Florida. She taught in Minnesota, Florida, Bangkok, Thailand and Beirut, Lebanon. She loves reading, cross-stitch, traveling, and embracing multiple cultures. Kathleen has five children and eleven grandchildren.

Judy Salcewicz loves being a grandmother, a gardener, and a volunteer. After a satisfying teaching career, she's excited about pursuing her lifelong love of writing. Judy is a cancer survivor who believes in miracles and has experienced more than one.

Karen Sargent is the author of *Waiting for Butterflies*, the 2017 IAN Book of the Year. She is awaiting publication of her latest novel, *If She Never Tells*. A recently retired English teacher, Karen gets her teaching fix by presenting writing workshops and mentoring aspiring authors. Learn more at KarenSargent.com.

Troy Seate is an alumnus of Texas Christian University and lives in Colorado. His memoirs, essays, and fiction reflect his love of nature and its creatures.

Gail Sellers is honored to be a frequent contributor to the *Chicken Soup for the Soul* series. She enjoys writing, in particular, poetry, inspirational and animal (cat) stories. She is retired and enjoys spending time in her new home with her husband Tony and their three cats.

Patricia Simpson writes gothic, dark fantasy and paranormal suspense. She is a multi-published author who has written novels for thirty years. She lives in the Bay Area with her Scottish husband and two sweet dogs and is an incurable karaoke addict.

Award-winning writer **Linda Harris Sittig** was born in New York City, raised in northern New Jersey, and put down her adult roots in Virginia. A passion for history, and a belief that every woman deserves to have her story told, led Linda to create her internationally followed blog which can be found at strongwomeninhistory.com.

Shelly Sitzer is a graduate of Brooklyn College and a lover of anything creative. This includes endeavors in oil painting and acrylics. She also loves to create short stories and poetry and has had poems published in anthologies. She has worked in the field of vision therapy where she enjoyed working with children.

Kurt Smith has been a part-time writer for many years. He is the author of sixteen fans' guides to MLB ballparks, and he has contributed to multiple magazines, blogs, and websites. His current website, "A Great Number of Things," features many pieces he's written over the years, including some humorous Amazon reviews.

Diane Stark is a wife, mother, and freelance writer. She is a frequent contributor to the *Chicken Soup for the Soul* series. She loves to write about the important things in life: her family and her faith.

Eleanore R. Steinle has experienced being a caregiver and advocate for her daughter through cancer treatment and terminal lung disease. She shares her writings hoping to encourage and inspire others. She lives in New York with her husband, son and their many pets. E-mail her at EleanoreRSteinle@gmail.com.

A storyteller at heart, **Barbara Eppich Struna** bases her four suspenseful historical novels, *The Old Cape* series, on history, myth, Cape Cod legends, and her personal experiences. Mother of five, grandmother of four, Barbara is a curious explorer wherever she travels. She and her husband live on Cape Cod in an 1860 home.

After an extensive career as medical auditor and teacher, **Judy Sutton** is enjoying her husband and six grandchildren under the warm sun in South Carolina. Judy quilts, gardens, writes content for medical websites and never ceases to be amazed by the world around her.

Deborah Tainsh, the widow of a U.S. Marine and mom to two sons, the older one killed in action in Iraq, is a published author of four military family books and one children's book. Deborah enjoys giving inspirational talks, teaching writing workshops, mentoring at-risk youth, traveling, camping, hiking, and continuing to write and learn.

Susan Traugh lives in Oregon with her family. She frequently contributes to the *Chicken Soup for the Soul* series, has written a novel about a bipolar teen, contributes to a blog on parenting kids with mental illness, published dozens of magazine articles and an extensive workbook series for teens on adulting. Learn more at susantraugh.com.

Constance C. Turner is a career educator who helps others to experience the fullness of their faith. She has raised three fantastic kids with her husband and currently lives in Oregon. She loves long walks, hot Americanos and great conversation. She is a member of hope*writers and is working on new ways to share her stories.

Lynne Turner, who lives near Mount Forest, ON, enjoyed a long career in community journalism. Her writing has appeared in the *Chicken Soup for the Soul* series, *Canadian Living* magazine and several local publications and websites. She is celebrating twenty-five years with the man whose mother saved "The Photo in the Paper."

Darci Werner resides in rural Iowa with her husband, along with chickens, ducks and a variety of other animals. She has spent her adult life in various farming venues and loves the country life. She is a proud mom, finance coordinator at a community college, and freelance writer for various publications.

Mary Whitney has stories published in more than thirty *Chicken Soup for the Soul* books. She loves being a part of the Chicken Soup for the Soul family. Mary lives with her husband, John, and their little dog, Max, in Leavittsburg, OH. She loves her morning walk and talk with God, gardening, and visiting her grandchildren.

Jamie J. Wilson received her MBA from Baldwin Wallace University in 2004. She has two precious sons and works in the banking industry. Jamie enjoys biking, playing piano, creative writing and animal rescue. She plans to publish motivational and humorous parenting books.

Patti Woods is a freelance writer based in Connecticut. Her work has been featured in *The Boston Globe*, *Business Insider*, *The Christian Science Monitor*, *Health* and many more publications. She's the author of *Lost Restaurants of Fairfield* (The History Press) and the owner of Sandy Hollow Tarot found at www.sandyhollowtarot.com.

Debra Zemke is a songwriter and music publisher in Nashville, TN. Songwriting since 1992, with dozens of recorded songs, she found a second love of writing in short stories and is grateful to have contributed multiple times to the *Chicken Soup for the Soul* series.

Meet Amy Newmark

Amy Newmark is the bestselling author, editor-in-chief, and publisher of the *Chicken Soup for the Soul* book series. Since 2008, she has published 174 new books, most of them national bestsellers in the U.S. and Canada, more than doubling the number of Chicken Soup for the Soul titles in print today. She is also the author of *Simply Happy*, a crash course in Chicken Soup for the Soul advice and wisdom that is filled with easy-to-implement, practical tips for enjoying a better life.

Amy is credited with revitalizing the Chicken Soup for the Soul brand, which has been a publishing industry phenomenon since the first book came out in 1993. By compiling inspirational and aspirational true stories curated from ordinary people who have had extraordinary experiences, Amy has kept the twenty-seven-year-old Chicken Soup for the Soul brand fresh and relevant.

Amy graduated *magna cum laude* from Harvard University where she majored in Portuguese and minored in French. She then embarked on a three-decade career as a Wall Street analyst, a hedge fund manager, and a corporate executive in the technology field. She is a Chartered Financial Analyst.

Her return to literary pursuits was inevitable, as her honors thesis in college involved traveling throughout Brazil's impoverished northeast region, collecting stories from regular people. She is delighted to have come full circle in her writing career — from collecting stories "from the people" in Brazil as a twenty-year-old to, three decades later, collecting stories "from the people" for Chicken Soup for the Soul.

When Amy and her husband Bill, the CEO of Chicken Soup for the Soul, are not working, they are visiting their four grown children and their grandchildren.

Follow Amy on Twitter @amynewmark. Listen to her free podcast — Chicken Soup for the Soul with Amy Newmark — on Apple Podcasts, Google Play, the Podcasts app on iPhone, or by using your favorite podcast app on other devices.

Chicken Soup
for the Soul